CHRISTA JOO HYUN D'ANGELO

—

FATAL ATTRACTION

who is the
monster.
↓
who haunts you

in these dreams?

This publication is a collection of works that culminate several years of fun, bad taste, failure, heartbreak, discovery & above all curiosity. Sometimes this curiosity has brought me to strange & uncomfortable places that force me to confront unsettling truths. It is my hope that the reader is inspired by the works in this publication that ultimately tries to make sense out of such bizarre & extraordinary experiences that help us to propel forward with greater insight & empathy. I would like to thank the entire team behind this publication who have held my hand through the entire process of making this book.

Thank you so much Mousse Publishing & to Ilaria for taking this publication on! It has been an intense & crazy time! Thank you to the readers of this book also & for spending time getting to know my work & the last few years of my life

Much love Christa xxx

"It's all HER fault—!"

Collage and Confrontation: On the Work of Christa Joo Hyu D'Angelo

Travis Jeppesen

I have been following Christa Joo Hyun D'Angelo's work for more than a decade, over the course of which I have found myself constantly surprised by her work—not just its consistent quality but the places it takes me, for I can never predict where the ride will lead. When I first met her in Berlin, where we both ended up in the 2000s, she was mostly engaged in two-dimensional collage work. The quintessential Surrealist practice, and one of the originary art forms of the previous century, collage elevates the act of editing to the plateau of creation, allowing the artist to comb the landscape of premade imagery and put forth her own novel composition. D'Angelo's collages, often collected in bound volumes, showcase a sensibility characterized by a punkish embrace of chaos, and an eye-brain that orders that chaos into rhythmic splinters of joy and anger, and above all awareness. For D'Angelo's sensibility is very much attuned to the world we live in—in particular its injustices, which she confronts and rails against in her work.

It is the formal device of the collage, I would argue, that undergirds her work. In spite of the seeming randomness with which collage artists—particularly those working in the Dada tradition—often pursue their craft, D'Angelo combines the savviness of a formalist aesthete with a research-intensive process that at times can appear obsessive, as the artist masters each subject she tackles. Through this approach, she traces the emotional economy behind difficult topics of abuse, racism, and exploitation to their roots in all-too human conditions such as vulnerability, fear, and uncertainty.

In the mid-2000s, D'Angelo began to turn to video, often showing the works in immersive installations that illustrate the multi-hyphenate nature of her practice. (Trained as a painter, D'Angelo is equally adept as a sculptor, scenographer, designer, and filmmaker.) In an early video work, *Past Present Tense* (2015), D'Angelo made a radical break with her collage practice to take a straightforward documentary approach in exploring the issue of racism in contemporary Germany, her chosen home. To paraphrase one of her interviewees, Berlin's status as a hedonistic, anything-goes nightlife capital frequently gives visitors the false impression that all the social ills afflicting more conservative cultures have been resolved here. On the contrary, the lived experience of many of D'Angelo's interviewees, combined with the artist's own personal experience as an American of Asian descent, attests to the fact that racial bias is still alive and present in the German capital.

Unearthing such discomfiting truths has, of course, long been the task of the artist—and especially an artist working in D'Angelo's vein, for whom transgression is the natural by-product of the act of unveiling. If the work is confrontational— and there is no doubt it is—the way D'Angelo chooses to present these topics is also compelling. This is rooted, I believe, in the authenticity of D'Angelo's own experiences of displacement and outsiderdom. Born in South Korea and raised in New York City, D'Angelo chose to continue her education at the Academy of Fine Arts in Kraków after a brief stint at the Maryland Institute College of Art, where she studied with the art historian T. J. Demos, before moving to Berlin in late 2006, where she has been based ever since. This lived experience of otherness has compelled her to seek out subjects that, though not directly linked to her own autobiography, share the unease that accompanies a trajectory of difference.

As an extension of her intense involvement with Berlin's queer community, D'Angelo began researching the epidemic of HIV/AIDS and other sexually transmitted diseases in early 2017, an issue that has impacted many of her close friends and collaborators. She became interested in the ways in which the stigma attached to this disease affects women of color, who do not resemble those usually afflicted. This resulted in *Protest and Desire* (2019), a video installation that focused on the plight of immigrant women with HIV in Germany. In the work, also executed using the direct documentary approach found in *Past Present Tense*, D'Angelo's subjects reveal the double standards they're exposed to by a national health system that essentially positions them as second-class citizens.

The racist and nationalist hypocrisy of the "us and them" scenario unwittingly authored by the German authorities is made clear as one of D'Angelo's subjects discusses a meeting for migrants on the topic of HIV and AIDS prevention. During the session, she was compelled to raise her hand and ask the doctor why nothing had been said about PrEP, a medication well known in the gay community in Europe and the US that helps prevent the transmission of HIV through sexual contact. The doctor replied that PrEP was a "different" topic from the one they were meant to discuss— that is, HIV and the (presumably heterosexual) immigrant community. Disagreeing, she asked why the gay community was "allowed" to know about the medication, while it was not considered appropriate for the immigrant community?

D'Angelo's relentless gaze is directed at the power imbalances that proliferate in society, wherein the most disempowered are expected to trust those in positions of authority, in the legal or medical sense. She likens this to an abusive relationship, whose intricacies are frequently mis-understood by those on the outside. D'Angelo took such a scenario as a subject for *A Lover's Touch* (2022), a five-channel video installation that plumbs the painful depths of domestic abuse within interracial relationships. The work takes the form of a fictional psychotherapy session with two characters, a white German man and his Japanese-Brazilian girlfriend, members of the same dance company. The powerful minimal score by Hans Appelqvist and the evocative imagery projected across five panels form a haunting backdrop for the characters' confessions, which address issues of racial fetishization, the common need of heterosexual men to feel like the dominant partner in a relationship, and the resulting power imbalances that can culminate in violence.

Elsewhere, D'Angelo turns her lens to the detritus of popular culture, from which she excavates—particularly from its more cringe-inducing or horrific moments—gold nuggets that contain the entirety of a worldview: the ugly, dark, shadow-casting side of contemporaneity. In two of her shortest and most playful videos, *Cool Girl* and *Bitches and Witches* (both 2019), the collage aesthetic that was present at the start of her career pronounces itself, but this time in the form of moving imagery. *Cool Girl* intersperses footage from the Tina Turner biopic *What's Love Got to Do With It?* (1993), which narrates the singer's doomed romance with Ike Turner and her success in liberating herself from that abusive partnership, with scenes from *Kill Bill* (2003), *Street Fighter* (1994), and *Waiting to Exhale* (1995), to highlight various ways in which Hollywood, prior to our current moment of so-called wokeness, so often worked to caricaturize and exoticize women of color. *Bitches and Witches* asks: What happens when women refuse to behave according to the gender roles that have been assigned to them? The hilarious video uses footage from Hollywood movies such as *The Witches of Eastwick* (1987) and TV shows like *Sex and the City* (1998–2004) to provoke an answer. In doing so, D'Angelo problematizes these generic engagements with issues related to gender oppression. Bad romance, indeed!

This brings us to one of my favorite recent works by D'Angelo. It is, in my estimation, her most elusive, which is why I find it among her most compelling: *MOTHERNIGHT* (2020). Here, she turns her collage practice to the task of poetic narrative, knitting her own story from the footage of several South Korean films, including Park Chan-wook's *Lady Vengeance* (2005) and Kim Ki-young's *The Housemaid* (1960). Told from the perspective of three female vampires reflecting on their time among the living, the meta-narrative makes use of an intertextual range of sources—Japanese nursemaid lullabies, a traditional Chinese village-ghost opera, and the myth of the shamanic goddess Princess Bari—to explore female ostracization and the violence of colonialism. With an act of domestic murder at its core, *MOTHERNIGHT* ultimately rejects the normative construc-tion of lifelong monogamous relationships, as well as its biological-family equivalent, suggesting that the monsters we fear most are closer to home than many of us want to acknowledge. The surreal trajectory of the work touches on many of the themes that have preoccupied D'Angelo through the course of her career, including transracial adoption, serial violence against women, suicide, and shame.

Shame, of course, is distinct from guilt. Not tied to any one event, it is rather an all-pervading feeling of alienation, a sense that something is fundamentally wrong with the self. Shame can be seen as the emotional reality that anyone afflicted with a stigmatizing sense of difference—whether racial, sexual, tied to one's health status or national identity—must grapple with and ultimately overcome in order to function, let alone thrive.

To heighten an empathetic awareness and engagement with these works, D'Angelo chooses to shroud the audience in darkness, a key element of her installations. She insists on showing the videos in pitch-black rooms, particularly her latest works. Darkness, of course, helps alleviate feelings of shame—especially important, one might argue, considering the confrontational nature of much of D'Angelo's work—yet it also heightens the immersive experience, allowing the viewer to become more receptive. (Such an approach contrasts with the bright, sterile nature of the white cube, in which no one can hide—in such a scenario, you are not just a viewer but an object under scrutiny.) Rather than viewing darkness as scary and negative, the place of danger and lost innocence, D'Angelo reinvigorates it as a site of intensive engagement. Darkness as a space for contemplation and reflection, a darkness that poses a challenge to the racial imaginary: a place of intimacy with the self, whence new, positive associations might emerge.

In her sculptural installations, D'Angelo explores many of the themes of her videos in a more oblique way. Her 2021 work *Into the Drift and Sway*, shown that year in the Berlin art space Bärenzwinger, a site notorious in the early twentieth century for gay cruising, featured silver plaster arms and hands attached to chains hanging from the ceiling; on the wall behind them, her LED panel work *I Just Can't Stop Loving You* (2021) flashed aggressive demands for abuse with clichéd invitations for romance: "wine me dine me" is followed by "intrude me contempt me dismiss me starve me." In D'Angelo's worldview, every possibility comes enshrouded with its opposite, the threat of violence and manipulation. Remaining cognizant of the imbalances that pervade every exchange, whether erotic or romantic or otherwise, is the only means by which one can remain empowered.

Here, the juxtaposition of the elements—the hanging limbs, the textual fragments—gives the viewer a jolt, removing complacency. Again, D'Angelo's prowess as a collagist announces itself. Through a careful combing through, selection, and insertion of disparate elements, her work stages a frontal assault on conventional thinking and brings us face-to-face with the real. It can put you in a tough spot, but it is the very place in which we all need to spend time, as the task of transforming the world, with all its injustices, ultimately begins with the self.

Reparative Desires and Retributive Justice

Kathy-Ann

"These places of possibility within ourselves are dark because they are ancient and hidden; they have survived and grown strong through that darkness. Within these deep places, each one of us holds an incredible reserve of creativity and power, of unexamined and unrecorded emotion and feeling. The woman's place of power within each of us is neither white nor surface; it is dark, it is ancient, and it is deep."

—Audre Lorde, "Poetry Is Not a Luxury"

"Your body will be an apparition—hologram of your former self."

—Khalisa Rae, "Ghost in a Black Girl's Throat"

"A ghost is something only *you* can imagine and see." These words open Christa Joo Hyun D'Angelo's two-channel video *Protest and Desire* (2019). They are spoken by Lillian, the work's protagonist, who is captured across two screens that at moments mirror each other, as she discusses the inner struggle racialized subjects like herself have to deal with in a predominantly white society that perpetuates intersectional forms of discrimination. Using the metaphor of the ghost, Lillian describes how society in Germany views her, an HIV-positive Black female emigrant from Uganda, but does not really *see* her.

Instead, Lillian is interpellated by white Germans as a sexually and morally loose woman. Instead of being regarded as a precarious subject or a subject at risk, she is mistaken as a *risky* subject—one who carries and can potentially spread HIV. Lillian speaks candidly about the misconceptions and racist stereotypes attached to HIV, namely that sexually promiscuous people get infected through reckless and dangerous acts like unprotected intercourse. While HIV can be transmitted in other ways, public opinion still largely views it as sexually transmitted, which normalizes sex-shaming attitudes.

Lillian draws an analogy between structural racism and the insidious logic of colonialism: the colonized are forced into submission by state apparatuses that have them internalize the authority of colonial power, with the claim that they will be "protected" if they abide by the system. In the video work, Lillian addresses this dynamic that keeps former colonies in eternal bondage to the West, in a love-hate, codependent relationship that ensures and reproduces colonial entanglement. She also points to one of the many ways that women of color are discriminated against in the German healthcare system—they do not have the same access to the medication PrEP (pre-exposure prophylaxis) as white gay men.

Despite the very real challenges of Lillian's daily experience of discrimination, and her unflinching critique of the systemic racism involved in healthcare, there are moments of lightheartedness in D'Angelo's work.[1] For instance, sequences of a cheap music box in which a flimsy Japanese geisha figurine twirls are accompanied by the tinny notes of a whimsical melody. This image alludes to the exoticized and racialized fantasies and stereotypes of Asian and Black women in the eyes of white Germans, especially those who perceive themselves as white saviors of the "dark" continent of Africa. Challenging this racist stereotype, Lillian describes Africa as a complex continent

---

1	The video recalls one of D'Angelo's earlier works, *Past Present Tense* (2015) wherein a diverse group of artists, cultural practitioners, and scholars from "visible minority" communities in Germany provide firsthand accounts of their experiences of "difference," identity, and (un)belonging.

full of people who are, "amazingly, not depressed"—in
contrast to mainstream Western media depictions of Africa
as a continent ravaged by poverty, war, and disease.
The association of HIV/AIDS with Africa is a misconception
propagated by the West, Lillian points out, because it is
marketable. It is such misconceptions that drive the capitalist
logic of white saviorism that allows white guilt to be
assuaged by "charitable" acts such as donations or child
sponsorship. By extension, the cultural capital that white-led
institutions gain by claiming allyship with decolonial
and anti-racist movements is often driven by the same logic,
which simply reinforces and reproduces existing power
relations instead of challenging them.

What would it take for a paradigm shift to happen,
wherein the Global North—particularly geographies like
the US and Europe where late capitalism holds sway—
takes accountability for the ravages of colonialism and its
present-day forms of racial capitalism and systemic ex-
traction from the Global South? The answer is, as Lillian
makes clear: "The world is not yet open for that."

Protest and Desire was the centerpiece of *GHOSTS*,
D'Angelo's 2019 solo exhibition at Galerie im Turm in
Berlin curated by Sylvia Sadzinski. The show, which also
included four sculptural works, addressed how white heteropatriarchy continues to define and regulate female sexuality

through acts of violence, shaming, discipline, and punishment. Bathed in a reddish glow from the neon sculptures *Heart of Glass* (2018) and *It's Complicated* (2019), the gallery became an intimate space of encounter with the erotic—not only in a sexual sense, but also in Audre Lorde's sense of the word, as "an assertion of the lifeforce of women; of that creative energy empowered"[2]—and hence a space of personal and political agency.

"A ghost is something only *you* can imagine and see." The experiences and encounters Lillian recalls in *Protest and Desire* speak to a hollowing out of the self, a ghostly existence that does not allow one the opportunity to fully embrace oneself—and be embraced—for all that one is. This haunted existence and the exorcising of one's ghosts returns as a motif in D'Angelo's *MOTHERNIGHT* (2020), a three-channel video in English and Korean in which three female vampires from the past, present, and future recount their personal stories. Their intertwined narratives become part of the archive of folktales and fictional portrayals of the innumerable other East and Southeast Asian women who have taken retributive justice into their own hands instead of relying on a heteropatriarchal system that has failed them.

---

2 "When I speak of the erotic, then, I speak of it as an assertion of the lifeforce of women; of that creative energy empowered, the knowledge and use of which we are now reclaiming in our language, our history, our dancing, our loving, our work, our lives." Audre Lorde, "Uses of the Erotic: The Erotic as Power," in *Sister Outsider* (Berkeley, CA: Crossing Press, 2012), 55.

These range from the tale of the goddess Princess Bari, the first shaman in the Korean shamanic tradition, who was abandoned at birth because she was assigned female, to the tragic story of Myung-Sook, the protagonist of Kim Ki-young's film *The Housemaid* (1960), and the revenge tale of Lee Geum-ja, who, wrongly imprisoned for a child murder she did not commit, seeks revenge upon her release, in Park Chan-wook's film *Lady Vengeance* (2007). Sequences from these two well-known South Korean films are reproduced in *MOTHERNIGHT*.

While conveying the individual personal vendettas of these strong female protagonists, *MOTHERNIGHT* also articulates a larger collective critique of the ways in which female agency is often controlled and regulated by the patriarchal social institutions of marriage, family, and sexual reproduction, in both the East and the West. By extension, the work examines how notions of home, kinship, and racial and cultural belonging can be complicated and re-configured—for instance, by going beyond the normative understanding of lineage as that which is formed by blood ties. Alternative feminine, matrilineal ties of kinship and intimacy are formed, D'Angelo suggests, under the cloak of darkness, a darkness that, to recall the words of Lorde, runs "ancient" and "deep."

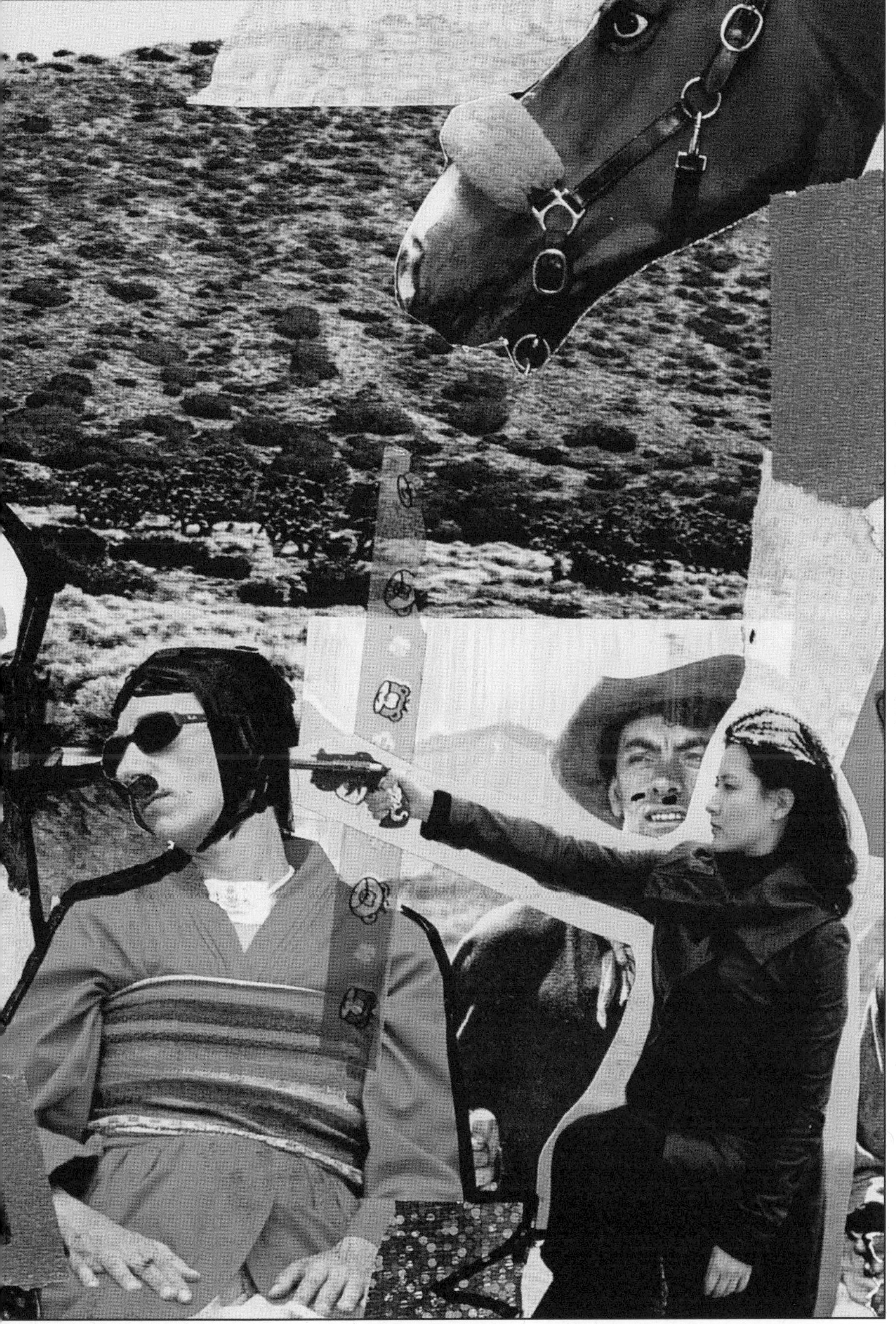

MOTHERNIGHT thus confronts and critiques the structural violence that heteropatriarchy enacts on the bodies of Asian women. It uncovers the horrific ways in which women's sexuality is tied to traditional understandings of honor, piety, and sexual monogamy—and the ways in which anyone who falls outside of that idealized image of docile womanhood is deemed a slut or a whore, even by other women. It is this form of incisive critique in D'Angelo's piece that reveals how women have internalized patriarchy, to the point where women from the upper classes reproduce violence on women they deem to be beneath them.

Based on folkloric mythology, the three Asian vampires in the video work are at once nowhere and everywhere. They are ghostly presences, their voice-overs recounting their own stories of betrayal, stigmatization, and ostracization, while they connect with the plights of the betrayed women depicted in the clips from the South Korean films.[3] Their tales speak of their search for forgiveness and redemption, as they attempt to come to terms with their pasts of murder, suicide, and domestic violence. Challenging the hypersexualization of both female vampires and Asian women, *MOTHERNIGHT* exposes upper-middle-class patriarchy as that which is remorselessly, viciously harmful in terms of the

---

3   Vampires were first regarded as female demons; the word comes from *upir*, which means sinner in Russian.

violence it enacts on women from less privileged backgrounds, who occupy more precarious positions in society.
The lack of care and empathy of the male lead in *The
Housemaid* parallels the lack of honesty and kindness
shown toward the female protagonist in *Lady Vengeance* by
her schoolteacher, who kills young children.

The work weaves together an oral and visual tapestry
of the voices of women who, defying societal norms,
carve out their own sense of agency, identity, and belonging in stories of their own telling. The tales of female
filmic protagonists are spliced together with the brazen
oral testimonies of the three vampires as well as dialogue
adapted from the lyrics of Japanese nursemaid lullabies and
a Chinese village-ghost opera. D'Angelo drew upon the
lullabies from a region of Japan where Korean prisoners
were held during Japanese colonial rule, from 1910 to
1945. They were sung by female nursemaids from the lower
classes as protest songs; sometimes they were about killing
the babies in their care. The government prohibited them,
and many of their composers, all women, remain unknown.
The Chinese village-ghost opera, banned during the Cultural
Revolution, tells the tale of a woman whose family forced
her to work in a brothel. She is raped a thousand times and
chooses suicide, later returning from the dead to seek vengeance on the men who raped her. In D'Angelo's work, the

lyrics form the dialogue spoken by the vampire in the future ("the ghost of thousands of men").

Protest and Desire and *MOTHERNIGHT* confront the realities of structural racism and heteropatriarchy that have built a world in which the other has no place, or only a designated place to serve the whims and fantasies of its "master." Yet D'Angelo's female protagonists also delight in satirizing the racist and sexist stereotypes of women of color who are objects of both disgust and desire within the white gaze. The female ghost, the bloodthirsty vampires, the siren, the femme fatale, the heartless bitch, the slut, the whore—rather than three-dimensional entities that exist in real life, they are the projections of our own fears, weaknesses, insecurities, and abjections, and hence a reflection of who we are at heart. Similar to how Sethe, the protagonist of Toni Morrison's novel *Beloved* (1987), is shunned by her community after she kills her daughter so the infant will not be enslaved, the female characters in D'Angelo's *MOTHERNIGHT* are stigmatized, ostracized, and pathologized for their life choices. Their acts of infanticide and suicide are understood by society not as ultimate sacrifices, but as horrific acts that cast them as demonic. It is the return of the ghost, in both Morrison's novel and D'Angelo's video work, that finally sets free the stream of "rememory" and repressed emotions that accompanies the female subject along the passage of her rebirth—this time "without shame," this time "shameless."[4]

In a civil society where rules are drawn up to regulate and control bodies, subjectivities, and sexualities that fall outside of the norm, it is unsurprising that these are the figures who are at the frontlines of revolution. The writer Heinrich Böll once claimed that the twentieth century would be remembered as the century of the refugee. Perhaps the twenty-first century will be remembered as the century of retributive as well as restorative justice, especially for women. Perhaps it will be a century characterized by the creation and not merely the reclaiming of spaces in society of greater freedom, equity, kindness, and empathy.[5] In an artistic context, it is the spaces of darkness, of deep creativity, and of unapologetic, unruly femininity that D'Angelo opens up and holds tenderly.

---

4 Sethe speaks these lines: "Some things go. Pass on. Some things just stay. I used to think it was my rememory. […] Places, places are still there." Toni Morrison, *Beloved* (New York: Vintage, 2004), 43. The last line from *MOTHERNIGHT* is: "I would like to be without shame, I would like to be shameless."

5 See bell hooks, *Belonging: A Culture of Place* (New York: Routledge, 2009).

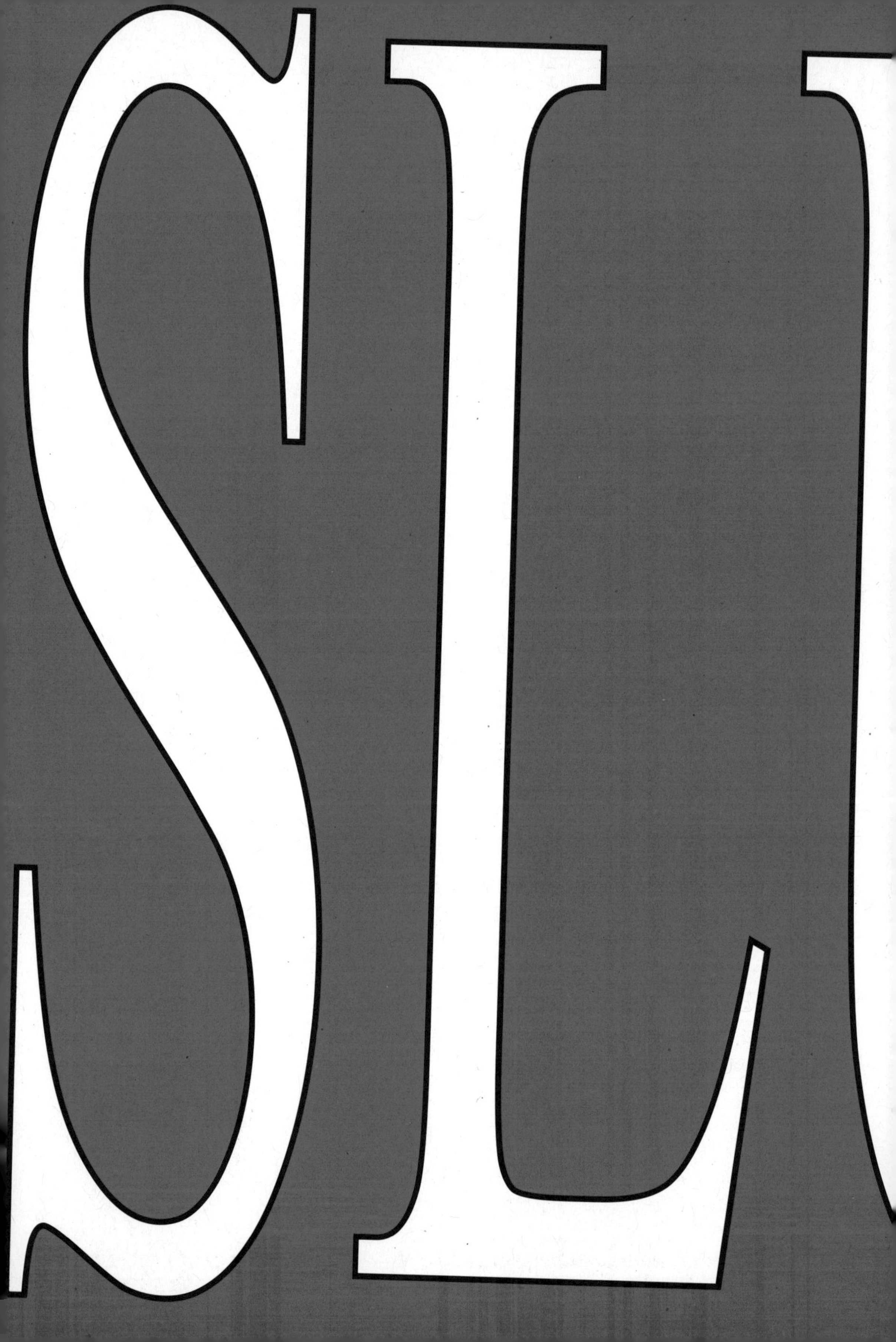

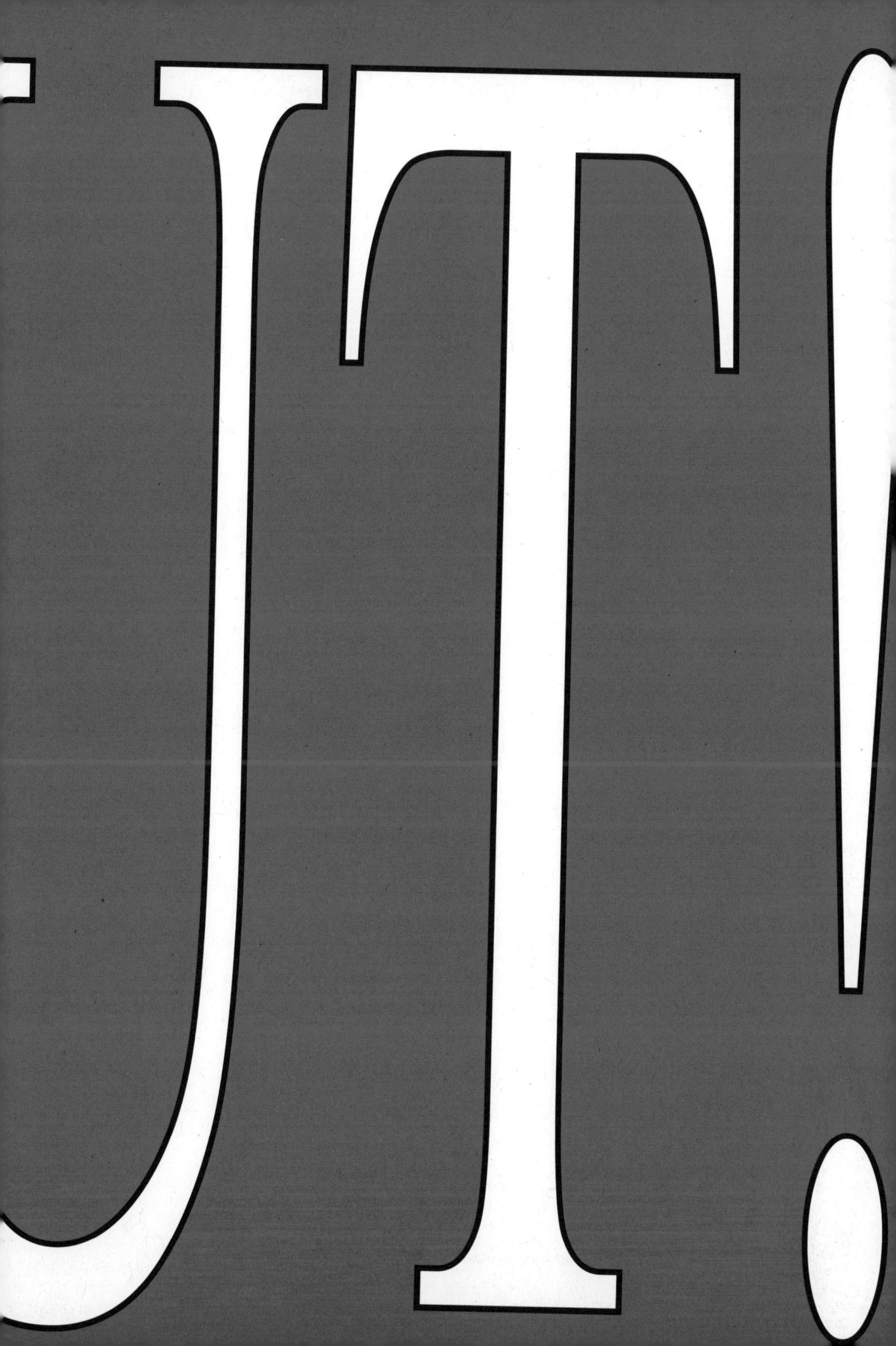

In the
Basement
Karina Griffi
in conversatio
Christa Joo H

n with
un D'Angelo

Karina Griffith: Your work accesses subconscious levels of lust, fetishism, and juvenile delinquency to explore the tensions between control and desire. At your 2022 show at SOMA in Berlin, I felt like I'd entered my parents' den, commanding the remote and flipping through late-night TV way past my bedtime. It felt dangerous and delightful and cozy and off-limits, all at the same time. Can you talk about the mise-en-scène of your installations and how your work taps into adolescent energy to tackle very adult subjects?

Christa Joo Hyun D'Angelo: My subject matter can be rather intimidating since I deal with taboo and uncomfortable topics. In order to make the audience feel more at ease, I try to eliminate the white cube as a space to see and be seen by creating the complete antithesis. I transform galleries and institutional spaces into suburban dens or windowless basements using cheap wall-to-wall carpeting, the kind that was popular in middle-class American homes in the 1980s and 1990s. The audience typically sits on the carpeting among kitschy silver pillows while looking up at the screens, like when you are playing video games or watching movies as a child, when the world is so much bigger than you. I find that people are more receptive in these grounded positions, because they are more comfortable and feel less observed. The white cube of the gallery can make people feel as if they do

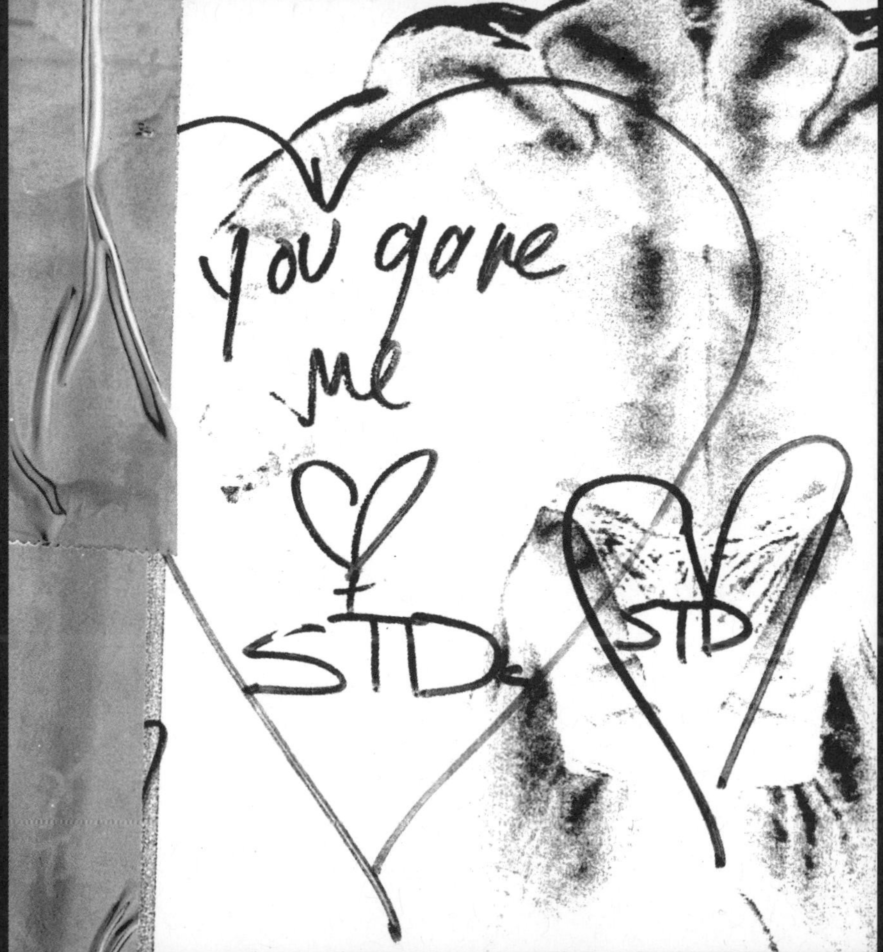
you gave me
STD
STD

not belong. Coming from a working-class family, I understand that art spaces can make people feel excluded. In high school, I started going to galleries and museums and realized the other visitors did not "look" like where I was from, meaning they didn't seem to belong to the same class as me. I find that people become hyperaware of appearances in art spaces, especially of those who are outsiders, because the culture sector is not made up of working-class perspectives or people. The mise-en-scène of my installations does resemble a basement, or even a darkroom or carnival house of horrors, due to the interplay of darkness and low lighting. As a result, the energy within these spaces becomes charged with erotic or sinister feelings of tension and desire.

KG: I'm reminded of a 1990s public service announcement from DARE (Drug Abuse Resistance Education) about Snake the drug dealer, who transforms behind a lamppost from a friendly Black man into a monster. Snake directly addressed the kids watching TV late at night. It is clear to me now that the racist tropes made the ad just as much anti-Black as it was anti-drug. I'm still scared by that commercial! It might be the reason I study moving images now. What early TV shaped your practice?

CD: Horror and sci-fi movies, as well as MTV and late-night commercials. As the youngest in my family, I watched a lot of movies I probably should not have seen when I was little, mainly horror films and thrillers. My most vivid memory, and my first feeling of absolute terror, came from watching *The Exorcist* (1973) with my older cousins in their basement during a Christmas party. I was nine years old and horrified by what I saw, and at the same time I could not look away. Also the *Nightmare on Elm Street* (1984) and *Child's Play* (1988) movie posters—I remember trying to hide from them when I went to sleep. I was mostly frightened by what my imagination conjured up. By not having access to a complete narrative, my imagination went into panic mode envisioning what could happen. Even now, I vividly remember these feelings of fear—it was the greatest adrenaline rush I've ever experienced in response to imagery. I think that's why I am constantly seeking intense experiences for both myself and the audience to explore. Artistically, I want to bring the audience with me to a place of unexpected terror, tragedy, loss, and contempt, universal feelings that, regardless of background, are also primal and intimate, bringing you face-to-face with fearful memories.

KG: Your later work often uses two primary colors: red and blue. The light cast from your neon signs gives the space a red-light-district vibe, sexy and scintillating. The twist is that the messages on your signs are anything but warm. Similarly, the blues in your work (for instance, the video work *Cool Girl*, 2019, and the LED sculpture *I Just Can't Stop Loving You*, 2021) flip expectations and often delve into intimate subjects, as opposed to the cold, impersonal topics we would expect from those tones. What makes you return to these colors in your work again and again?

CD: In early 2019, when I was in Stockholm working on the set of a Fever Ray music video, I met the lighting designer Jonatan Winbo. He became a close friend and collaborator, and got me to think critically about how to use light as a narrative tool, illuminating experiences and emotions according to what you do not see, what you chose to withhold. Along with my fascination with horror movies and the sensation of being scared by your own imagination, that propelled me to weaponize darkness in my work to push narratives that reveal people's unconscious fears and biases.

In Berlin, I spend a lot of time walking around the city at night, often in districts where sex work is common. I am both attracted to and repelled by such areas: they can be spaces of respite, insofar as they offer refuge and become a lifeline for many sex workers who come from precarious positions, but they can also be spaces of danger and shame.

Again, there is this feeling of disgust mixed with fascination, which brings me back to the sensation of watching *The Exorcist* as a child, that feeling of not being able to look away. Pink and red lights are usually associated with sex and are often found in "cheap" places like sex shops. I think my color palette tries to re-create this sense of danger while alluding to the seductive nature of such locations, inverting the audience's expectations to expose and illuminate their own fears and prejudices about sex, isolation, femininity, and class.

KG: Your found-footage films rely on precise editing—the match of eyelines, cuts, action, similar settings, the same actresses in different roles. What are you telling us about intimacy and media consumption in these works? What kinds of lineages are you drawing in your choice of footage?

CD: My academic background in painting has led me to view video as a modern form of portraiture. I didn't have much experience with video or editing when I started working on the video *Past Present Tense* (2015), but I was heavily influenced by the work of Michael Peters, the choreographer for the music video of Michael Jackson's "Thriller" (1983).

"No change no 3rd chance?
Hey can we talk or like what do you think
By the way? Do you like California Piz
kitchen?

I don't think that's
how you are supposed to like it

I'm really sorry!

I can't really say But I don't like
what you are supposed to be ...
Did you burn those papers?
HOW the hell?
OMG WTF OMG
SLUT SLUT SLUT!
ARNOLD! ARNOLD ARNOLD!

did that No way happen?
SLAY SLAY SLAY!

Peters was a pioneer in the choreography of moving images, and his work drew on pacing, body movement, and facial expression. His choreography is so precise and his compositions so unpredictable that you can't look away. I learned how to connect with the audience and construct a moving composition based on Peters's work, which is innovative, defiant, and informed by creative decisions that are both playful and serious.

In 2019, while I was struggling with the editing of *Protest and Desire*, I began to study the editing techniques of the cult vampire film *The Lost Boys* (1987). I wanted to learn how to both scare and move people through video editing, and *The Lost Boys* employs subtle, unusual editing techniques, specifically cross-fades. It is a bit outdated now, but when used effectively the cross-fade can convey a wide range of temporalities and emotions. With this narrative tool I wanted to learn how to take the audience to unfamiliar, potentially sensitive places, and compel them to see the unimaginable. I position the audience members within the narrative to avoid turning them into voyeurs or passive participants. The audience become victims of their own disillusionment.

KG: Is it fair to say you have a soft spot for bitches and witches? Smart, independent women who reveal our fetishes, on whom we project everything tantalizing and wicked?

CD: I think there is a lot to say about witches and sirens because they always seem to bring people, especially men, to their deaths. These strong female outsiders are the embodiment of everything society fears. We can see this in the outrageous amount of serial entertainment that continues to sensationalize and monetize violence against women and ethnic minorities. These characters somehow become emblems of danger: they represent the failings of patriarchal systems and heteronormativity. My video work *MOTHERNIGHT* (2020) was inspired by this phenomenon. The figure of the vampire was originally a female seducer of women—she brought disaster, spread disease, ate children, and destroyed families. So obviously I wanted to create a counternarrative. *MOTHERNIGHT* also came out of my eternal love affair with the movie *Vampire Hunter D: Bloodlust* (2000), which was based on the story of the first vampire, Carmilla, who even preceded Dracula. She was salacious, cunning, and bloodthirsty—in fact, no different than the vampires I created for *MOTHERNIGHT*, insofar as they are all archetypes of what society is drawn to while at the same time revels in destroying. I think our fascination with such characters, whom we invite into our private fantasies, becomes our greatest proxy for violence, perversion, and control.

KG: Returning to the tensions between control and desire: there is an interesting play with proximity in your sculptures and installations. The messages on the neon signs are intimate but can be seen from far away; the sculptures beckon us to come closer with their flirtatious humor and reflective surfaces. How are you pulling us closer and pushing us away, consciously and subconsciously, at the same time?

CD: Violence is accompanied by romance in all of my works. When I was working on the music for *A Lover's Touch* with the composer Hans Appelqvist, I told him that I wanted to have Guns N' Roses–style electric-guitar music, and he thought I was crazy. He was skeptical that I wanted to use this very white, crude masculine sound to narrate a story of domestic violence within an interracial relationship, because it seemed so far removed from romantic entanglement. However, that distance was something I was trying to accentuate; the threat of violence is always present in a codependent relationship, and I wanted this invisible tension to mount through the music. It makes sense to incorporate these polar opposites: each is dependent on the other. This duality is also evident in my neons and LED sculptures, which use formats like the run-on sentence or the "for your eyes only" private text message. Although they seem intimate, they also beg to be seen. They are words that cannot be spoken but compel us to scream, and in the LED sculptures they are arranged in a playful yet manic way.

My fixation on intimate relationships also extends to how machines express sentiment through touch, in particular the relationship between the teenager John Connor and the T-800 cyborg in the film *Terminator 2* (1991). My sculptures have a very *Terminator* feel, body parts cast in chrome to resemble humanoid machines that seek human contact. (All over my studio there are images of Arnold Schwarzenegger as the T-800 and Yul Brynner as the Gunslinger in the 1973 movie *Westworld*.) Many of my sculptures exist somewhere between this binary—machine and human, hard and soft, strong and weak. I want to implode these binaries, including gender binaries, through camp stereotypes to reflect our simultaneous repulsion and attraction to such extremes. Because danger and violence are always omnipresent, the artworks become a reflection of what we fear the most.

DON'T
TOUCH
ME

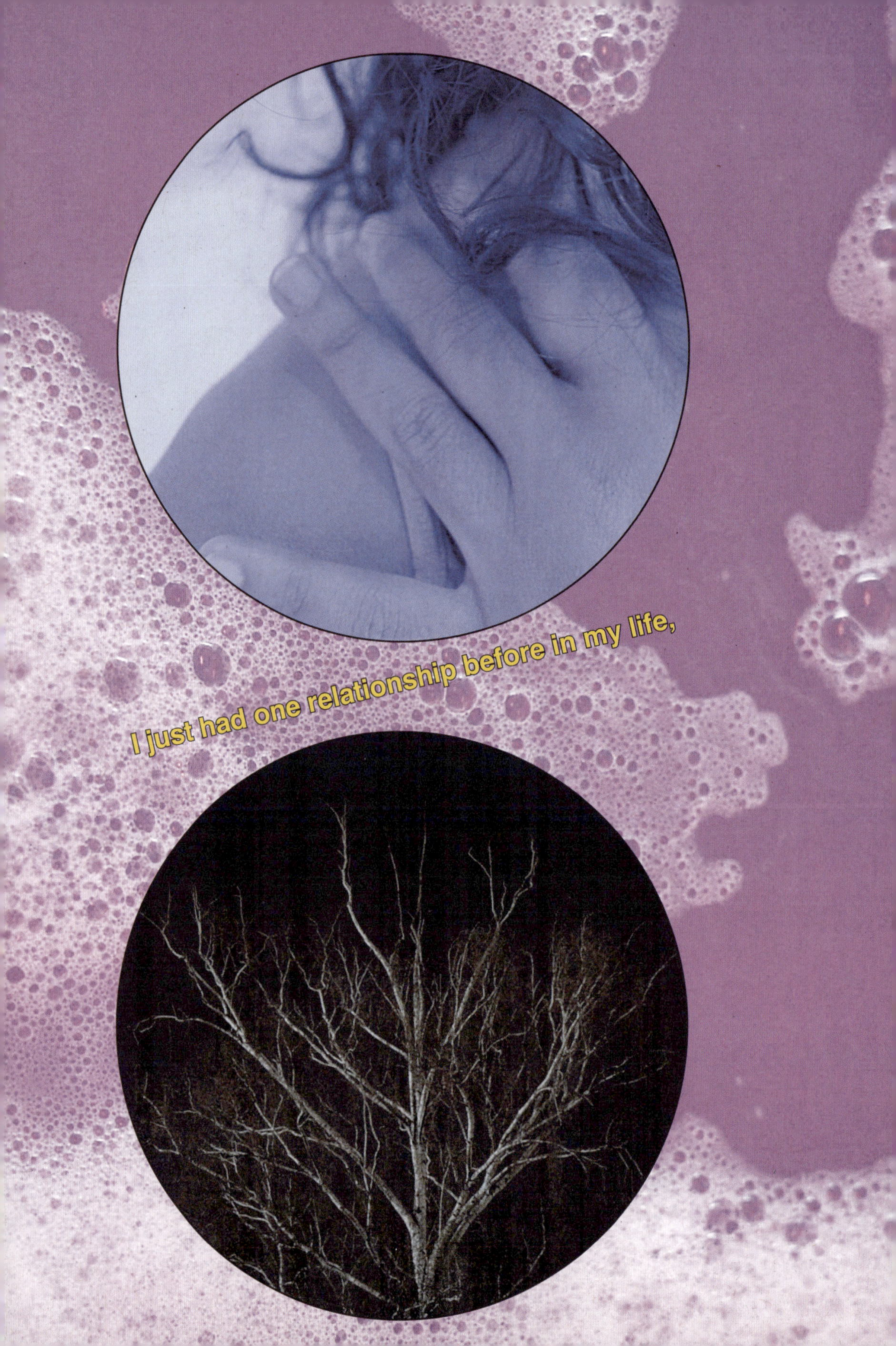
I just had one relationship before in my life,

Pg 129 — the desire for romantic intimacy.
↓ coming to terms with higher levels of anxiety
  shame, and stigma
↓ reclaiming stage from illness.
illness can lead us to live differently, accepting it
is neither easy nor self-evident.
— redefine the meaning of sexual health issues
↓ new label illness.

' lives up against her more educated, more powerful
than me,

— trauma will find you again + again

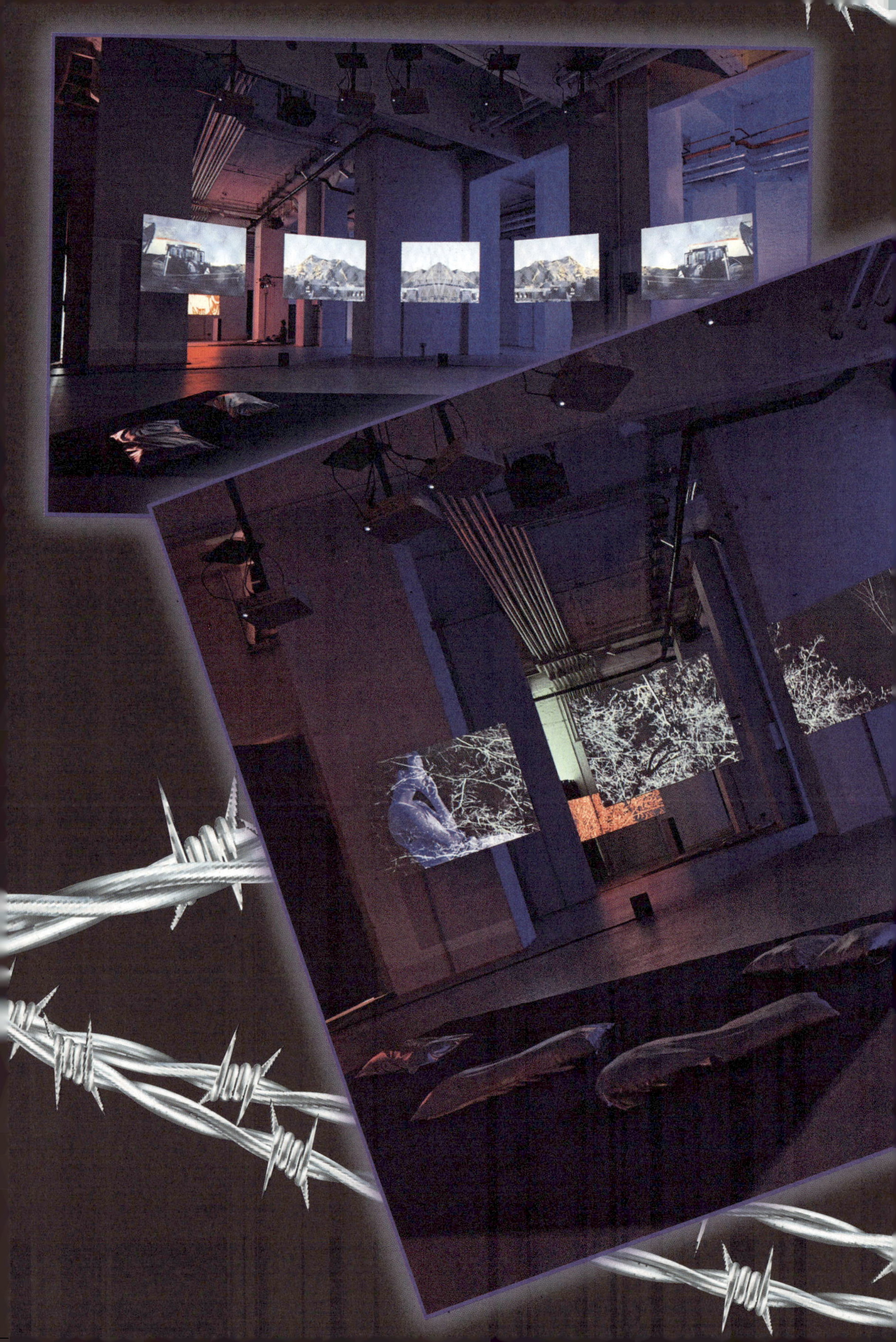

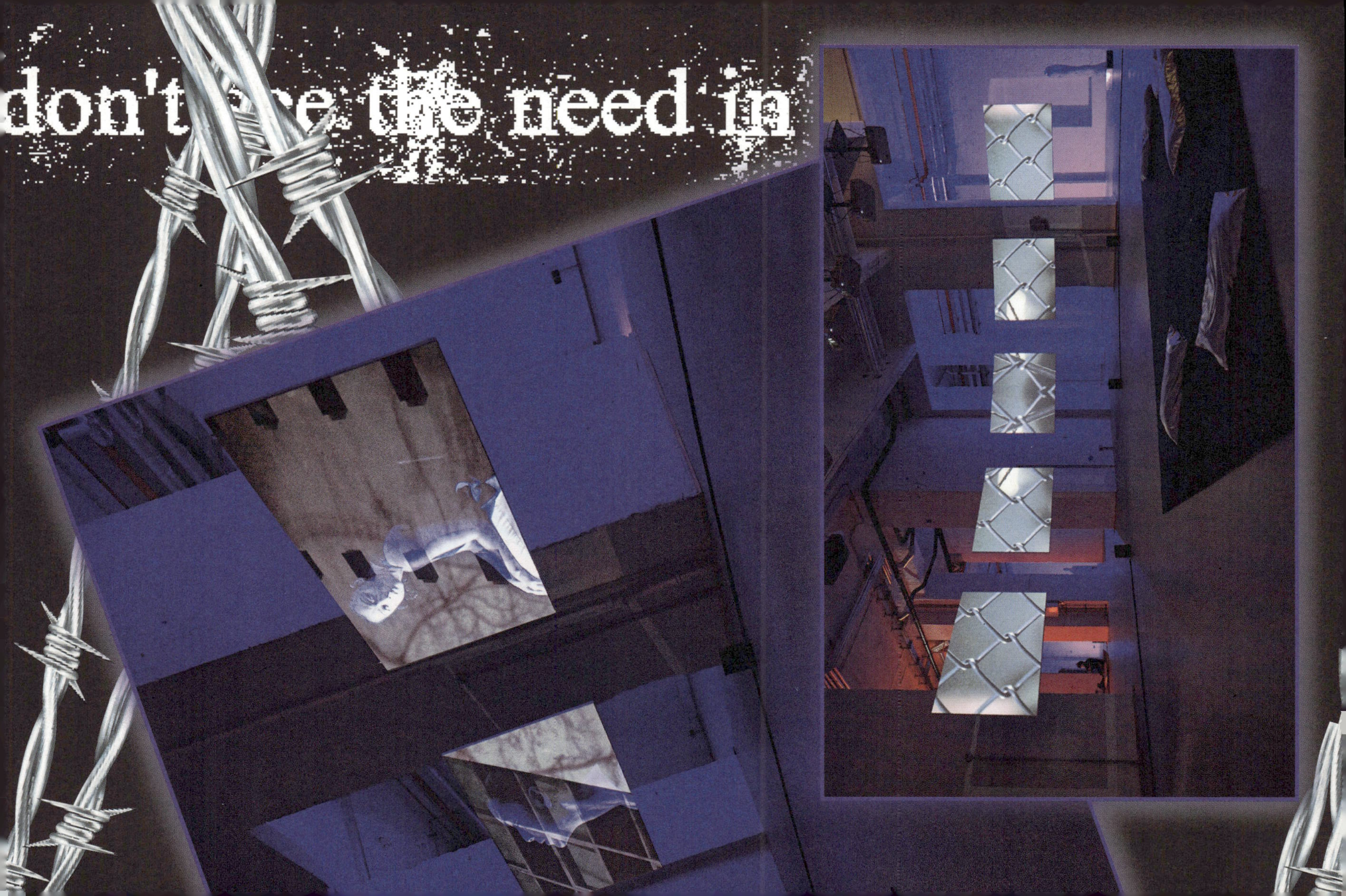
don't ... e the need in

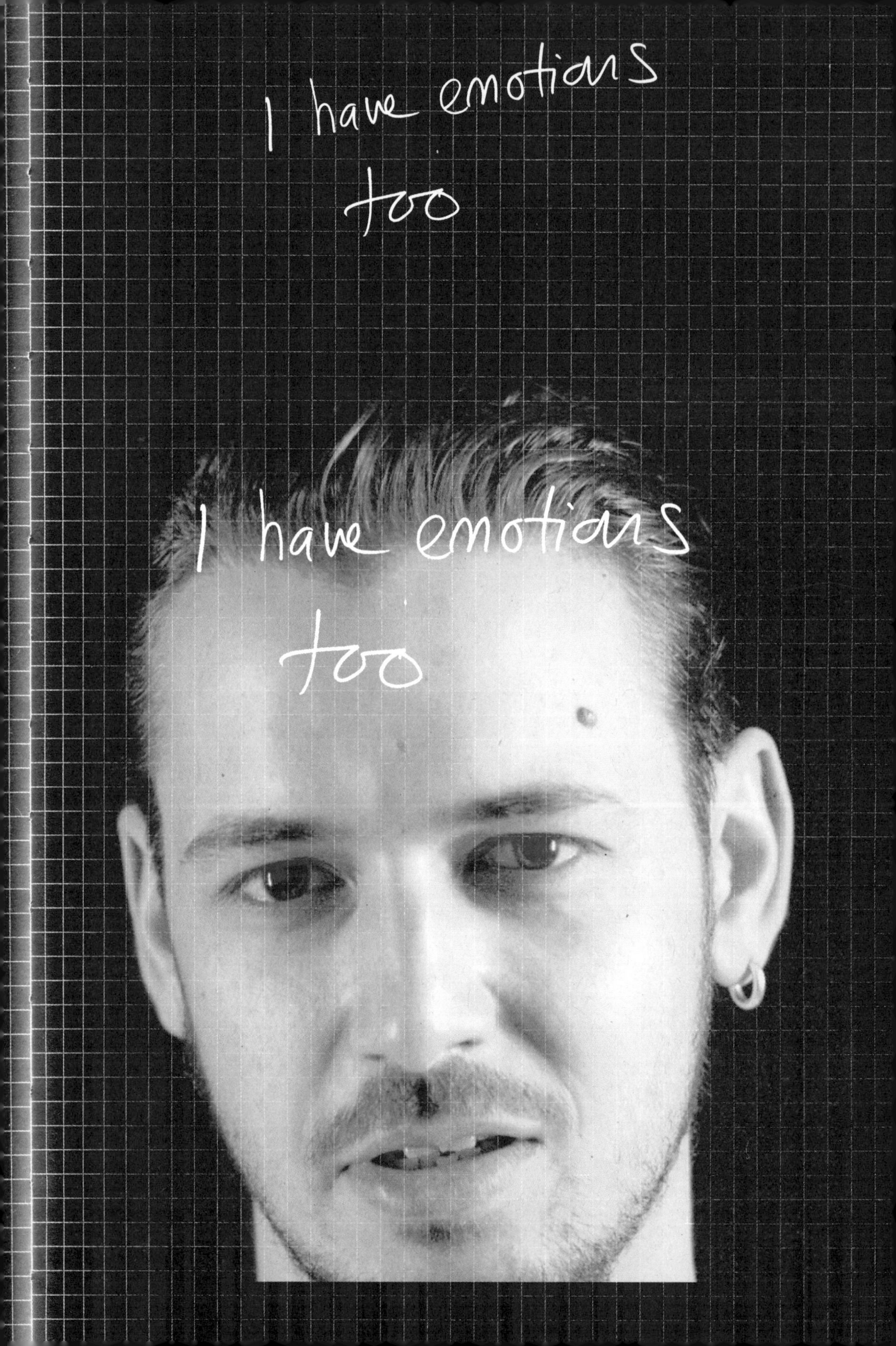

I have emotions
too

I have emotions
too

have a lot of sexual fantasies with. non white woman. This is one of the reasons why white men search for non white woman something ... and also being a white man. I think they have the being of being able to control and ... more power if they have a none white woman as girlfriend.

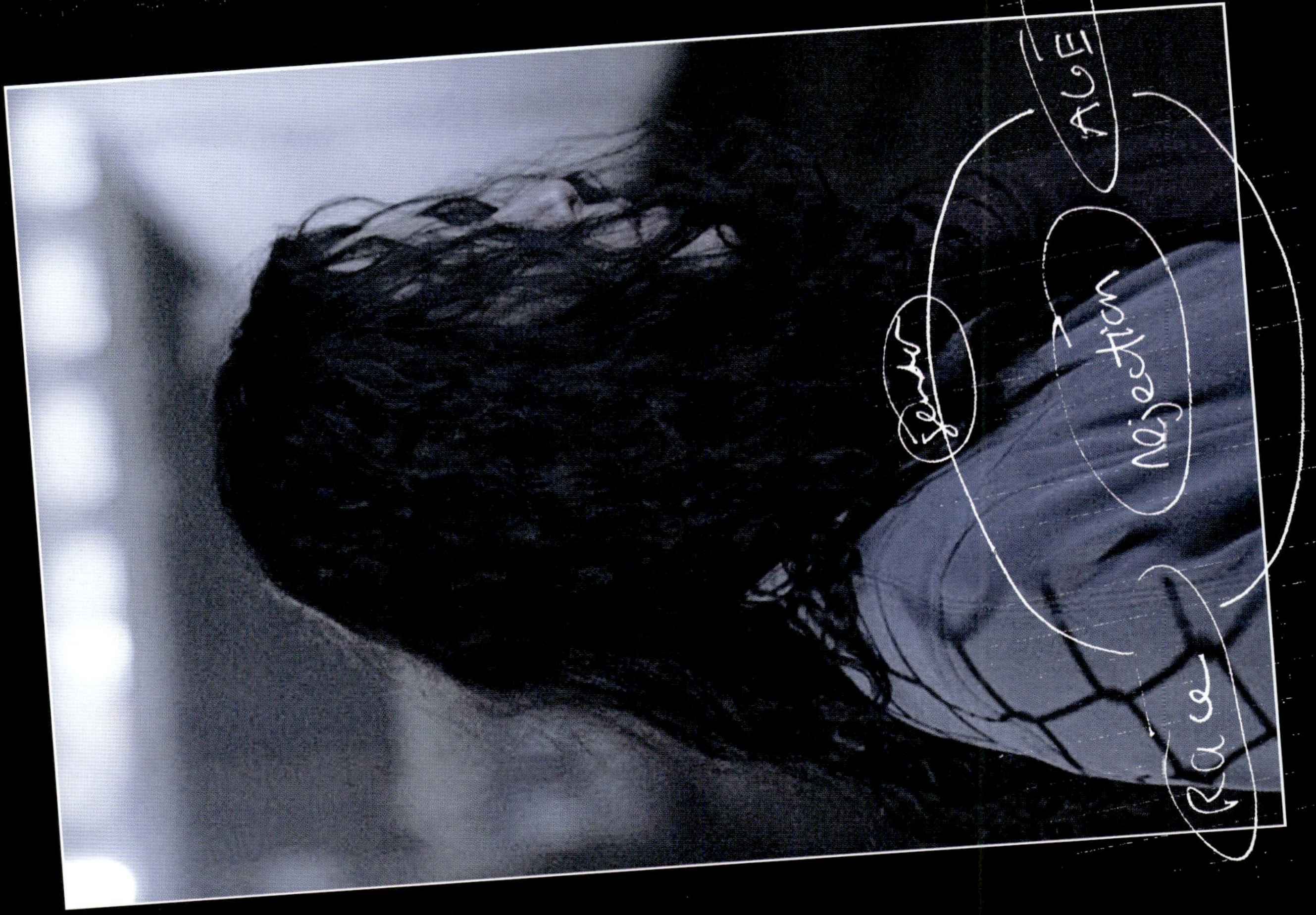

gender

Rejection

Race

AGE

cant

I hate you tok

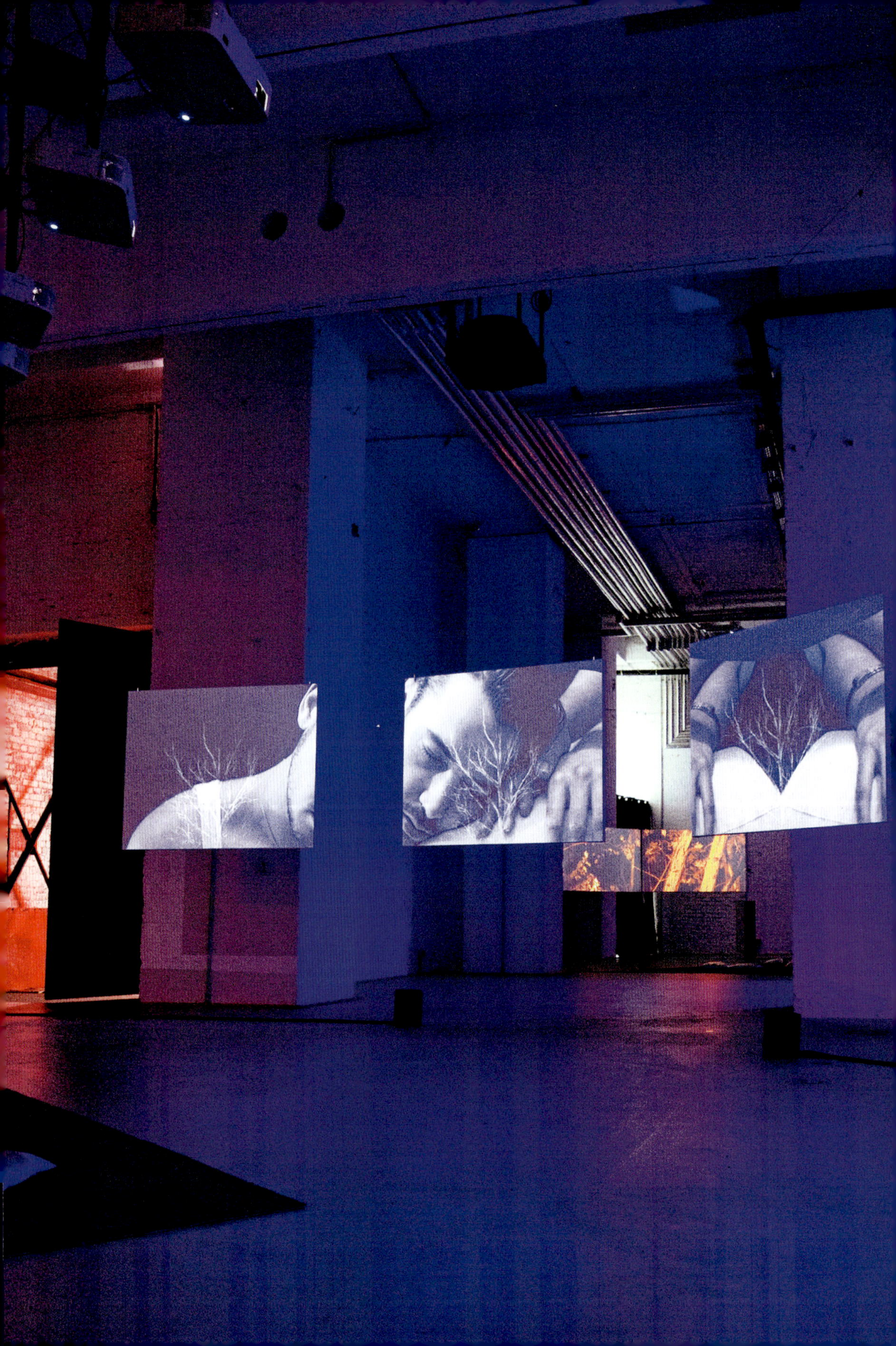

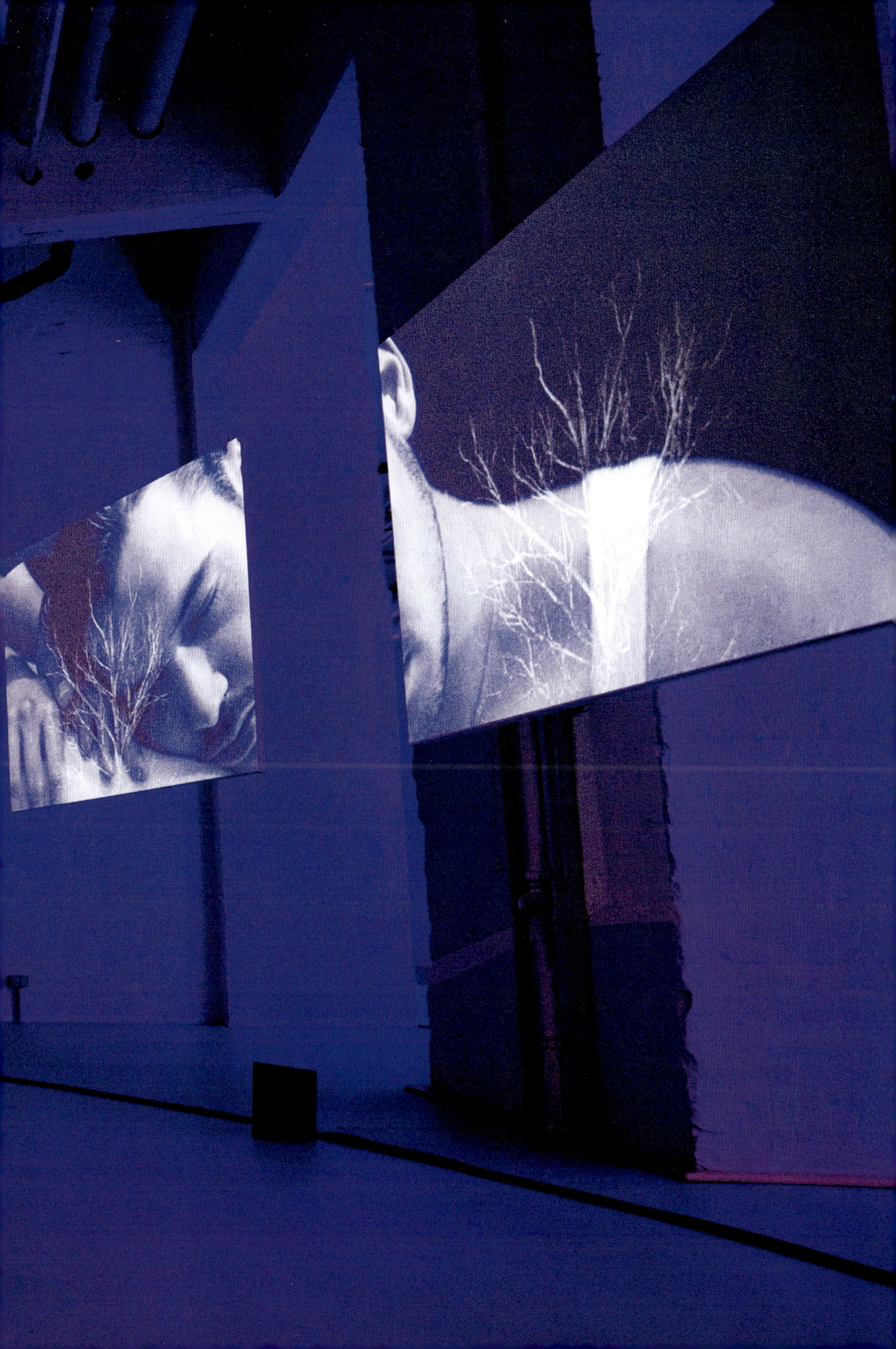

I'm always
again
afraid it can happen

OMG WHAT A SLUT WTF OMG WTF

6:17 This poor girl was on the verge of going mad.

6:24 But she tried to comfort herself in the thought that it happens to every woman sooner or later.

its really hard to trust MEN

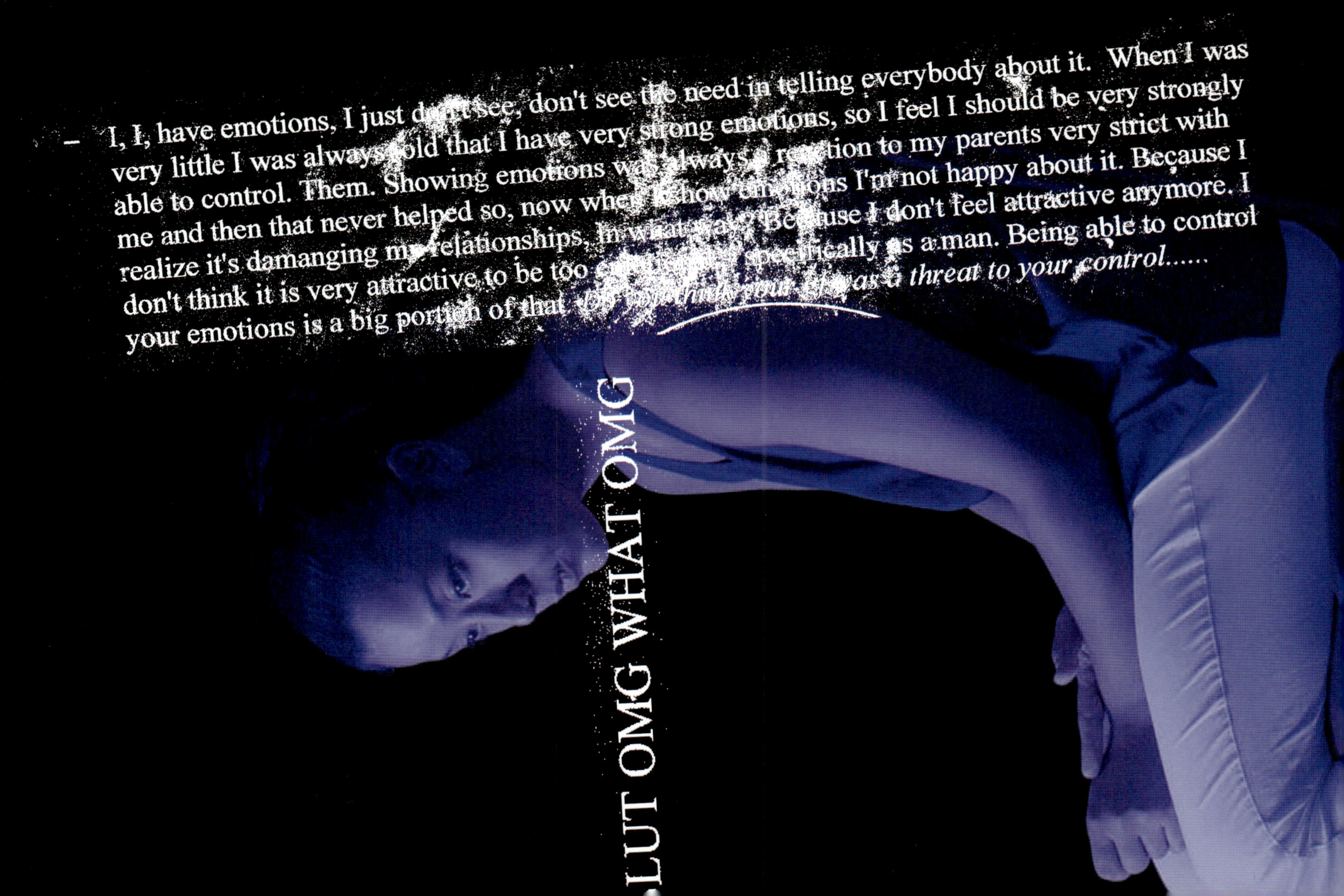

— I, I, have emotions, I just don't see, don't see the need in telling everybody about it. When I was very little I was always told that I have very strong emotions, so I feel I should be very strongly able to control. Them. Showing emotions was always a reaction to my parents very strict with me and then that never helped so, now when I show emotions I'm not happy about it. Because I realize it's damanging my relationships, in what way? Because I don't feel attractive anymore. I don't think it is very attractive to be too emotional, specifically as a man. Being able to control your emotions is a big portion of that. *Do you think your life was a threat to your control......*

LUT OMG WHAT OMG

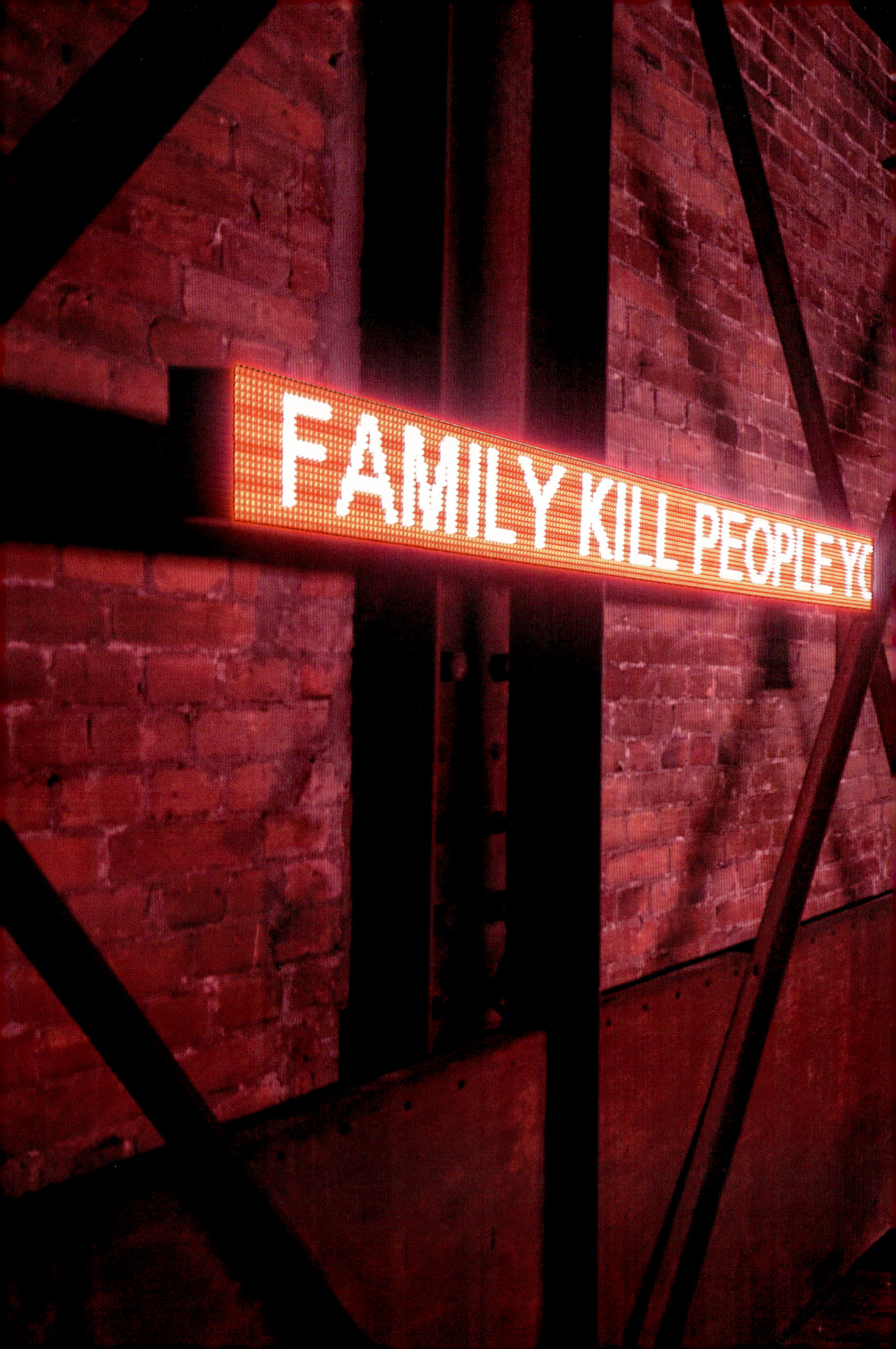
FAMILY KILL PEOPLE YO

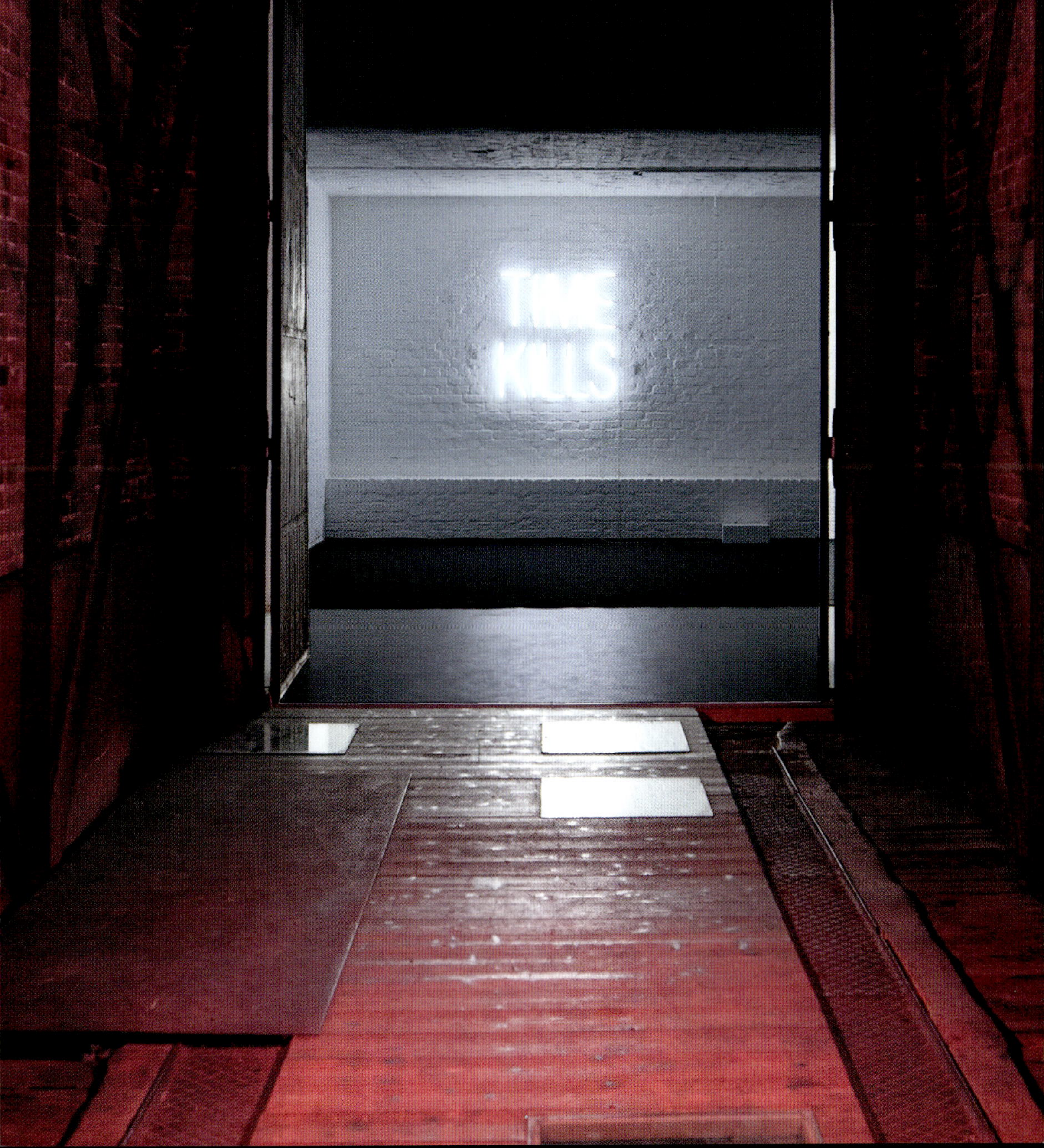
TIME
KILLS

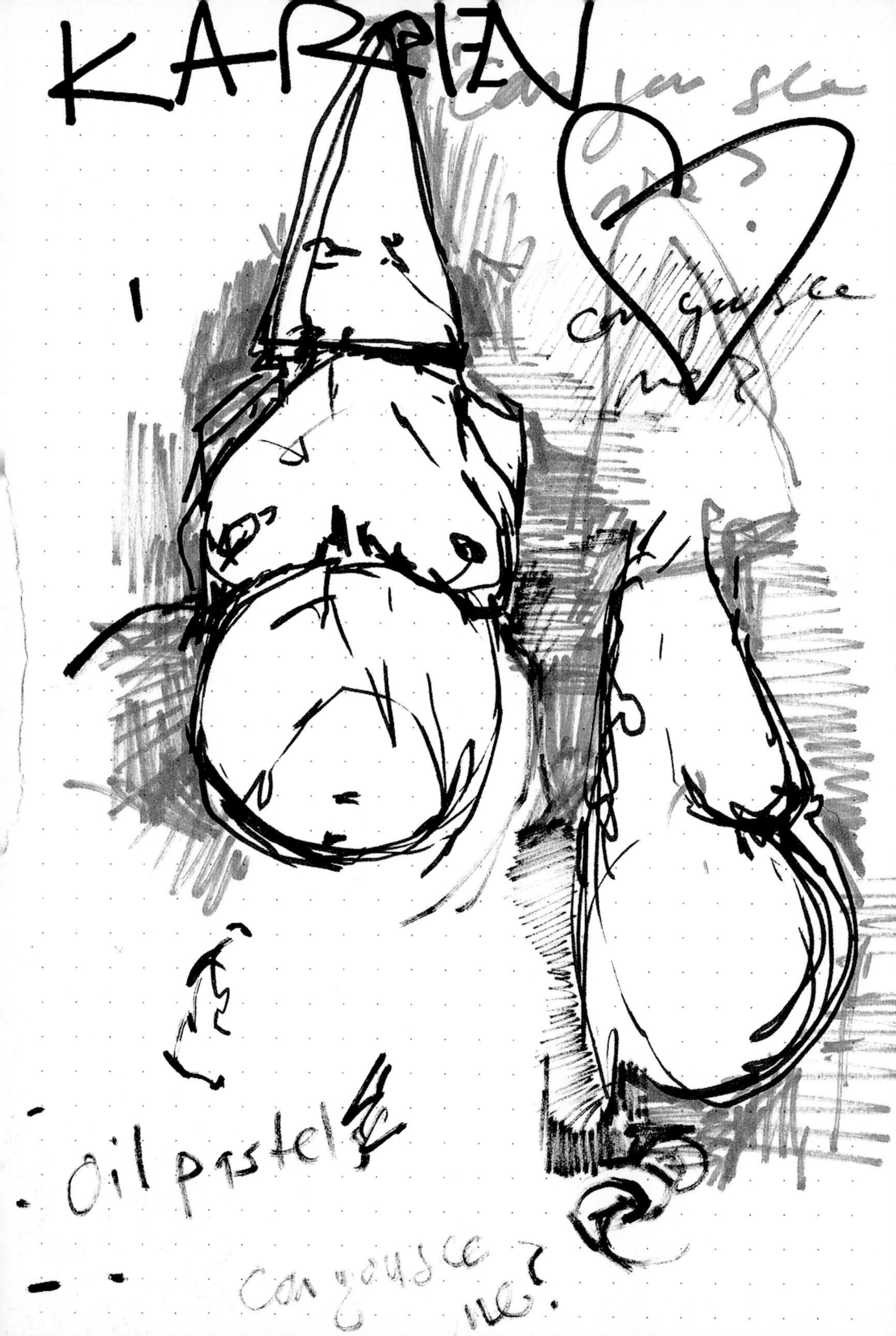

KAREN
can you see me?
can you see me?
can you see me?
Oil pastels
can you see me?

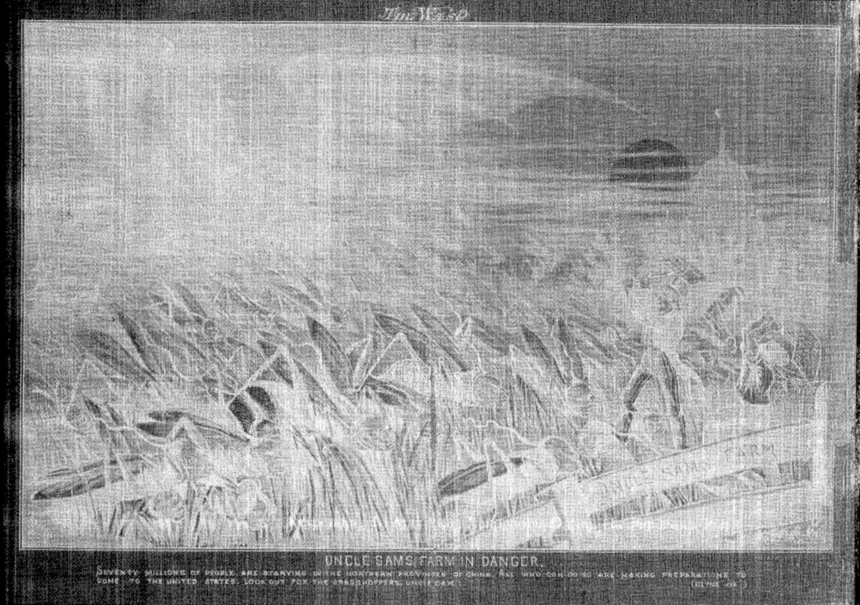

between the traditional ways of living and the now-dominant, hegemonic social order and values, inevitably contribute to the spread and response to this pandemic.

The biological concept of "foreign bodies" has been appropriated by right-wing politicians and conservative media to describe immigrants, portraying them as a disease that could infect the essentialist, monocultural social body defined by populist and nationalist rhetorics. We are in a moment when such mechanisms of hatred and exclusionary politics are gaining more traction. Fear of agents of difference has always found its base in dehumanizing the body of the Other, and the Other is perpetually fabricated.

Museums, curators, and other members of the art world must respond thoughtfully and creatively to help wider communities understand how systemic racism, the construction of racial prejudice, and cultural differences connect to fear, power, and violence. To reappropriate biological metaphors that have been much misused, the museum and the art field should welcome "foreign bodies" and let them actively

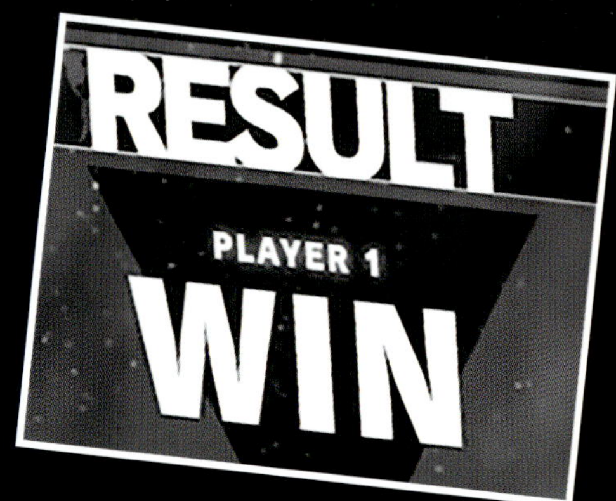

Past Present Tense

TEXT Mostly white people come to Berlin. Most likely more people who can afford it from good socioeconomic backgrounds, probably rather middle class and above, it's not like there very poor come here, in comparison to other cities it is still affordable. That is why it is still attractive.

3.20 – 4.27 It is a positive thing to see in Germany that we have discourse and critique that Germany is diverse and has cultural plurality in society and it is an important element in German society. And that we promote cultural diversity, which is correct and important. The question is then, is this cultural diversity showing itself in society and in institutions and will it name racism and try to develop and promote non- discrimination or be a branding image for the "beautiful" diverse Germany without changing pre-existing power structures that equal out "germans" and whiteness"

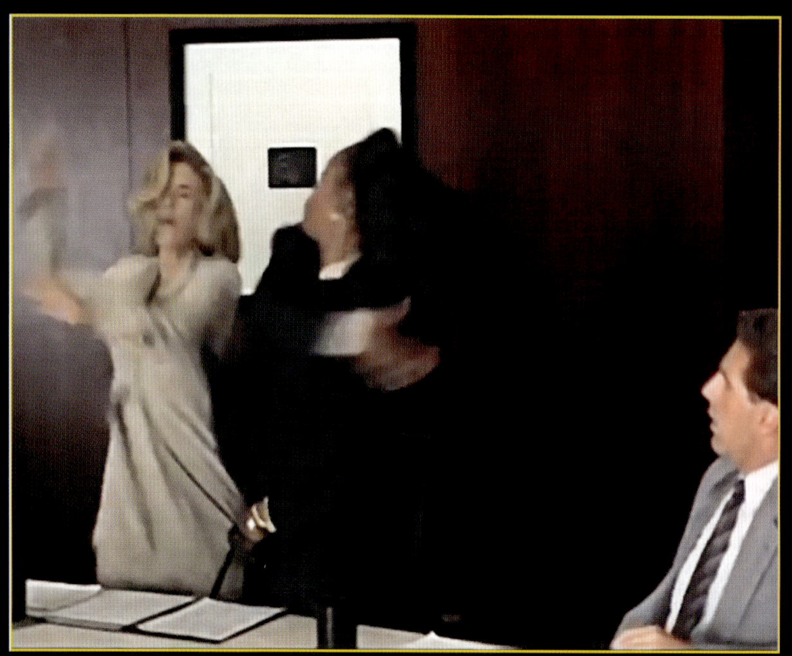

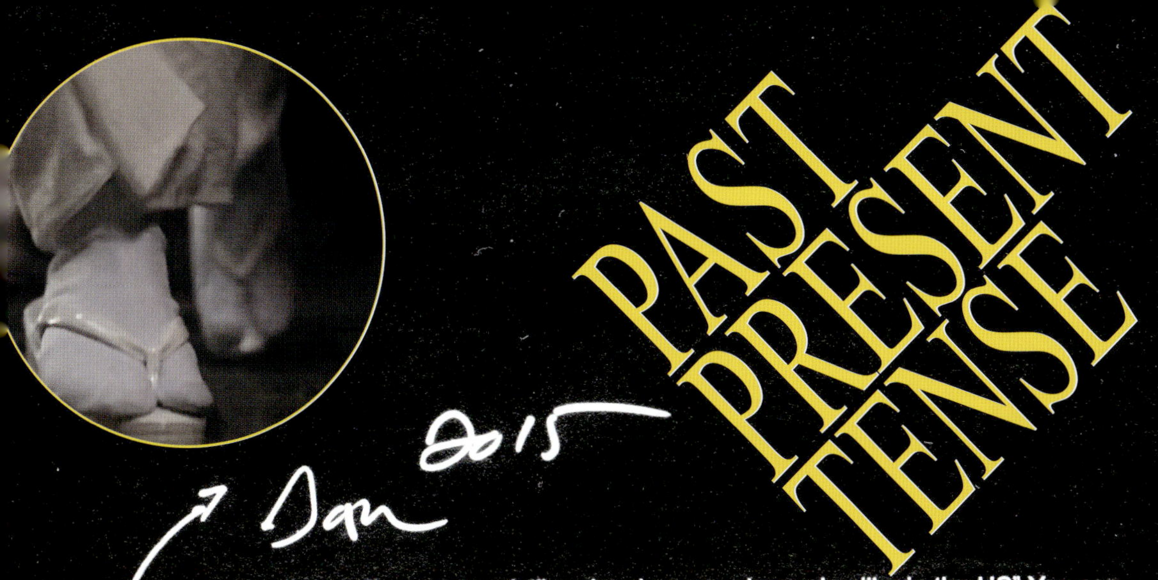

you can easily say "I am not racist" racism is somewhere else like in the US" You can get upset about it and even pretend to be "anti-racist" If you always see racism somewhere else and you don't deal with it yourself then there will be no groundbreaking changes in society.

10.27 – 11.03 But everyone, everyone has the possibility to know, why the Turkish came to Germany, the Vietnamese in the DDR or the Africans, or why the American GIs in West Germany. There must be some educational resistance when someone doesn't know anything. That is somehow stupid. The people have the possibility to inform themselves but they don't take any of these opportunities.

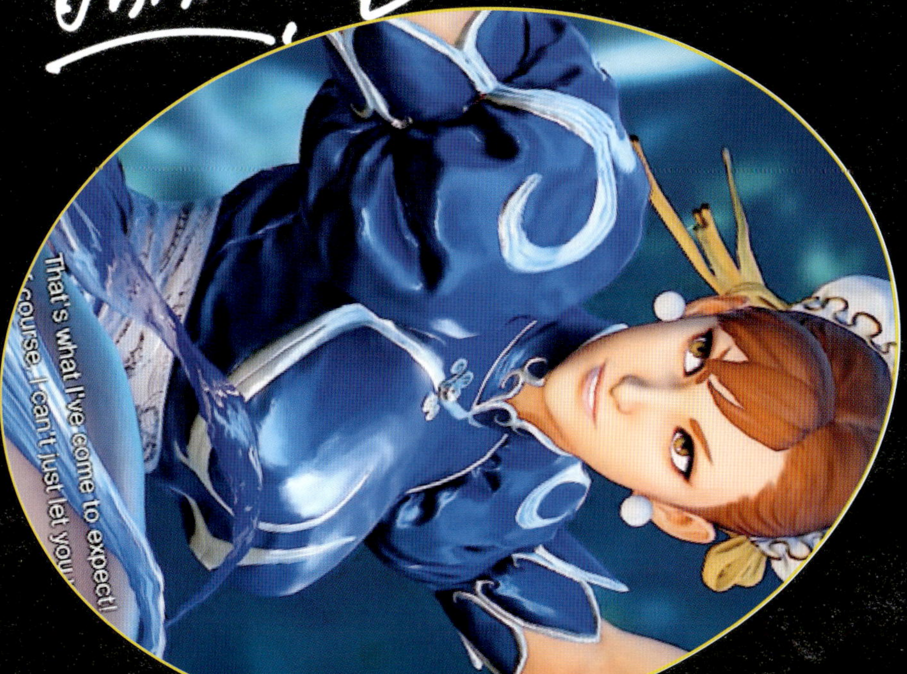

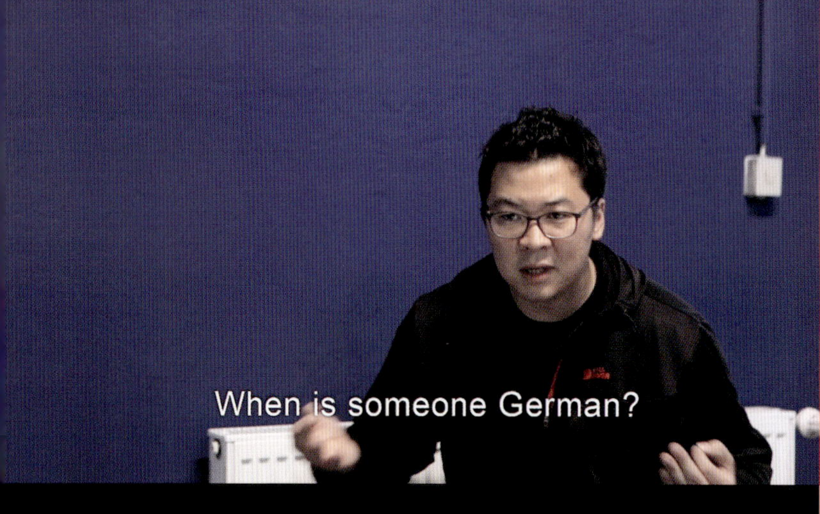
When is someone German?

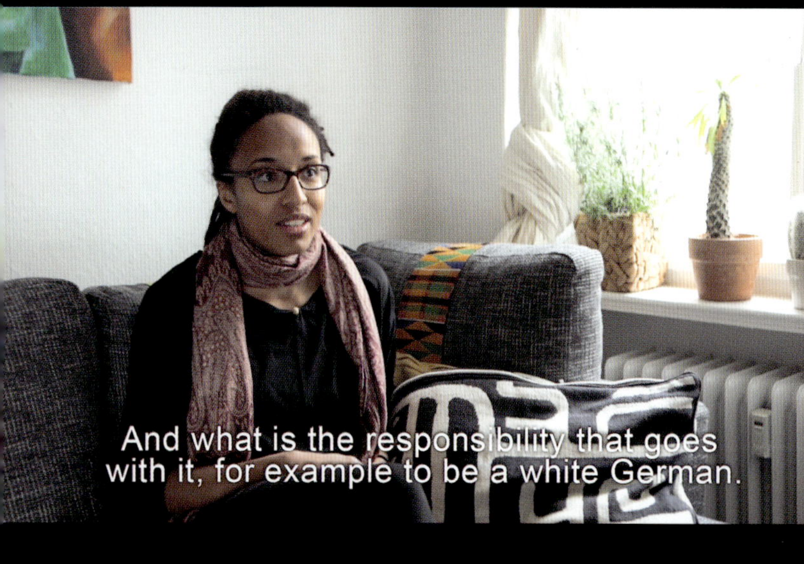
And what is the responsibility that goes
with it, for example to be a white German.

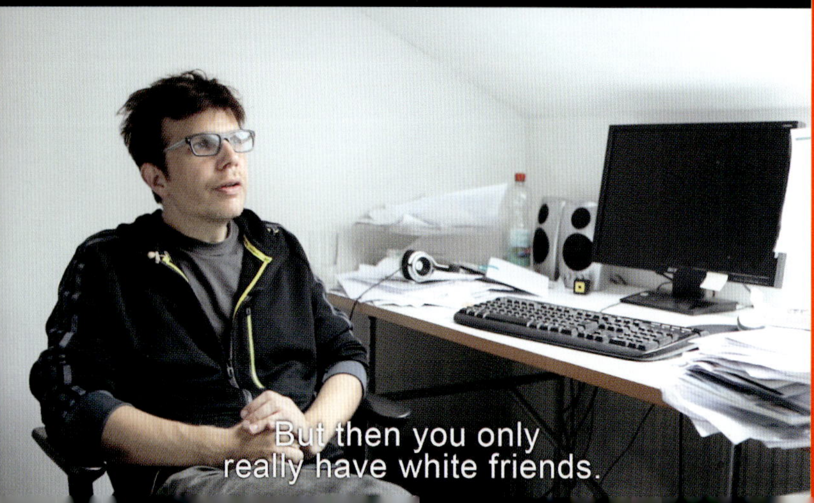
But then you only
really have white friends.

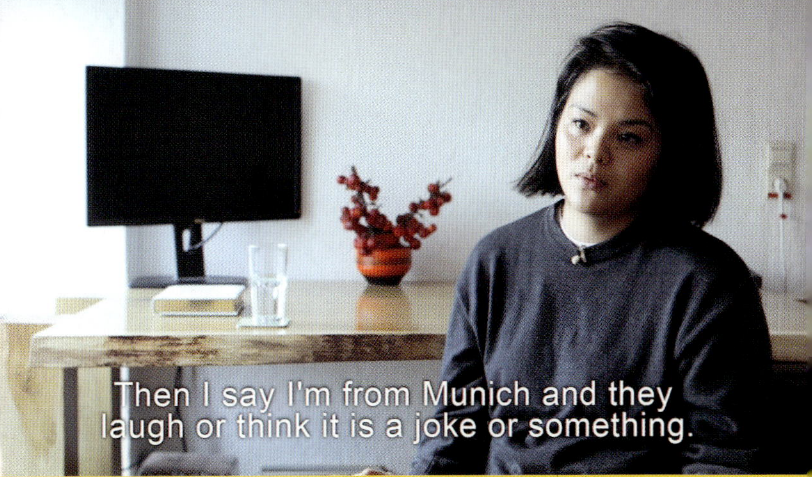
Then I say I'm from Munich and they laugh or think it is a joke or something.

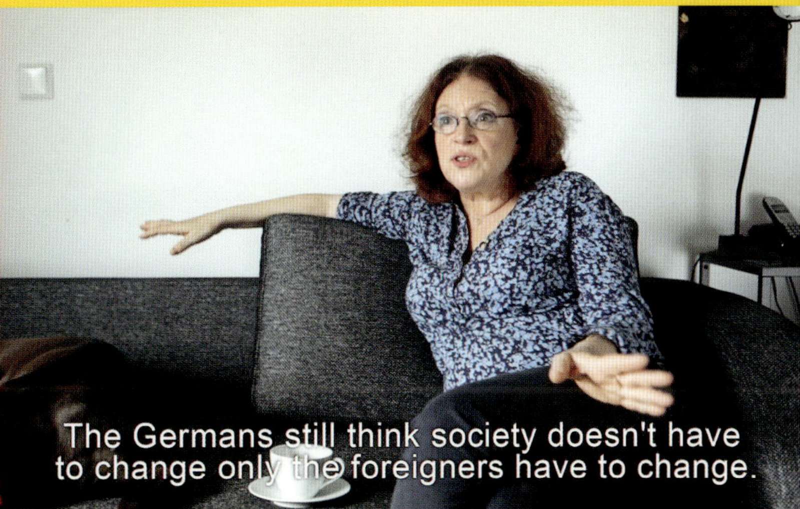
The Germans still think society doesn't have to change only the foreigners have to change.

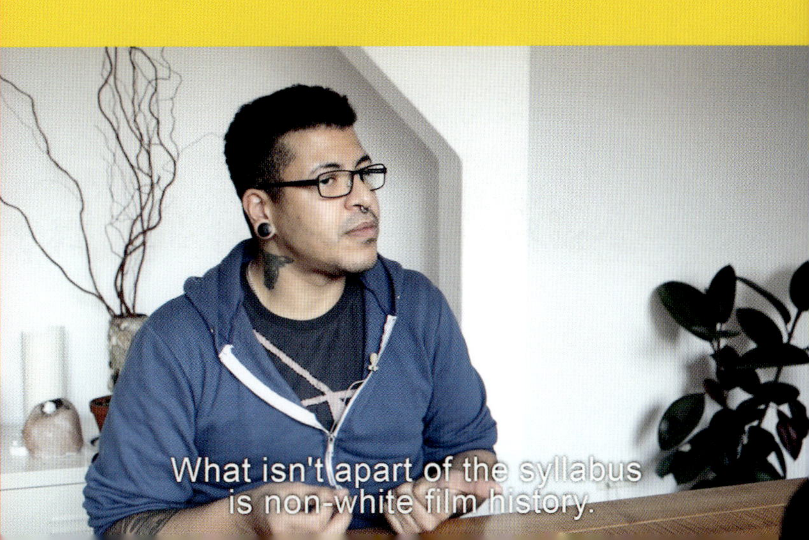
What isn't apart of the syllabus is non-white film history.

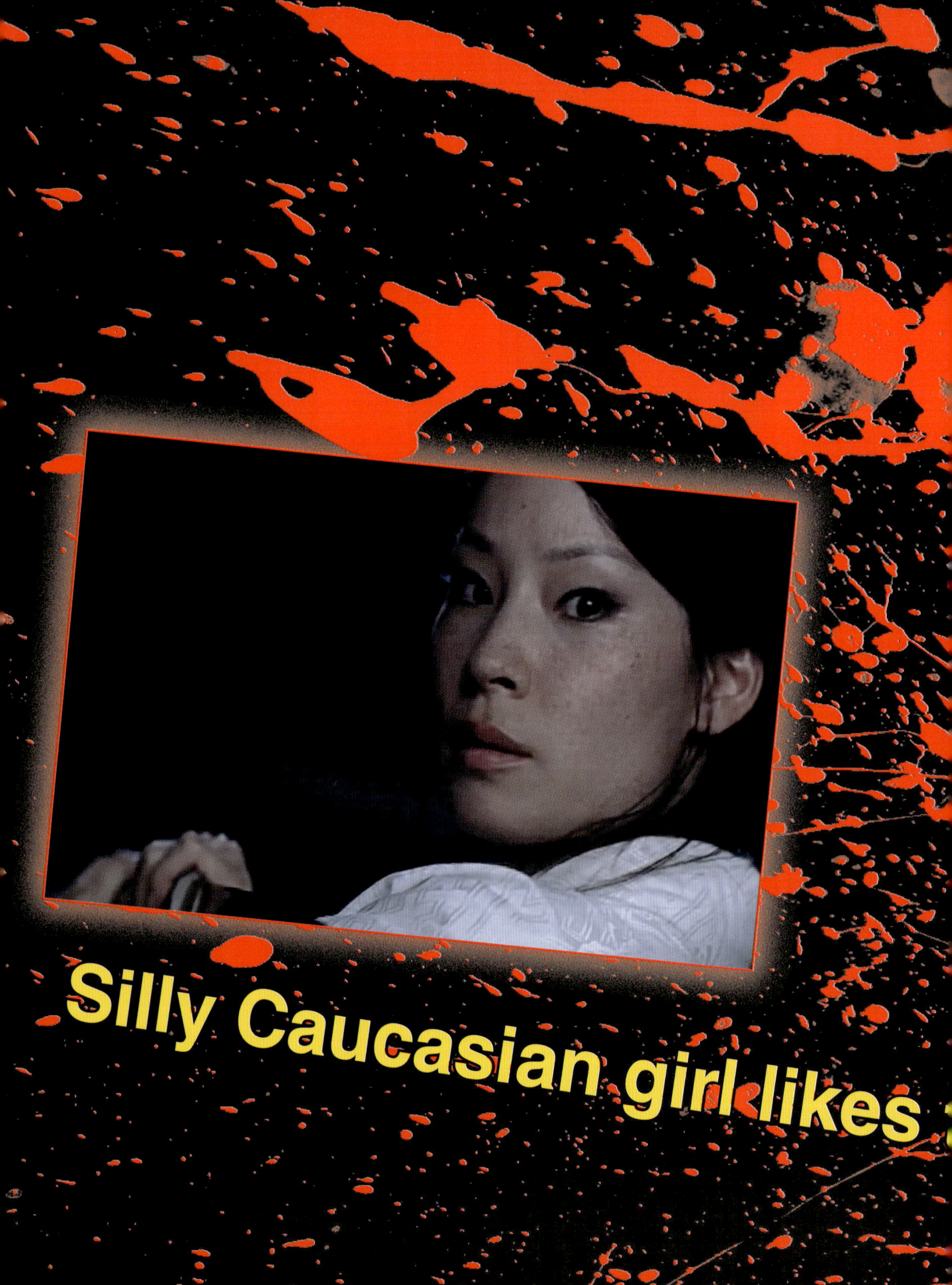
Silly Caucasian girl likes

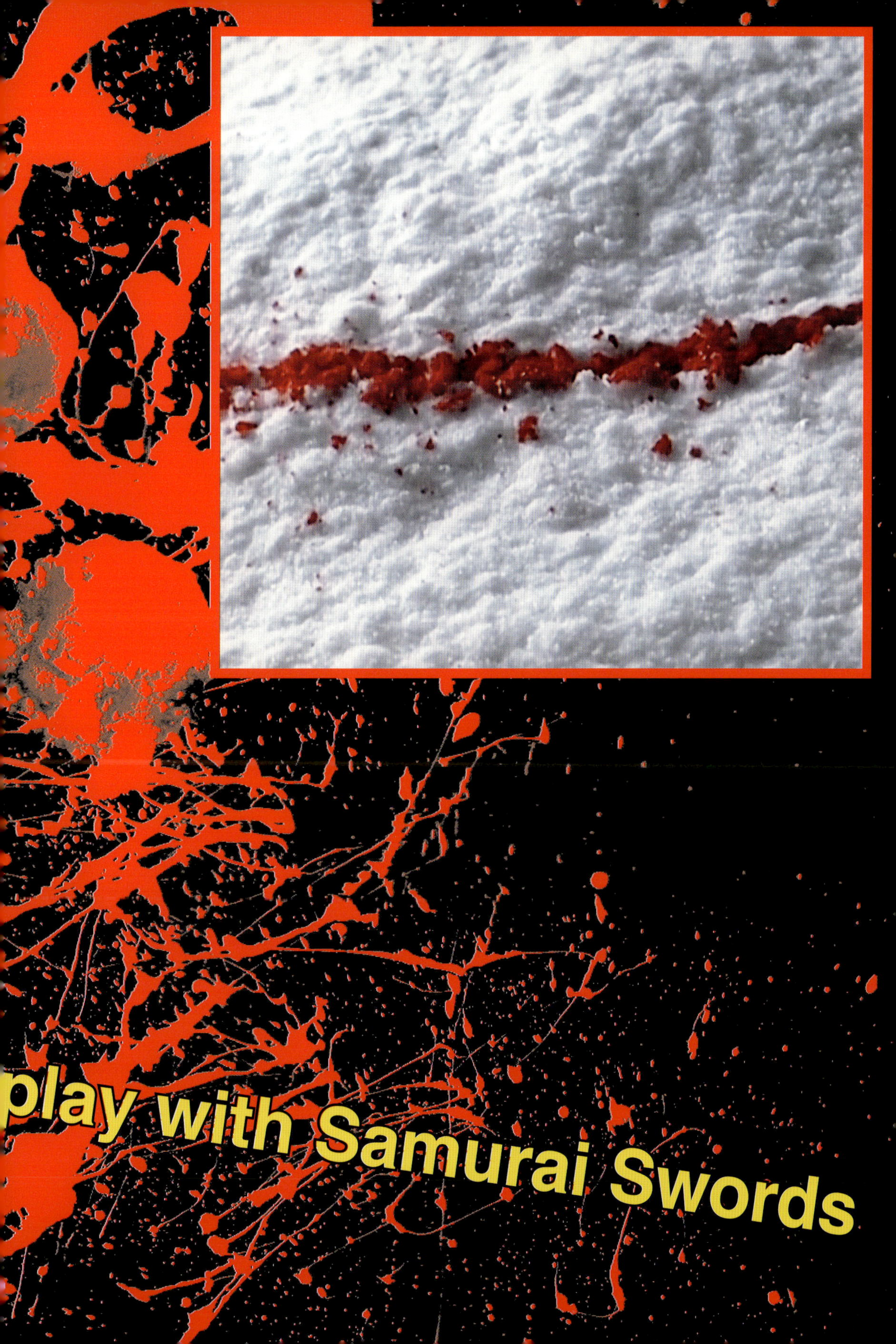

play with Samurai Swords

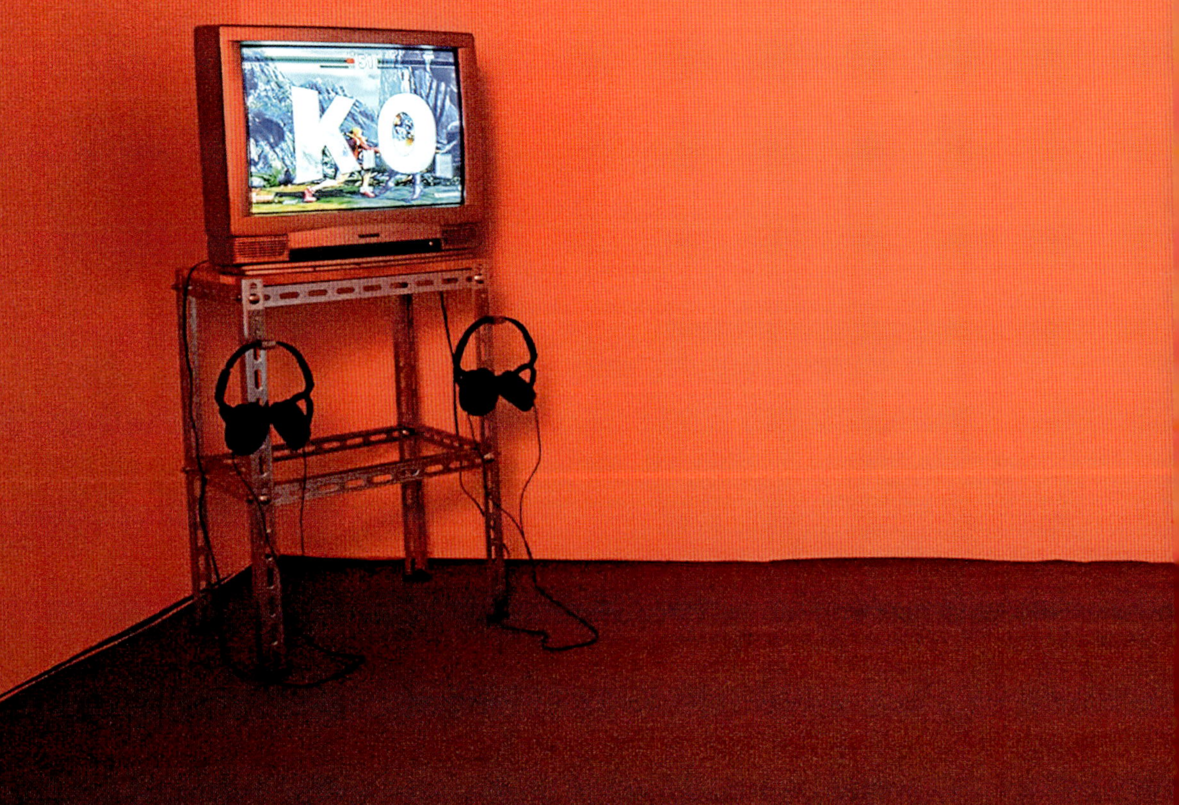

society and in institutions and will it nar
non- discrimination or be a branding im
without changing pre-existing SLUT str
SLUT OMG "
KO

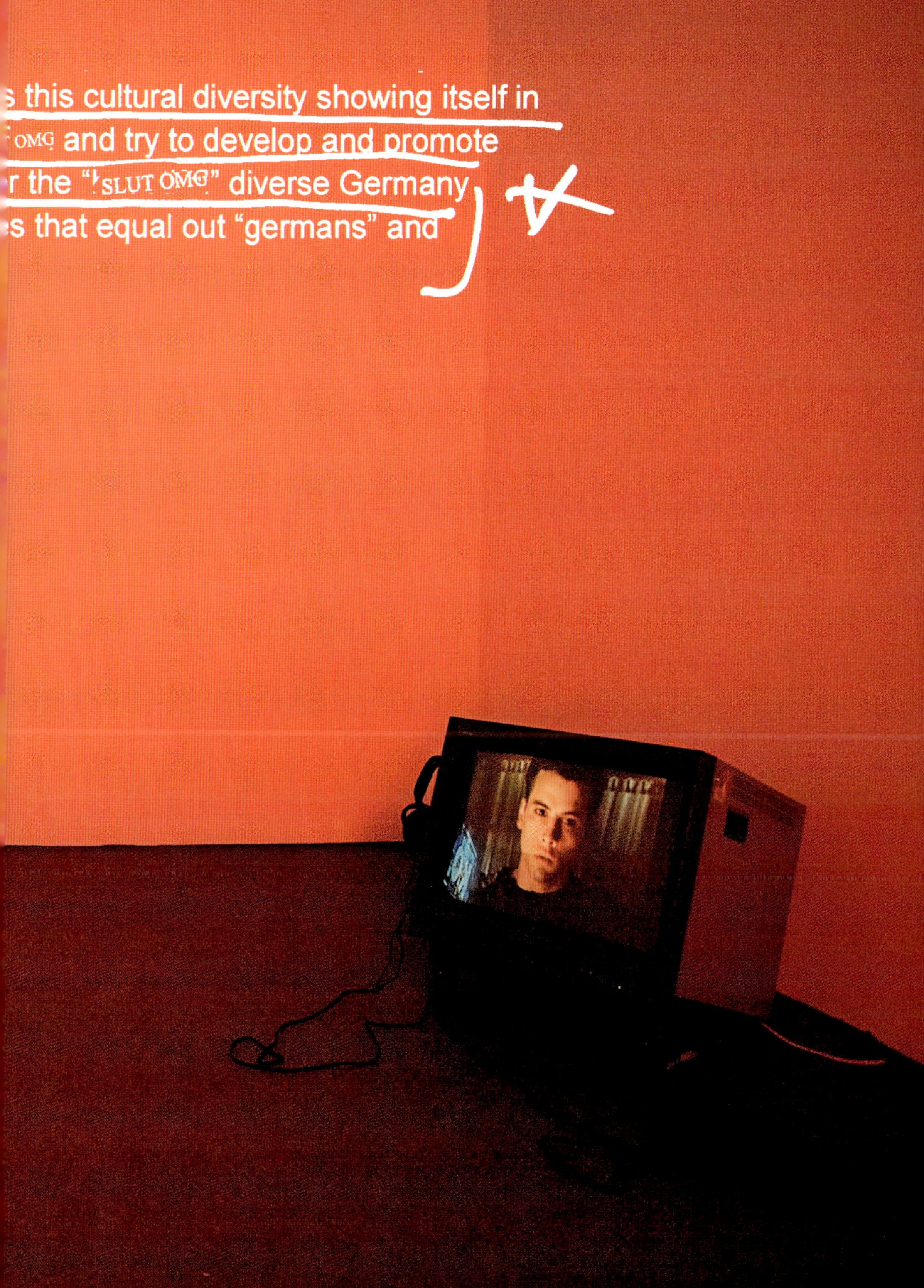
s this cultural diversity showing itself in
OMG and try to develop and promote
r the "SLUT OMG" diverse Germany
s that equal out "germans" and

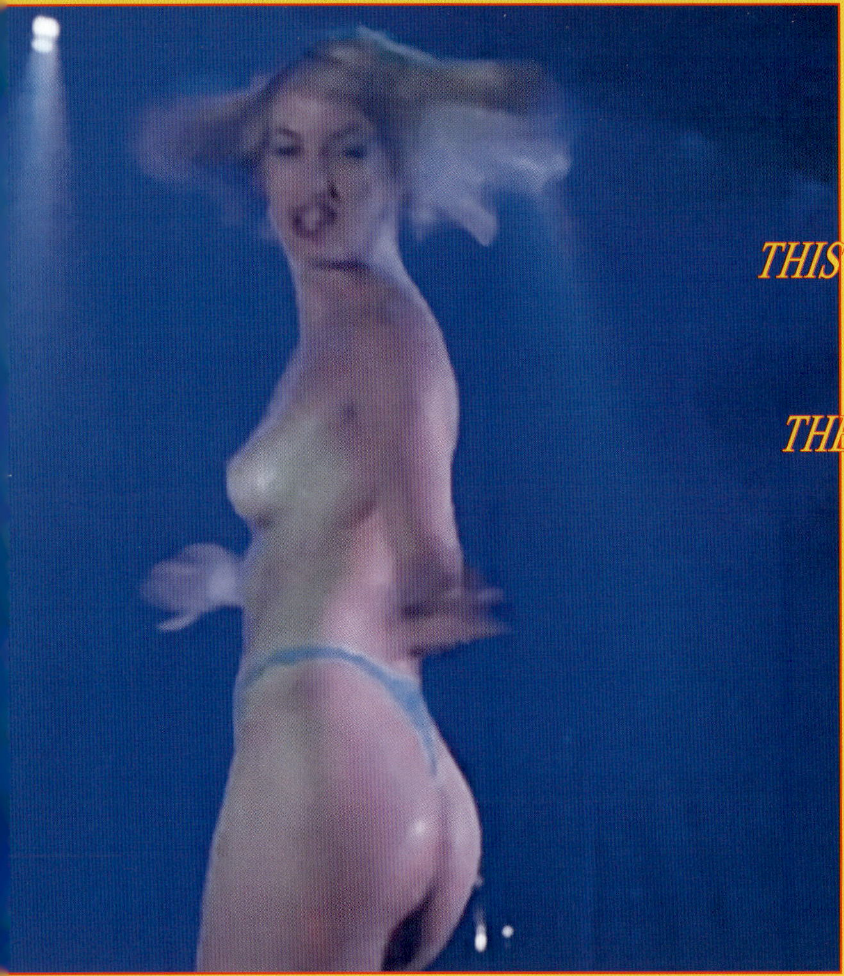

F OMG WTF A SLUT OMG W

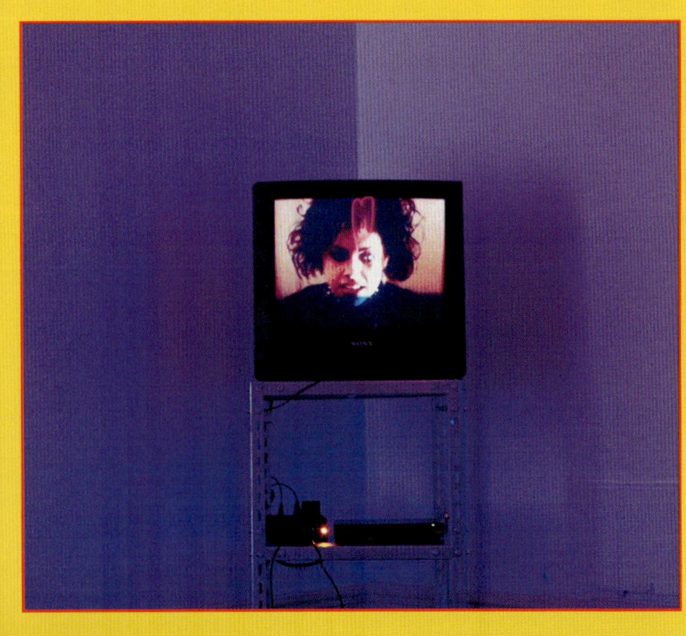

Kill
HIM
!

WTF
WTF WTF
WTF

Kill
HIM
!

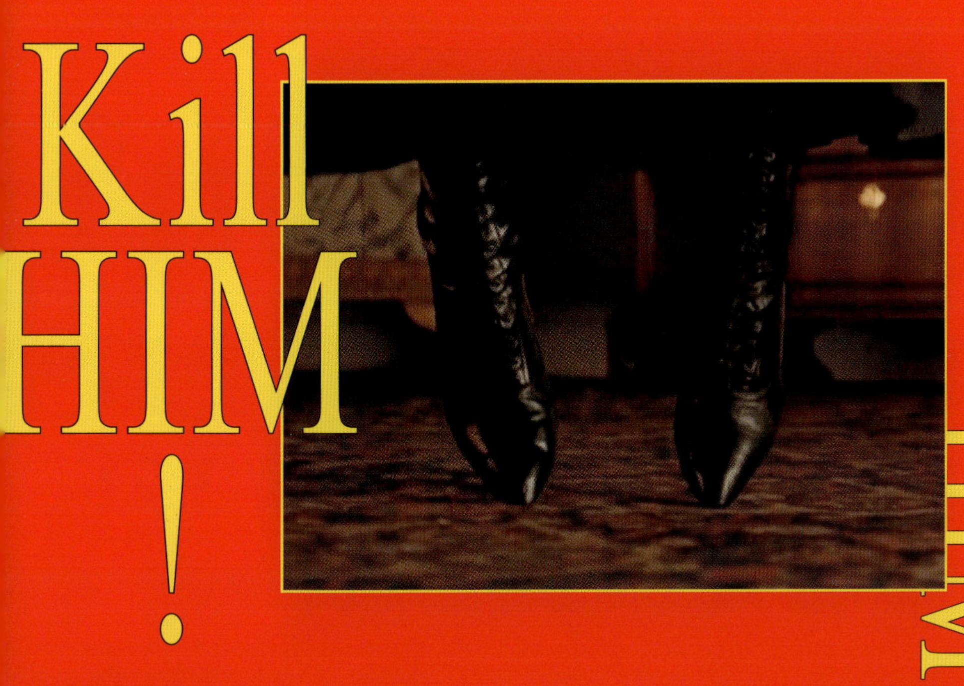

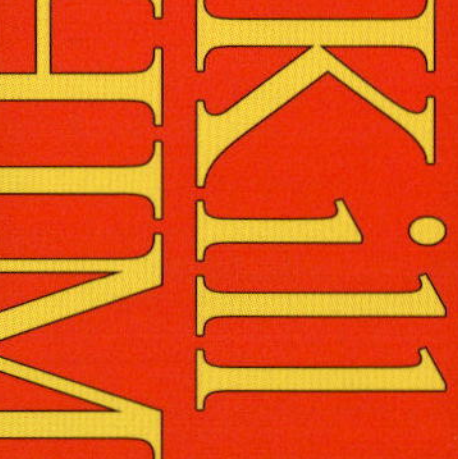

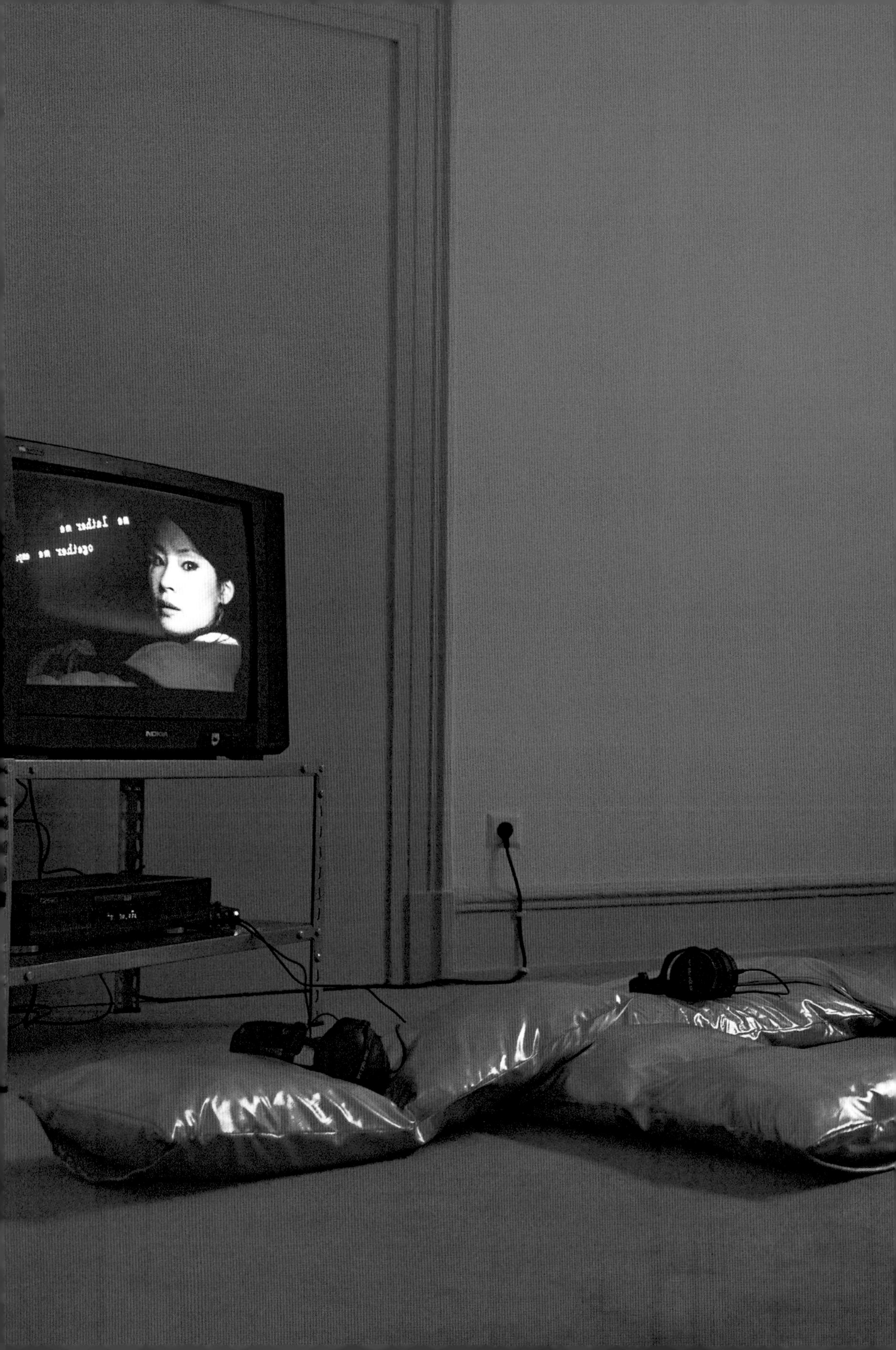

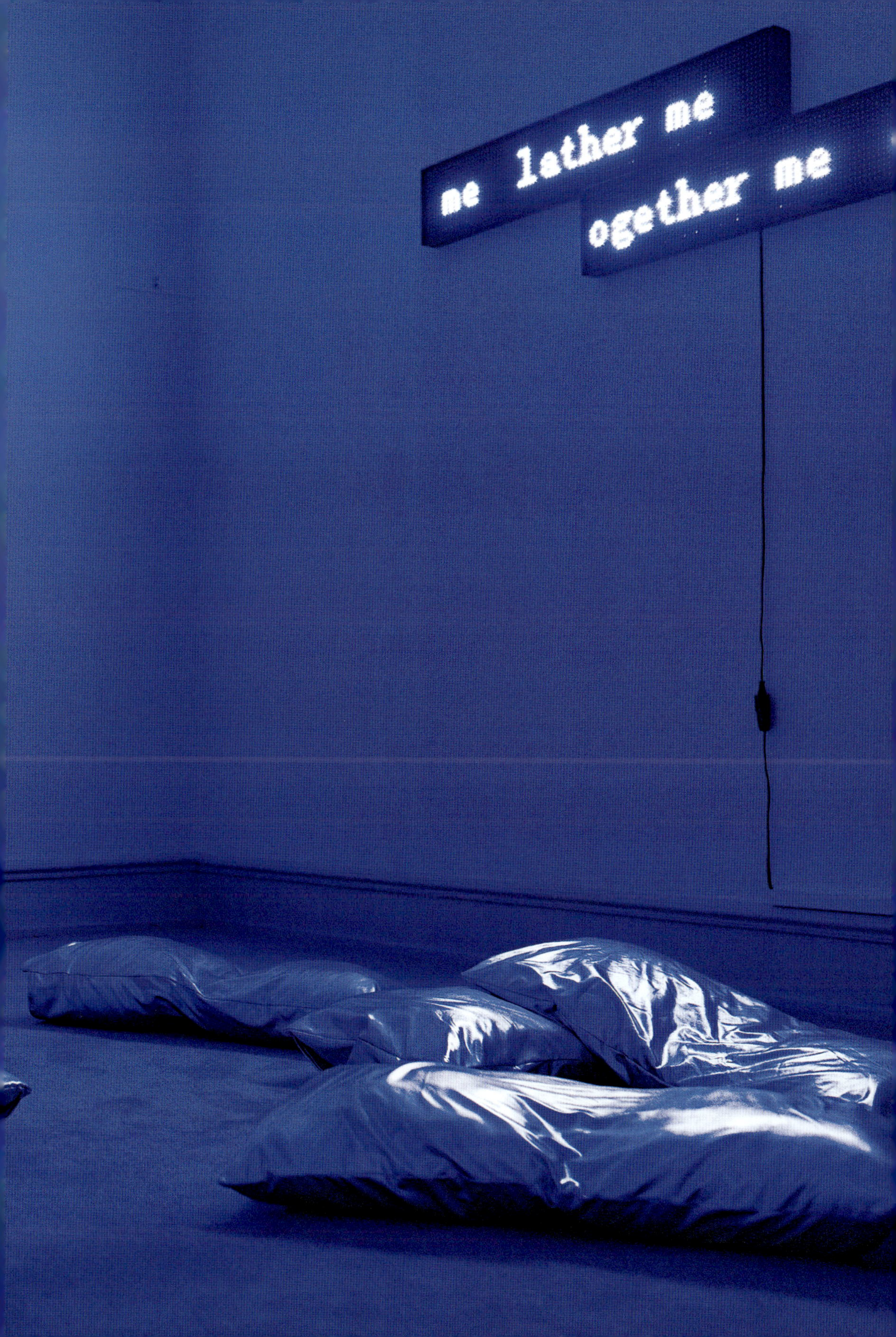
me   lather me
ogether me

Fear,
Shame,
Bl 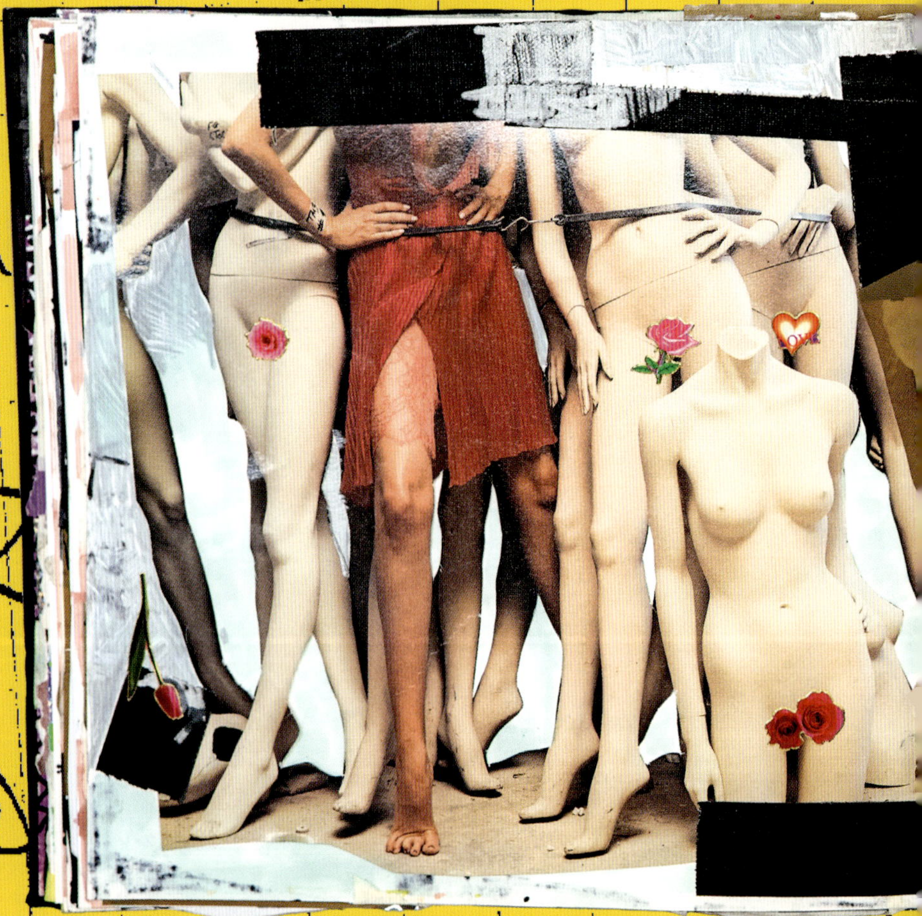
R
A
Sei,
Culti

TINA / BERNADINE - Angela Bassett
hun li / ⊕ - Ren Ishii → Lucy Liu
...es for Race
> same as John Harris's wife
"Revolt"
"Redemption"
"Final round"
The Secretary shredded

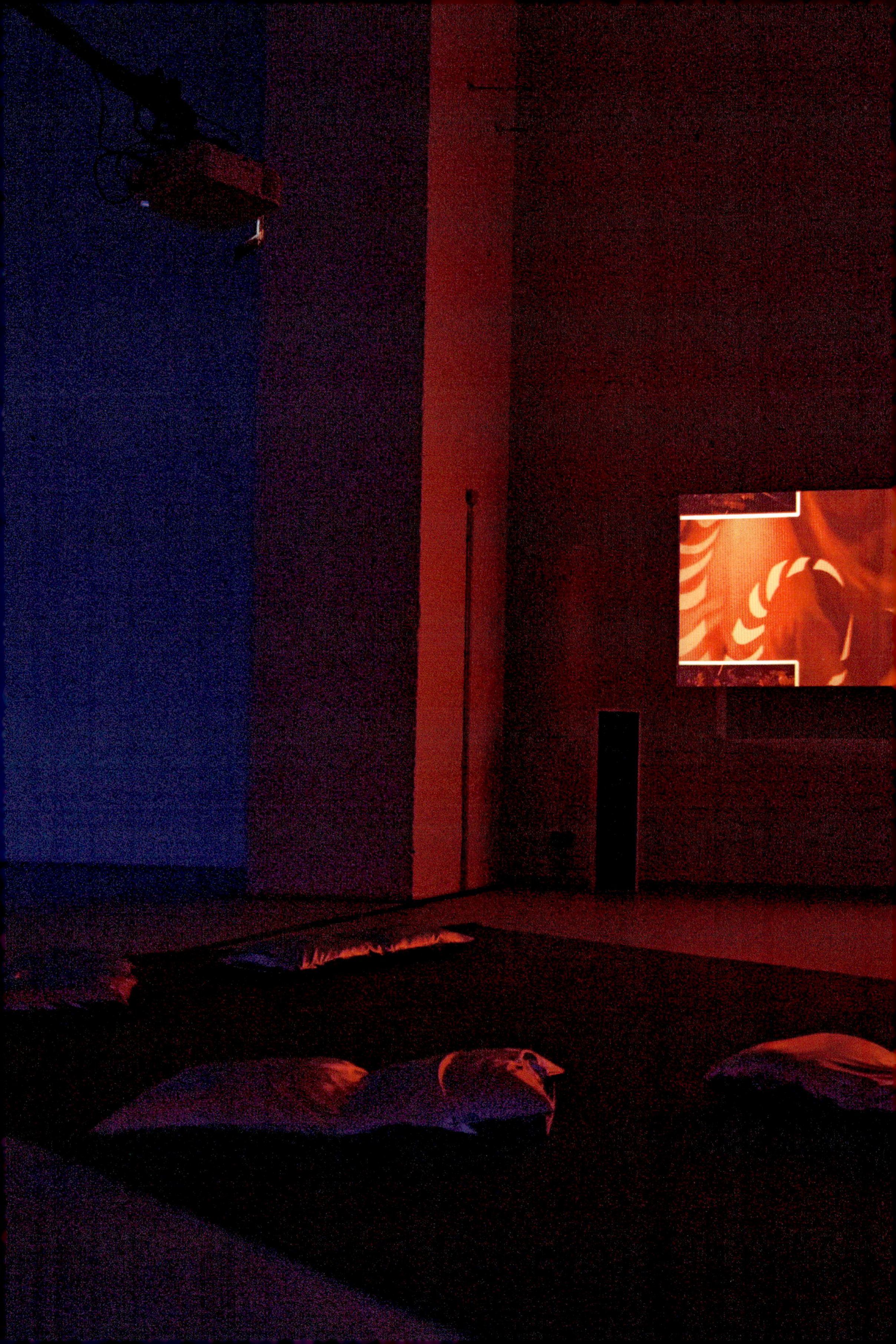

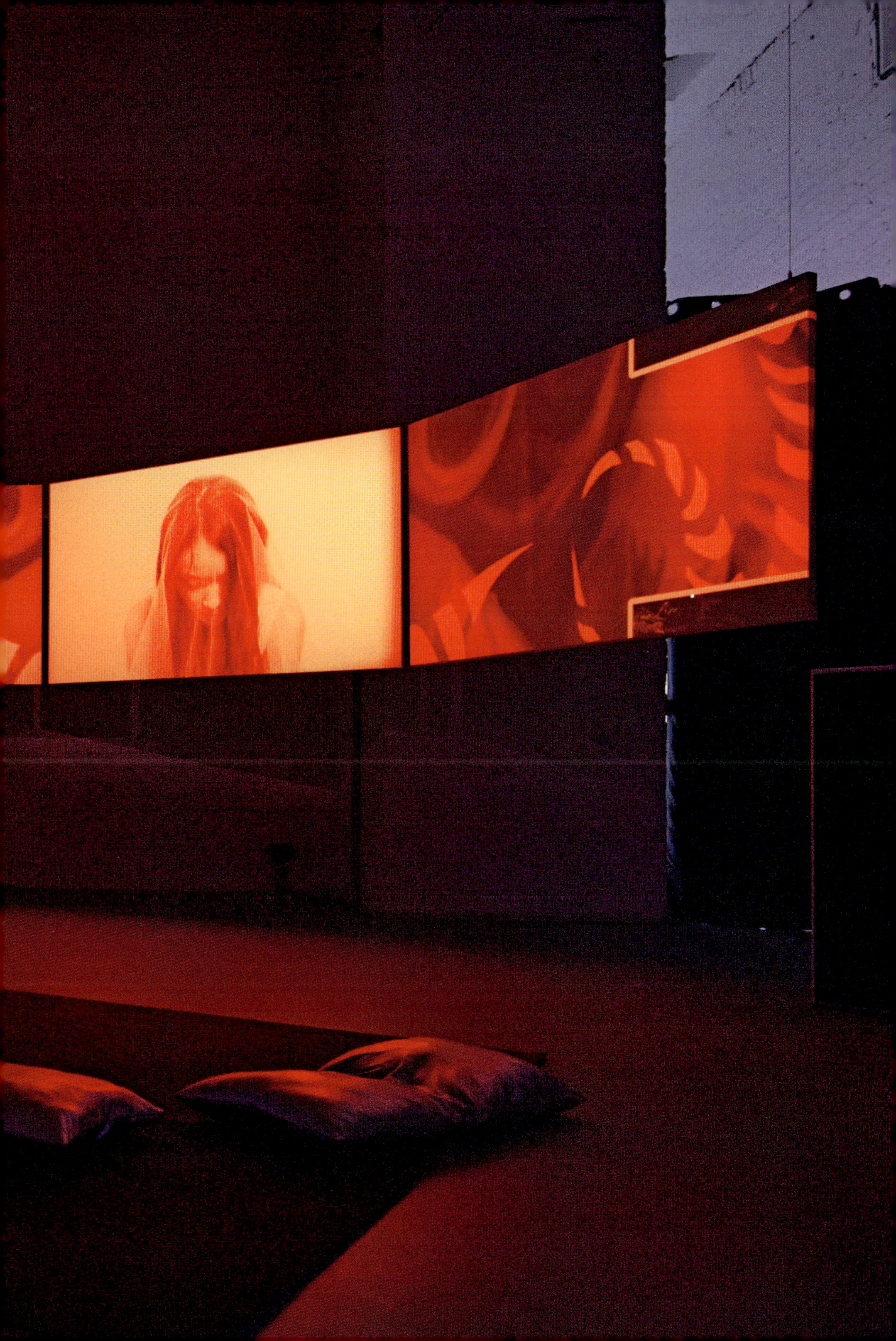

vampires rule the night

..but their numbers

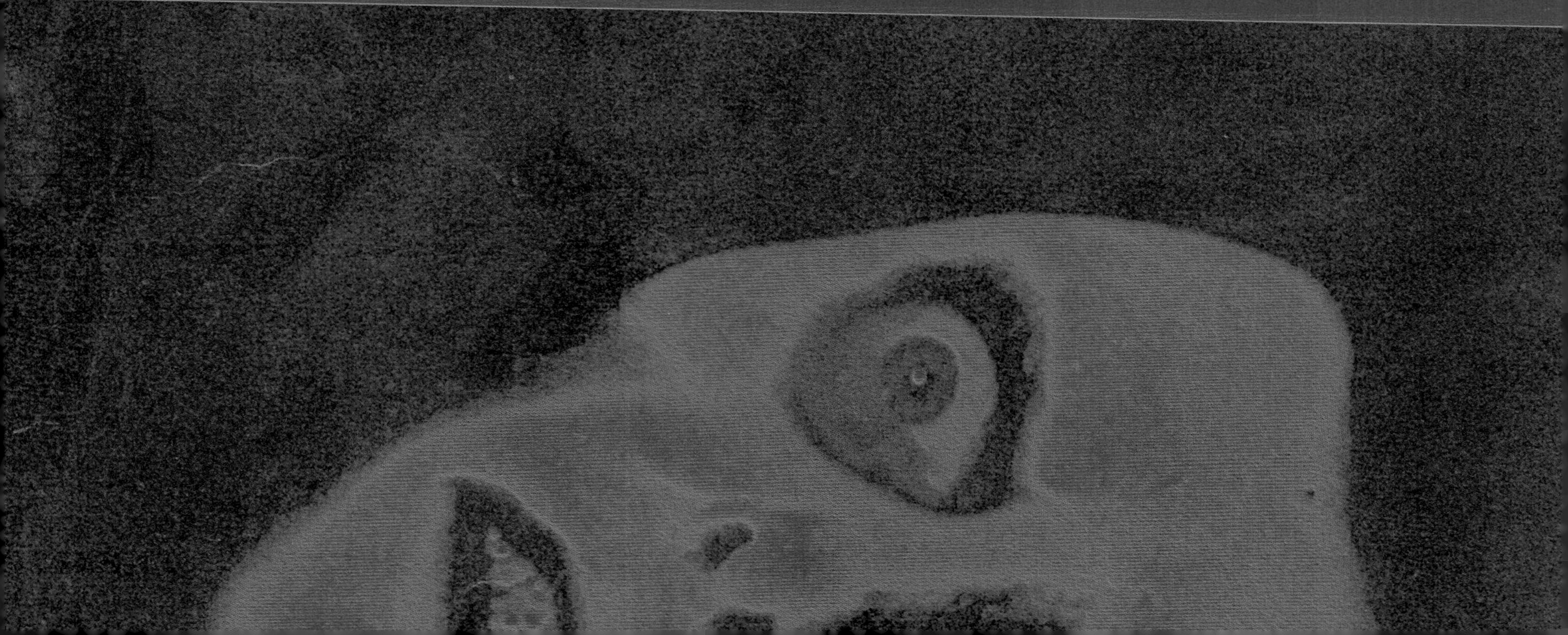

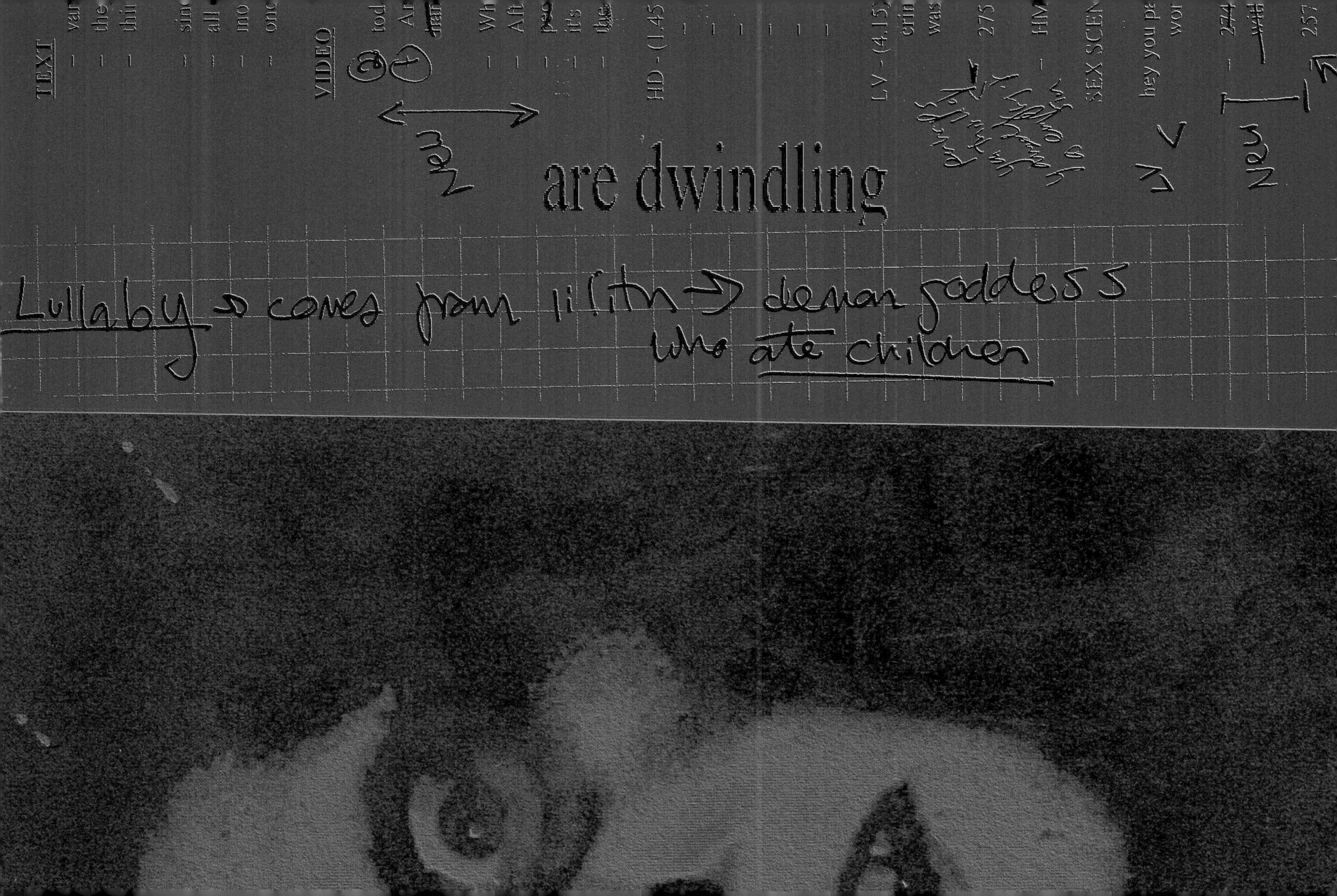

TEXT
var
the
thi
sin
all
mo
onc
VIDEO
tod
An
tran
Wh
Aft
pe
it's
the
HD - (1.45
LV - (4.15)
crin
was
275
HM
SEX SCEN
hey you pa
wor
274
with
257
New
are dwindling
Lullaby → comes from lilith → demon goddess who ate children
LV
New

将身缢死二十年
并无一人来替
苦海无涯，难挨朝，怎度夕
今日无亏痴心妇、烈心女
将奴身来替
笑今日苦尽甘来
讨替代，莫迟疑！讨替代，莫迟疑！

I died 20 years
No one substitutes me
The pain is endless, I cannot go through even the daytime, how can I live in the night
Thanks to the strong-minded woman who would substitute me
I laughed for the end of my pain
【Don't hesitate to find a substitute!】 x2

（寻死妇女的丈夫发现她上吊，后悔不已。）
The woman's husband found she killed herself and is regret.)

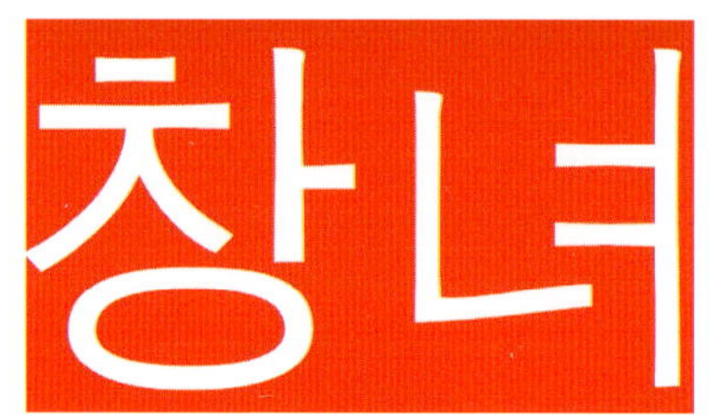

将身缢死二十年
并无一人来替
苦海无涯，难挨朝，怎度夕
今日无亏痴心妇、烈心女
将奴身来替
笑今日苦尽甘来
讨替代，莫迟疑！讨替代，莫迟疑！

I died 20 years
No one substitutes me
The pain is endless, I cannot go through even the daytime, how can I live in the night
Thanks to the strong-minded woman who would substitute me
I laughed for the end of my pain
【Don't hesitate to find a substitute!】 x2

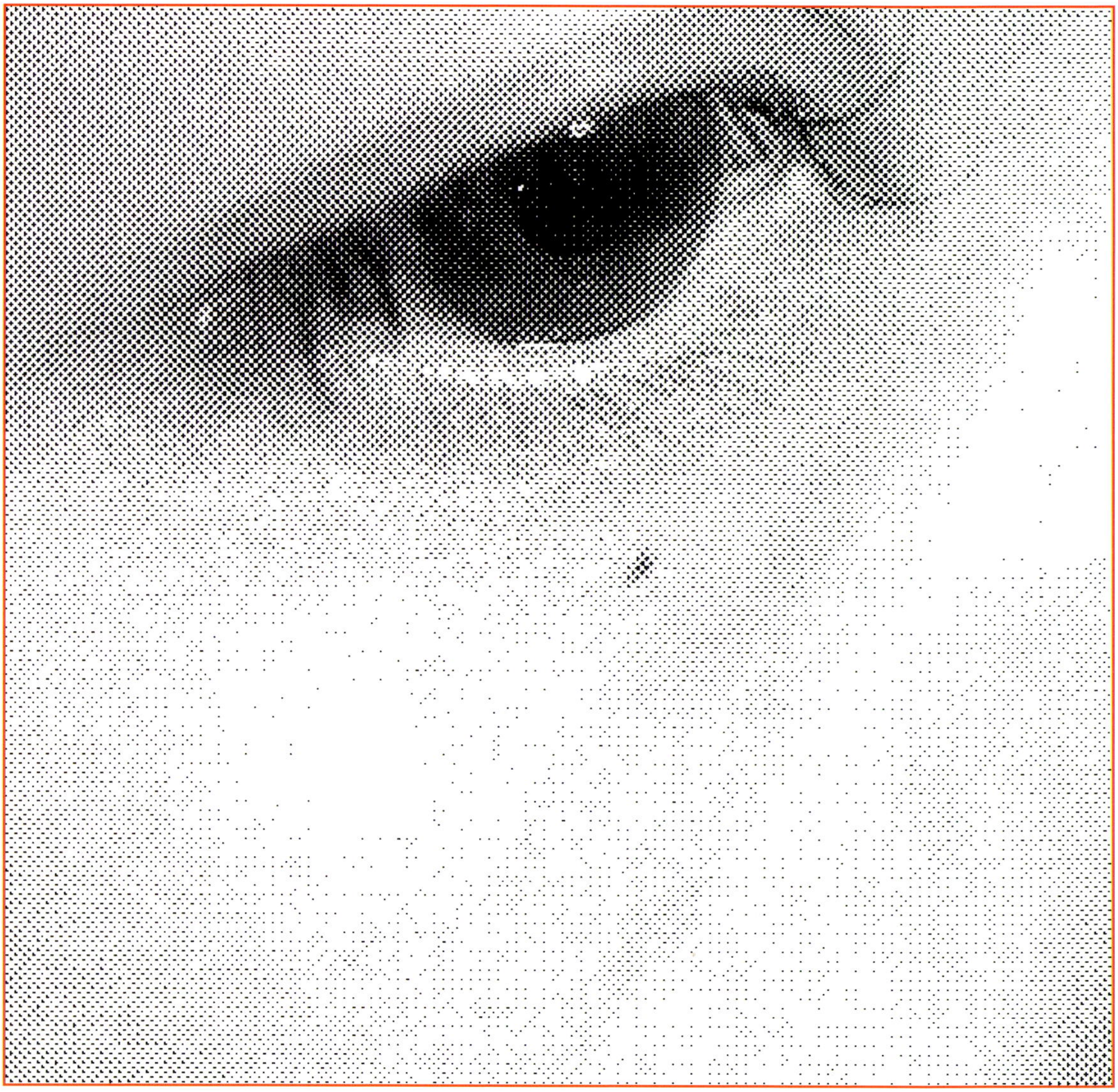

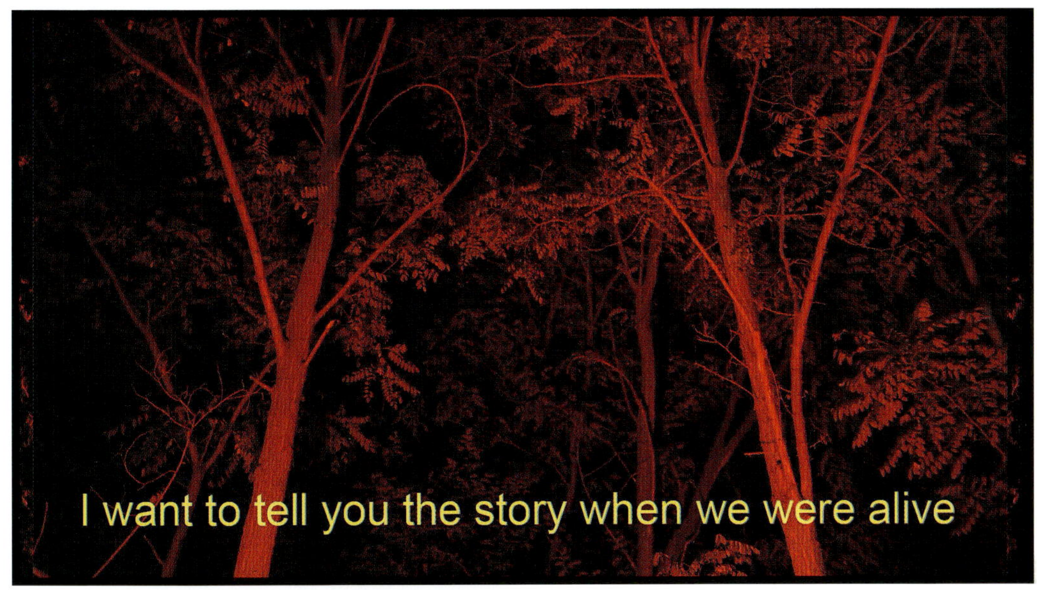

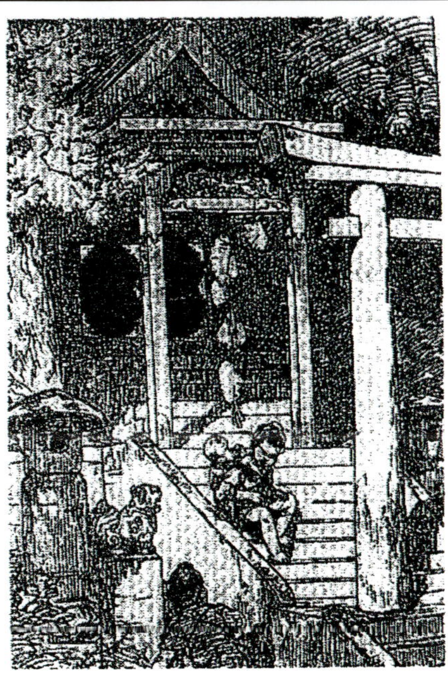

Nursemaids were banned from houses and farms. They usually stayed in the shrine yard. Other children also played there. Drawing by Felix Regamey, published in *Promenades Japonaises: Tokio-Nikko* (1880), cited in *Bakumatsu Meiji no Seikatsu Fukei [Japanese Life and Landscape in the19th Century]* edited by Isawo Suto (1995: 30).

It's hard to stay with a baby all day.
I have no place to avoid rain and wind.
If i stand under somebody's eaves,
I'm told "Go away, go there, not there, here."
They don't like me. They want to get rid of me.
This is how I spend days while serving as a nursemaid.

[Tochigi pref./ MKH:16]

It must have been very sad for a young person that everybody wanted her to stay away. A nursemaid expresses her feelings in a song with the image of mountains in

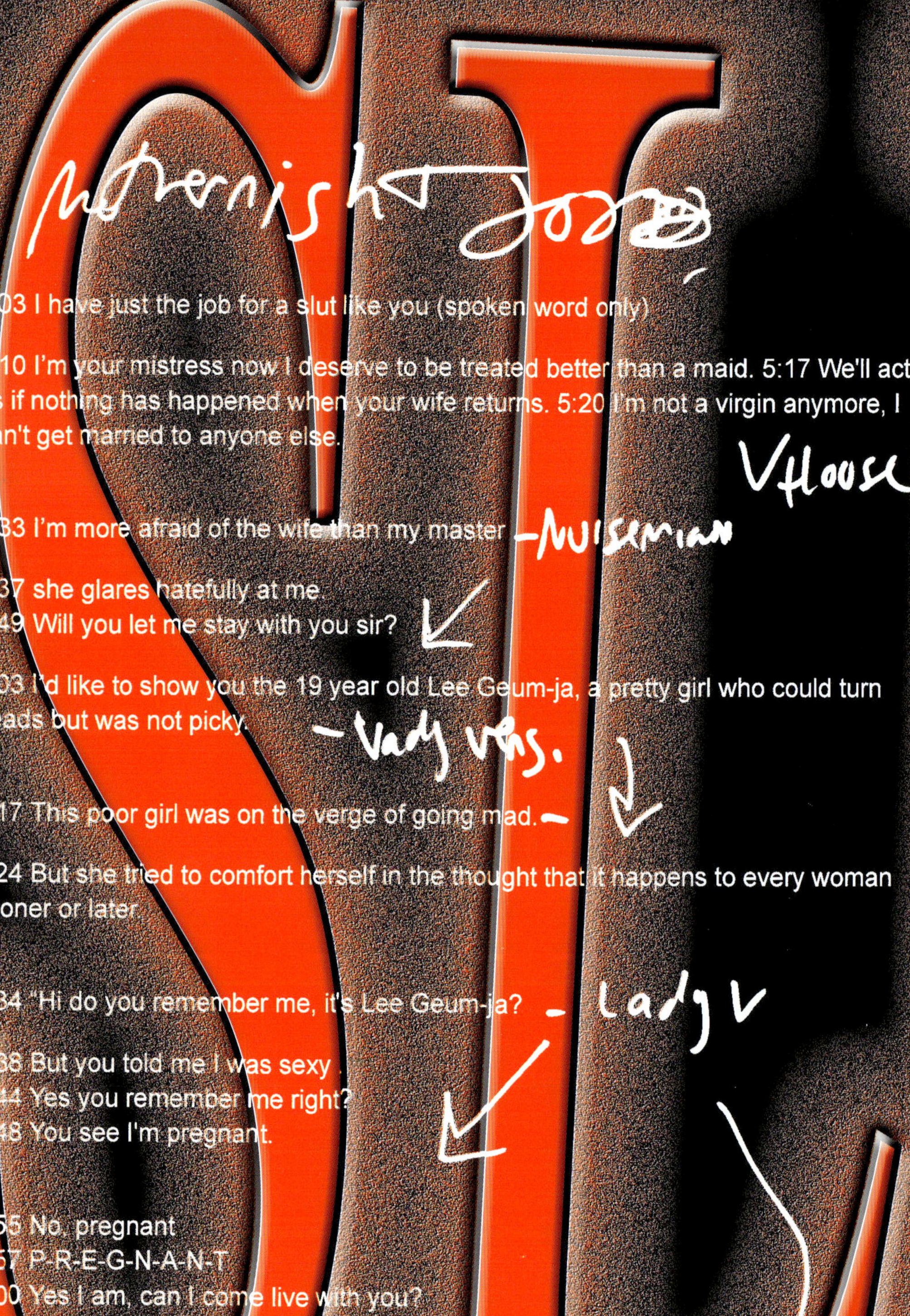
midnight joan

5:03 I have just the job for a slut like you (spoken word only)

5:10 I'm your mistress now I deserve to be treated better than a maid. 5:17 We'll act as if nothing has happened when your wife returns. 5:20 I'm not a virgin anymore, I can't get married to anyone else.

whoose me

5:33 I'm more afraid of the wife than my master — nuisemian

5:37 she glares hatefully at me.
5:49 Will you let me stay with you sir?

6:03 I'd like to show you the 19 year old Lee Geum-ja, a pretty girl who could turn heads but was not picky.
— vary vns.

6:17 This poor girl was on the verge of going mad. —

6:24 But she tried to comfort herself in the thought that it happens to every woman sooner or later.

6:34 "Hi do you remember me, it's Lee Geum-ja? — lady v

6:38 But you told me I was sexy
6:44 Yes you remember me right?
6:48 You see I'm pregnant.

6:55 No. pregnant
6:57 P-R-E-G-N-A-N-T
7:00 Yes I am, can I come live with you?
7:07 I can't go to my moms and it's even worse with my dad."
7:23 He was working as an English teacher for middle class families.
7:29 He was supposed to be sterile

无辜……奴身来替

The pain is painless
How can I let an innocent woman substitute
me?

You were wrong
If your parents in law beat you, it's just
domestic issue
If you argue with your husband, it's just
about bed and house
If you argue with your neighbor, it's just
about rumor
How can you kill yourself for that
if you listen to me
kill yourself
if you listen to me,
they look at you like now they're
me
avenged woman ghost

https://www.bilibili.com/video/BV1os411G7

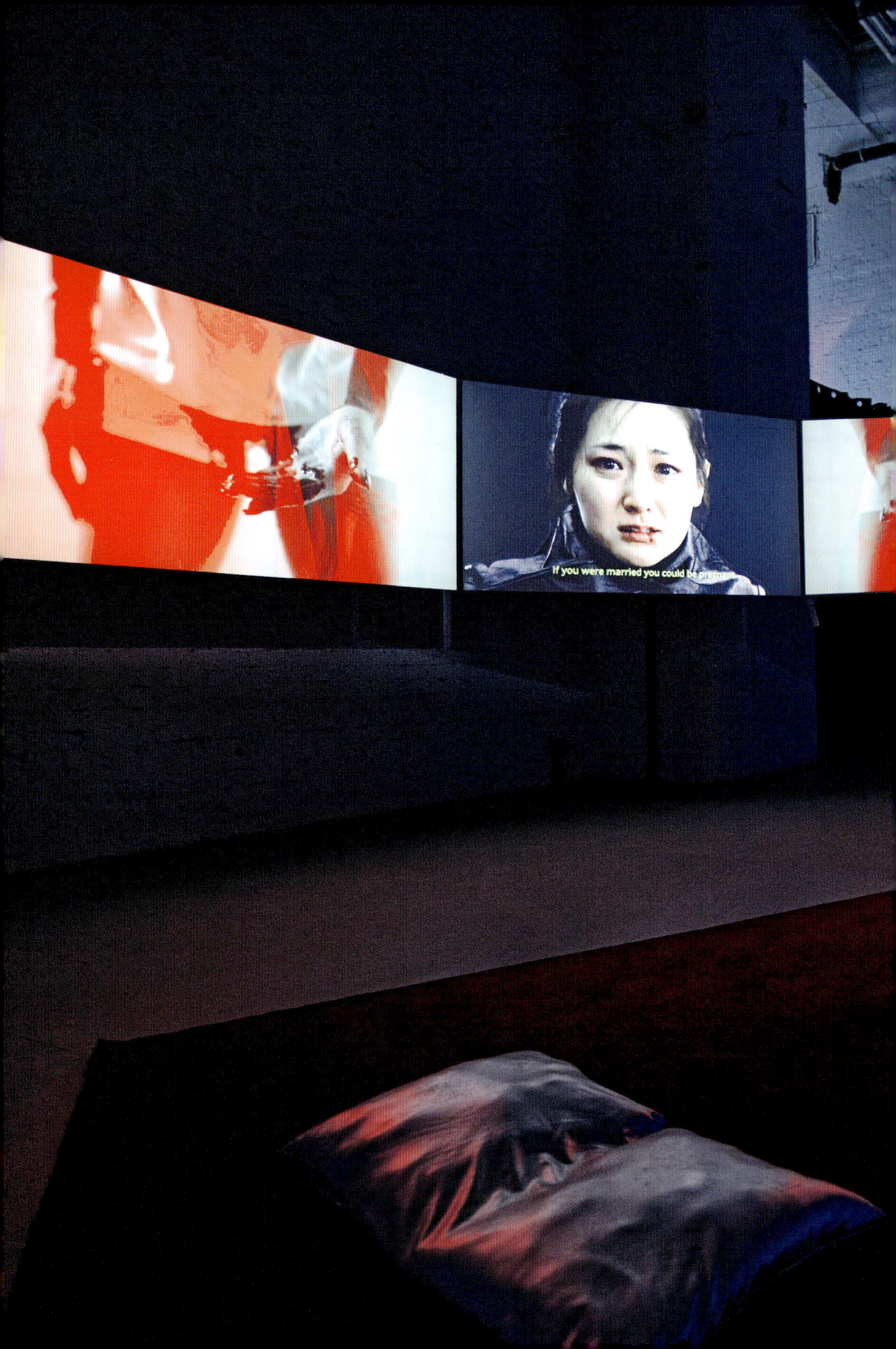
If you were married you could be pregnant

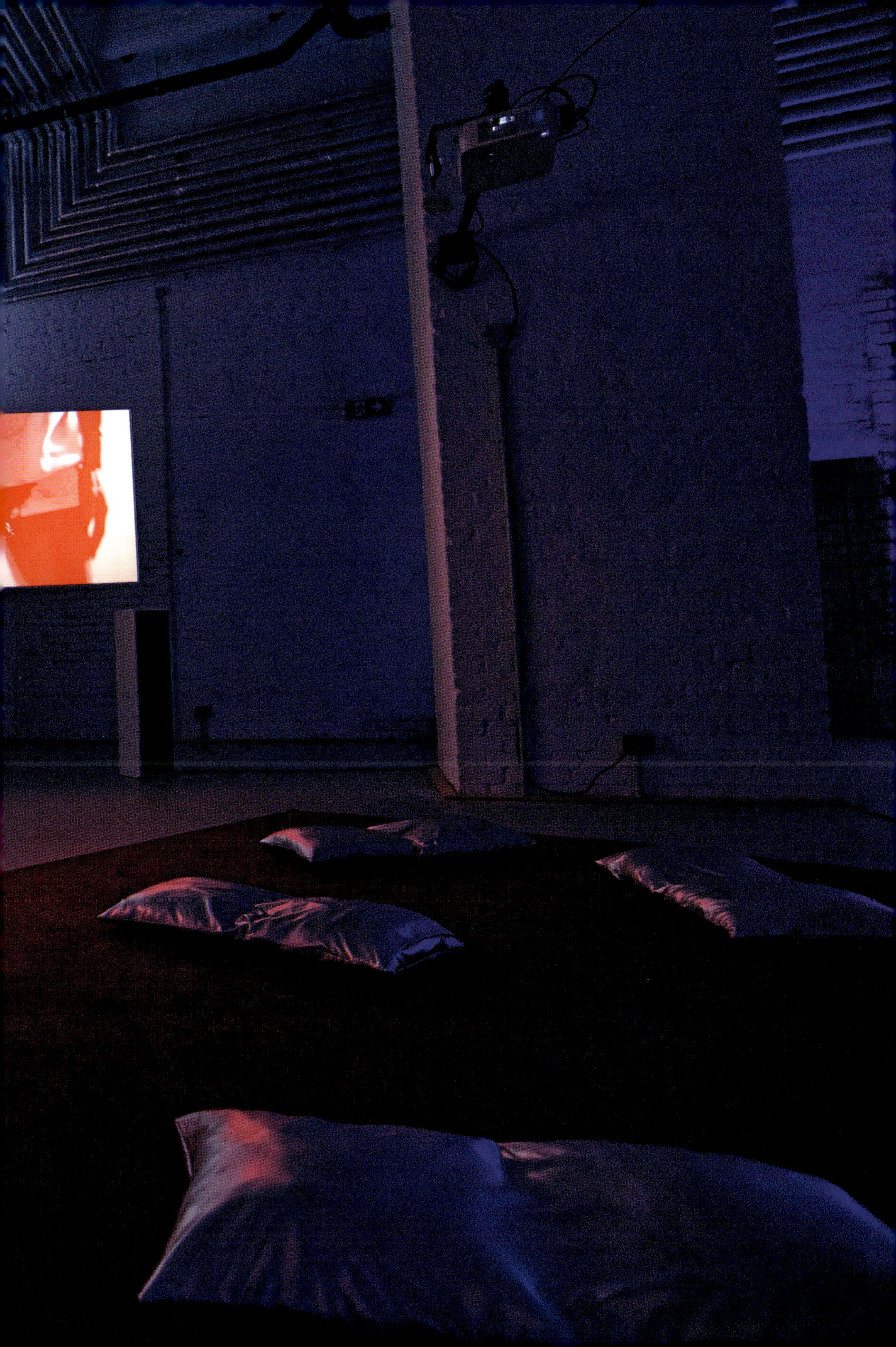

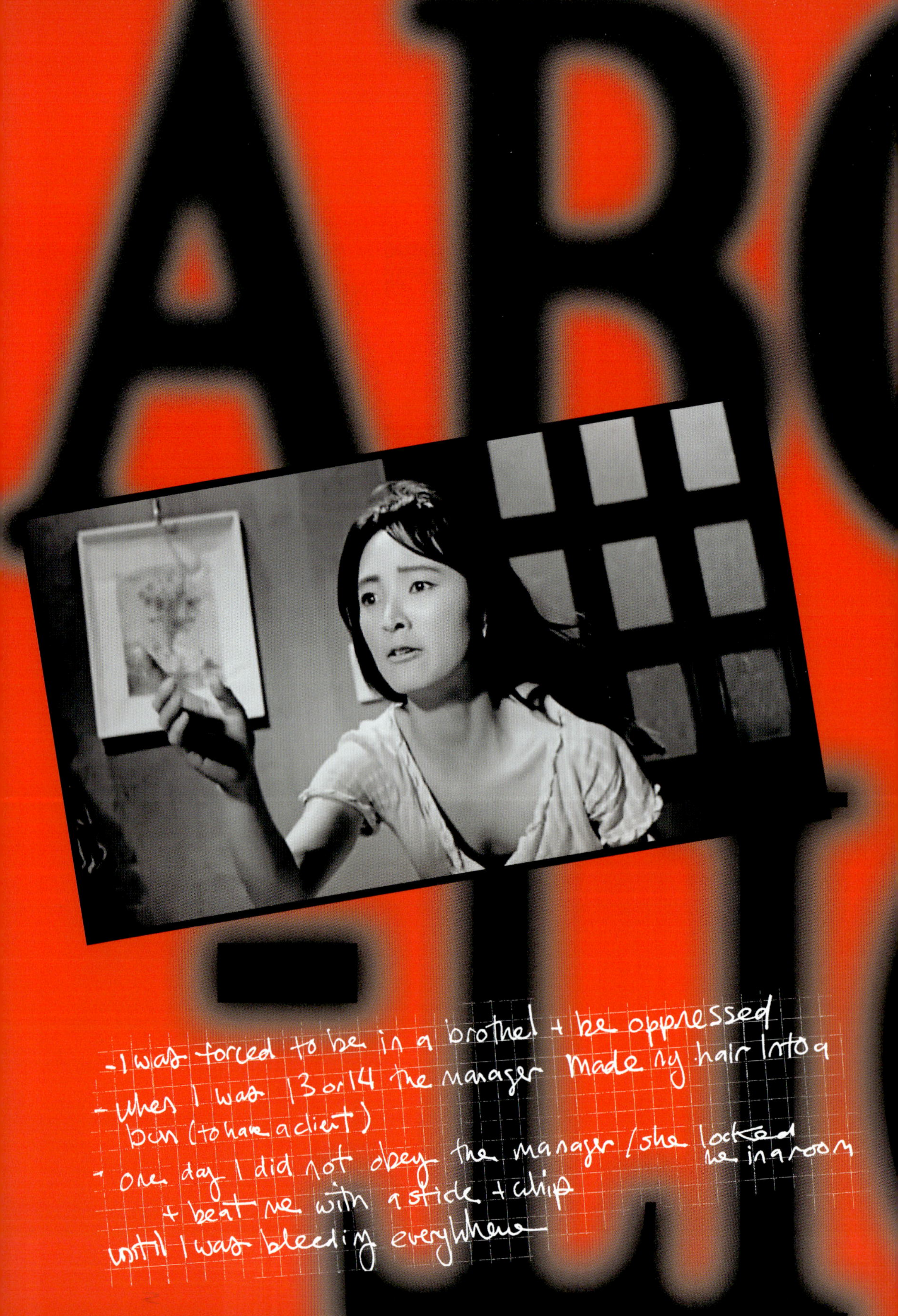
- I was forced to be in a brothel + be oppressed
- when I was 13 or 14 the manager made my hair into a
  bun (to have a client)
- one day I did not obey the manager (she locked
  me in a room
  + beat me with a stick + whip
until I was bleeding everywhere

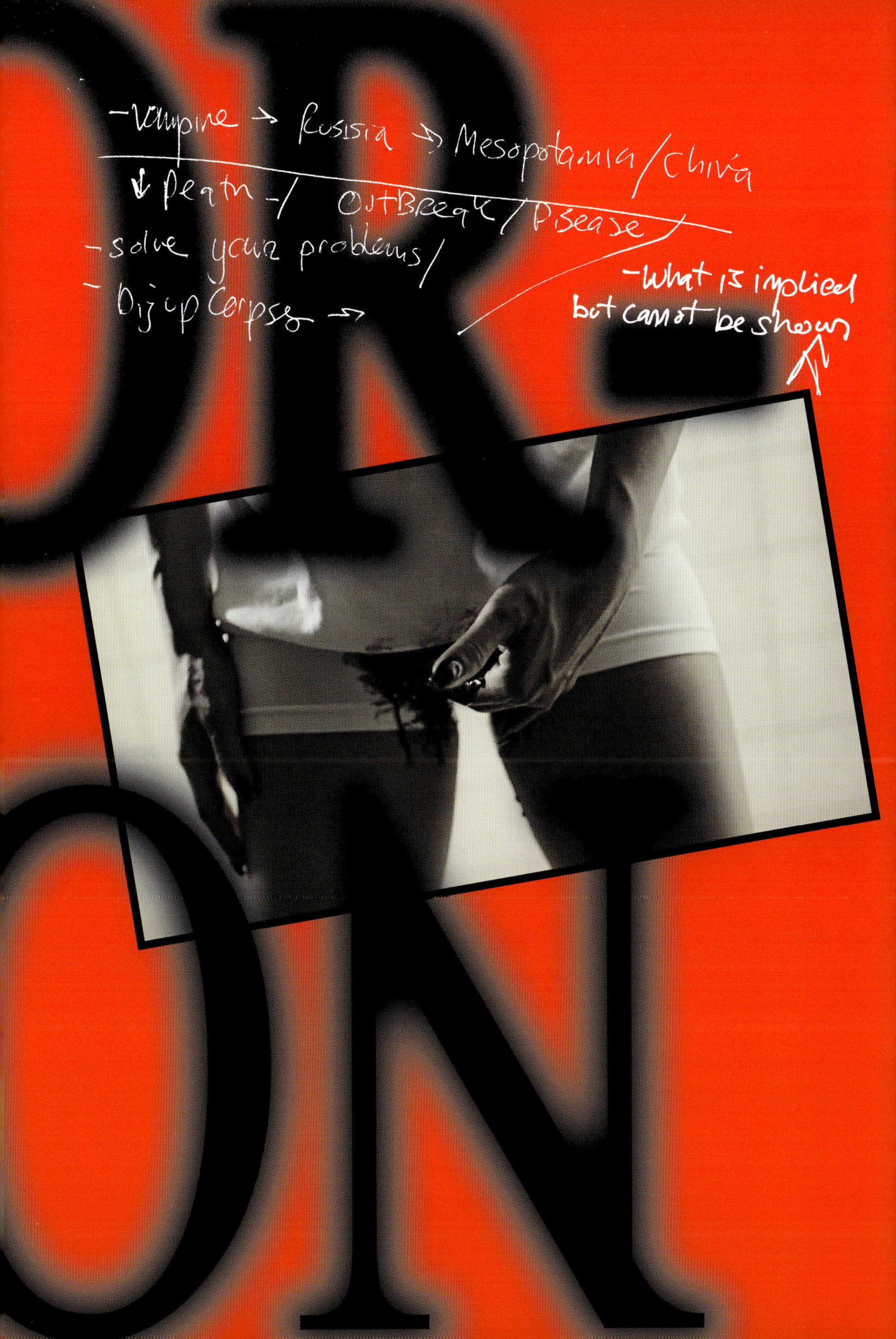

-Vampire → Russia → Mesopotamia/China
↓ Death - / Outbreak/Disease
- solve your problems /
- Dig up Corpses →
-what is implied but cannot be shown

~~I was 13 or 14 and my~~

l was my home then, i

are no such thi

A SLUT OMG WHAT

c or a deep n

der it she rea

l you Jenny, as you gr

uld celebrate your 1st

ld be happy to have y

manager put my hair

they let me go, where

as a sterile ma

OMG A SLUT OMG

enders   + wom

v in Ariel... I felt good lik

rthday I had to go to p

.... anyone would be h

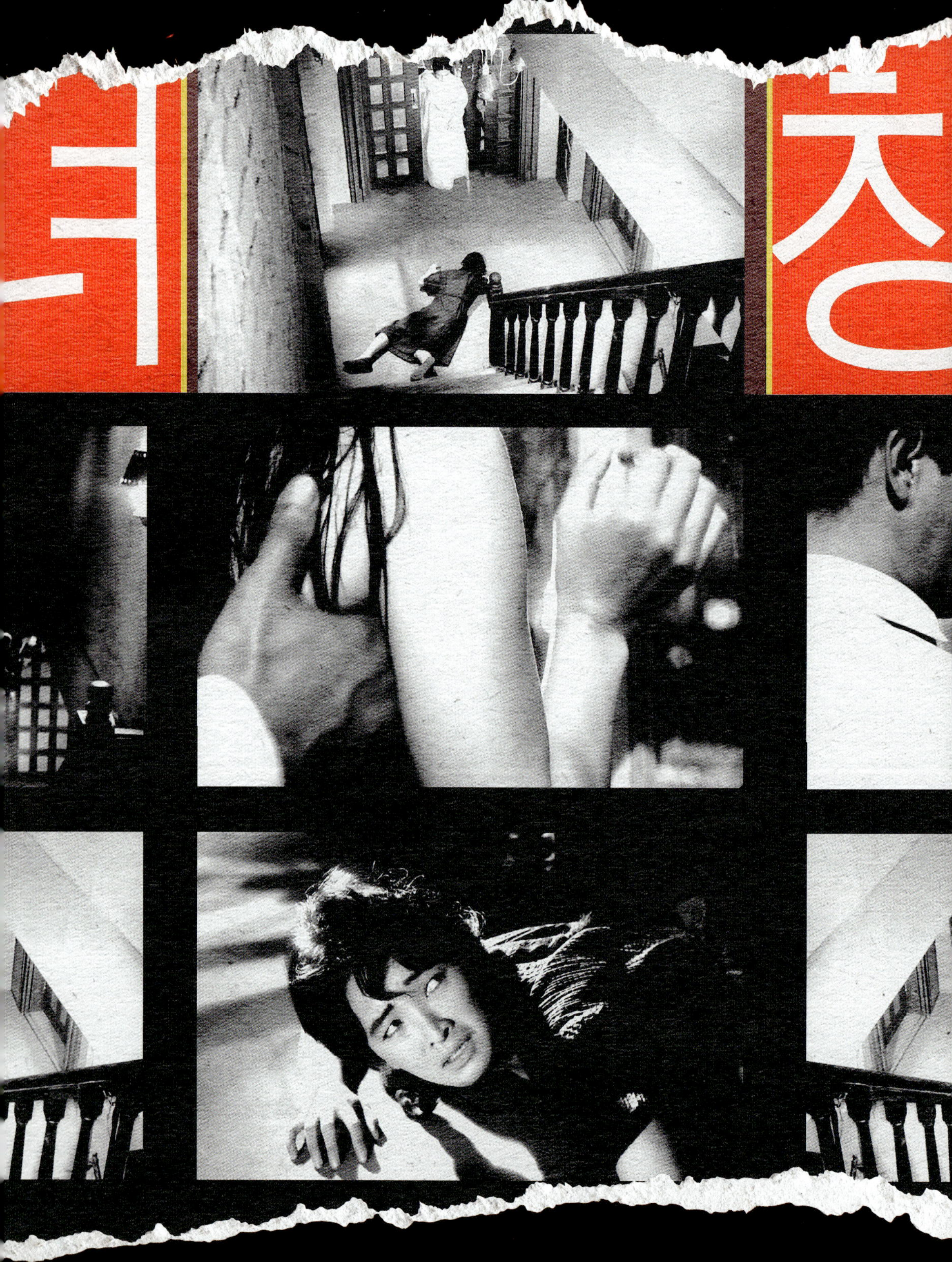

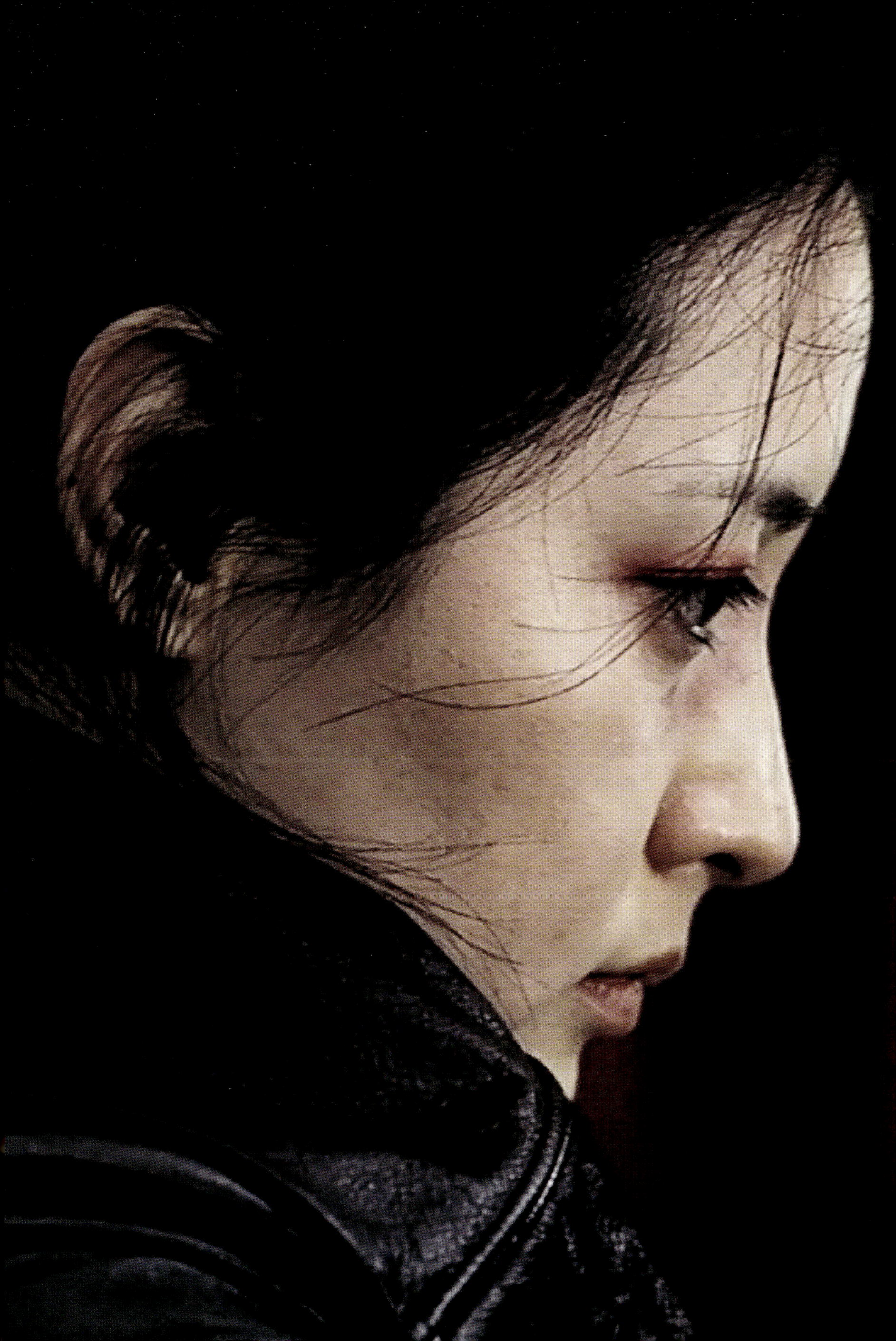

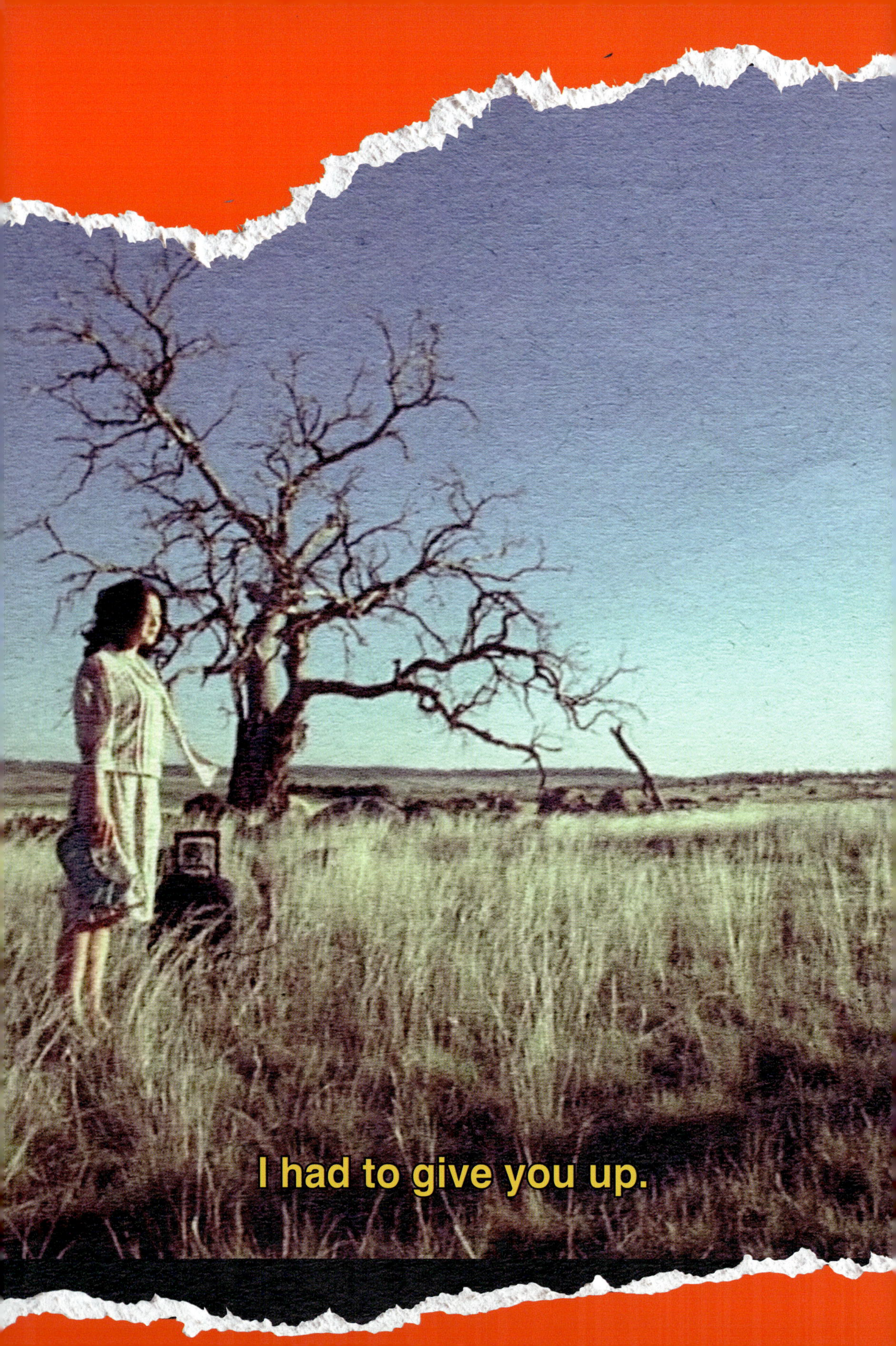
I had to give you up.

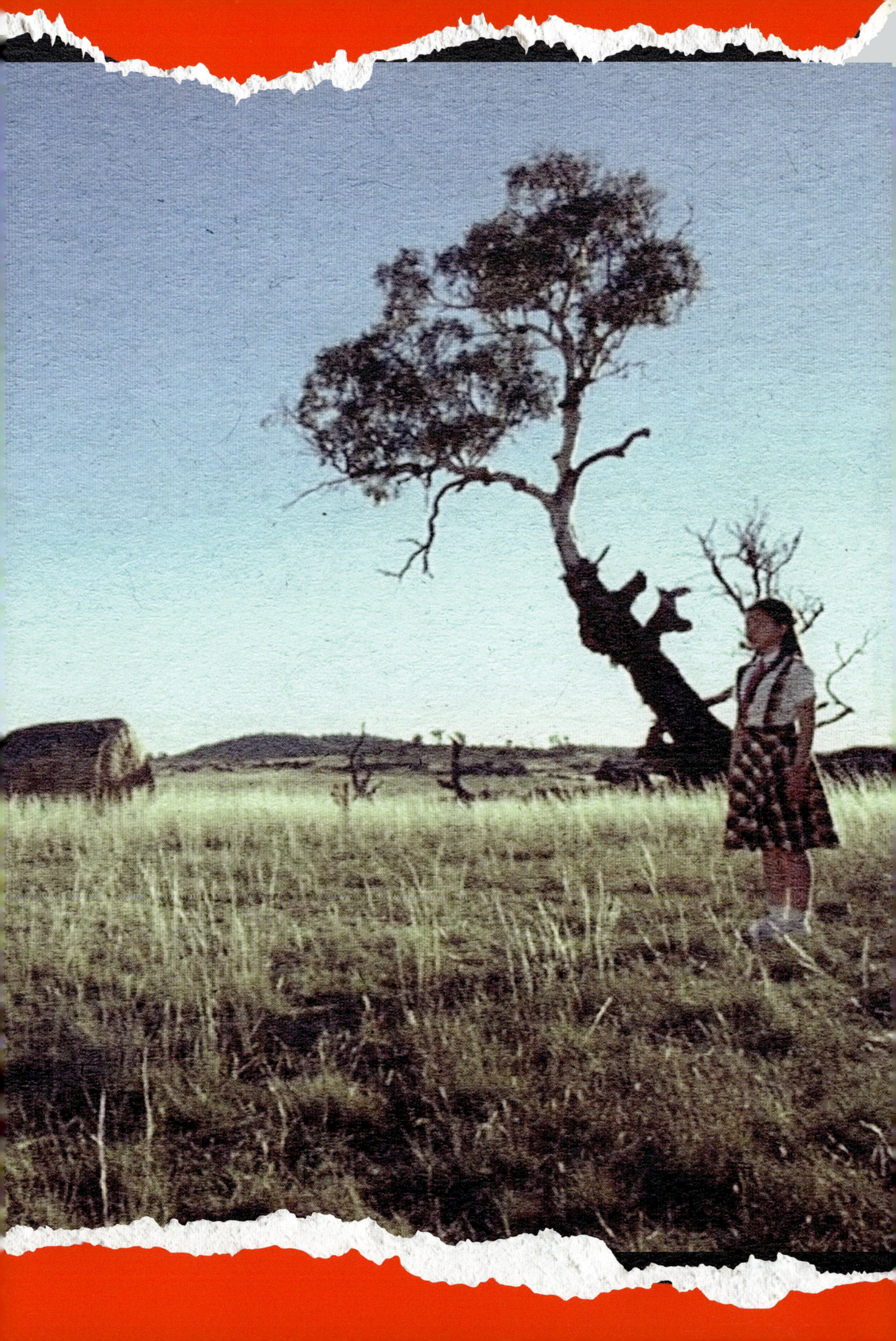

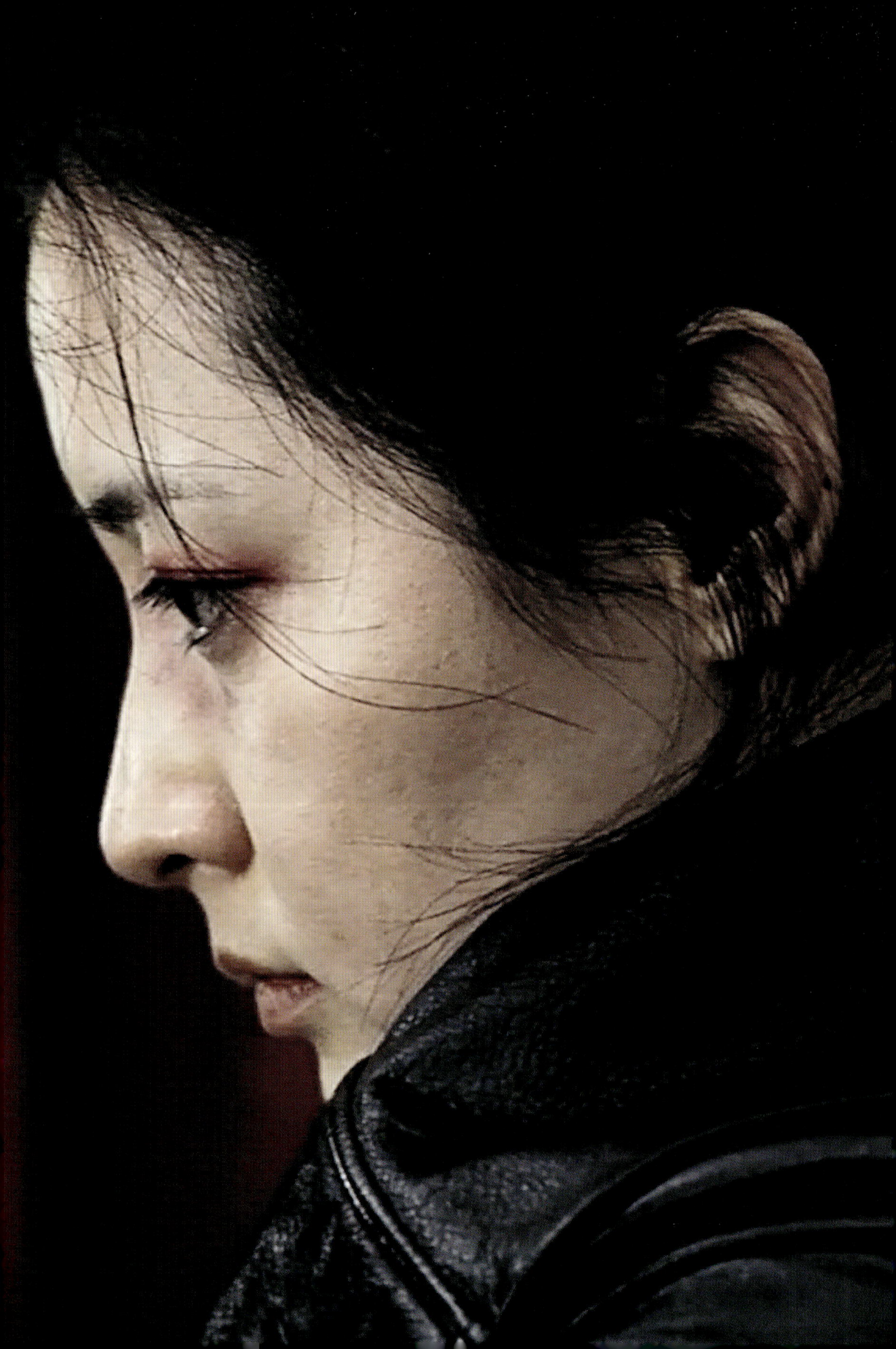

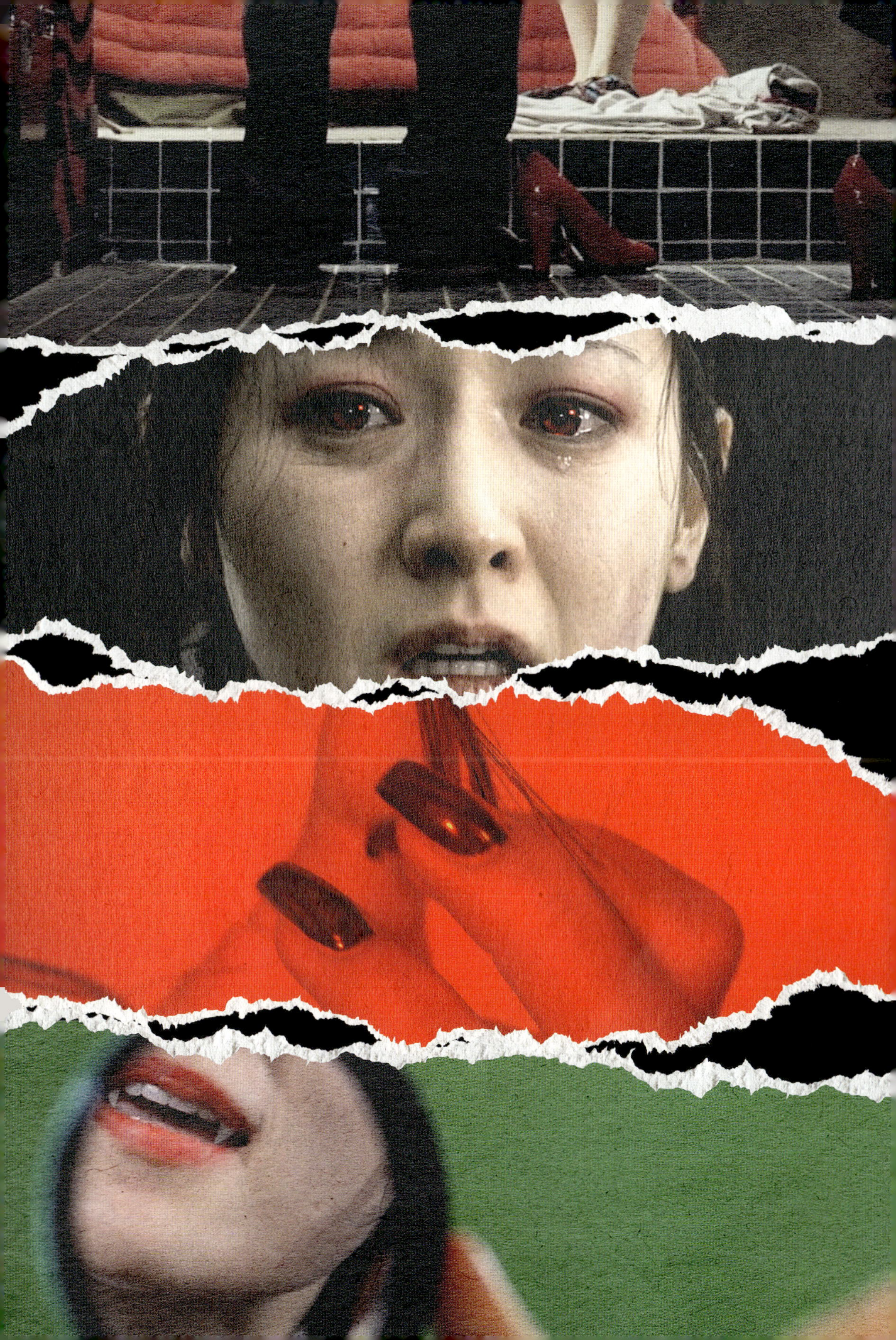

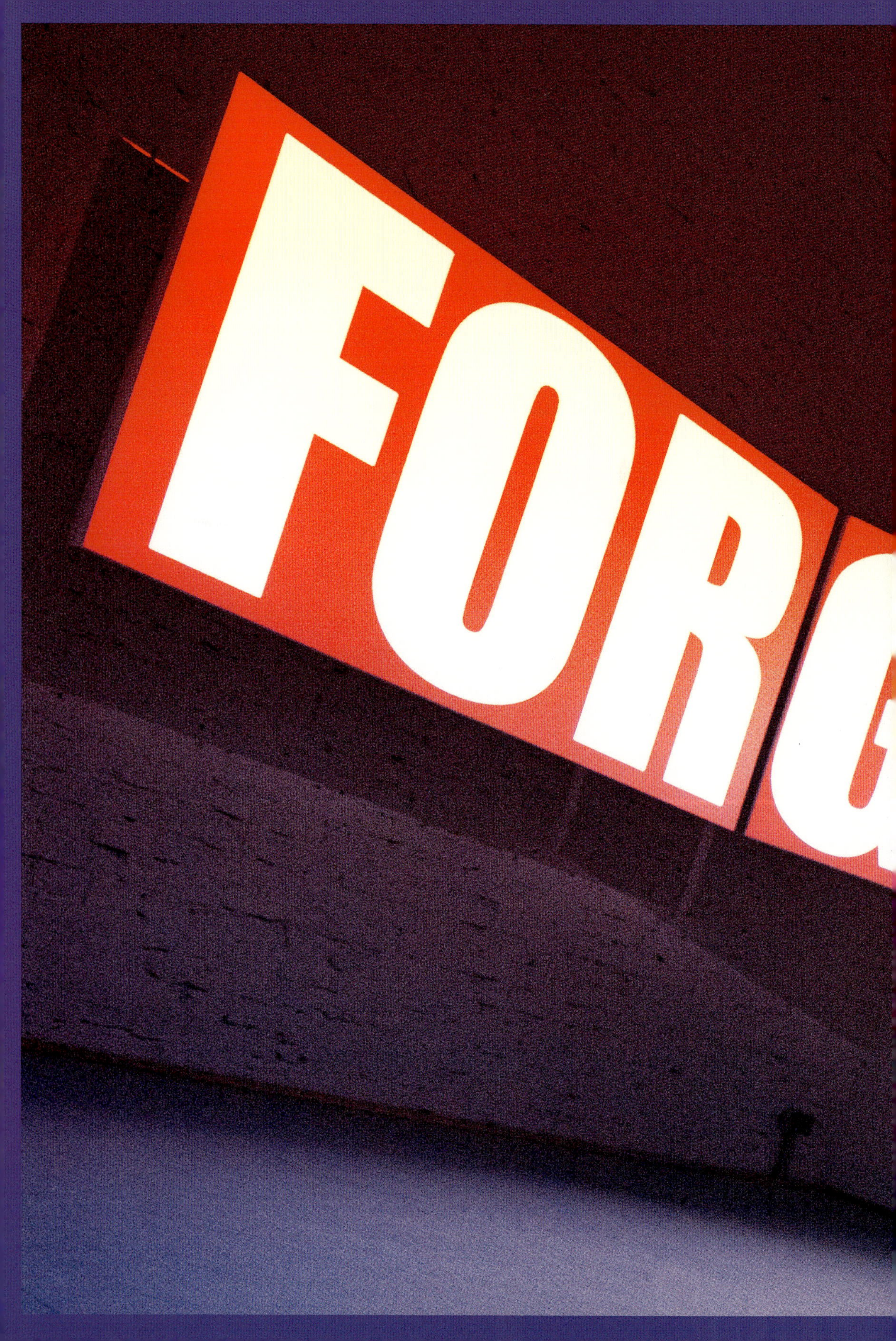
FORG

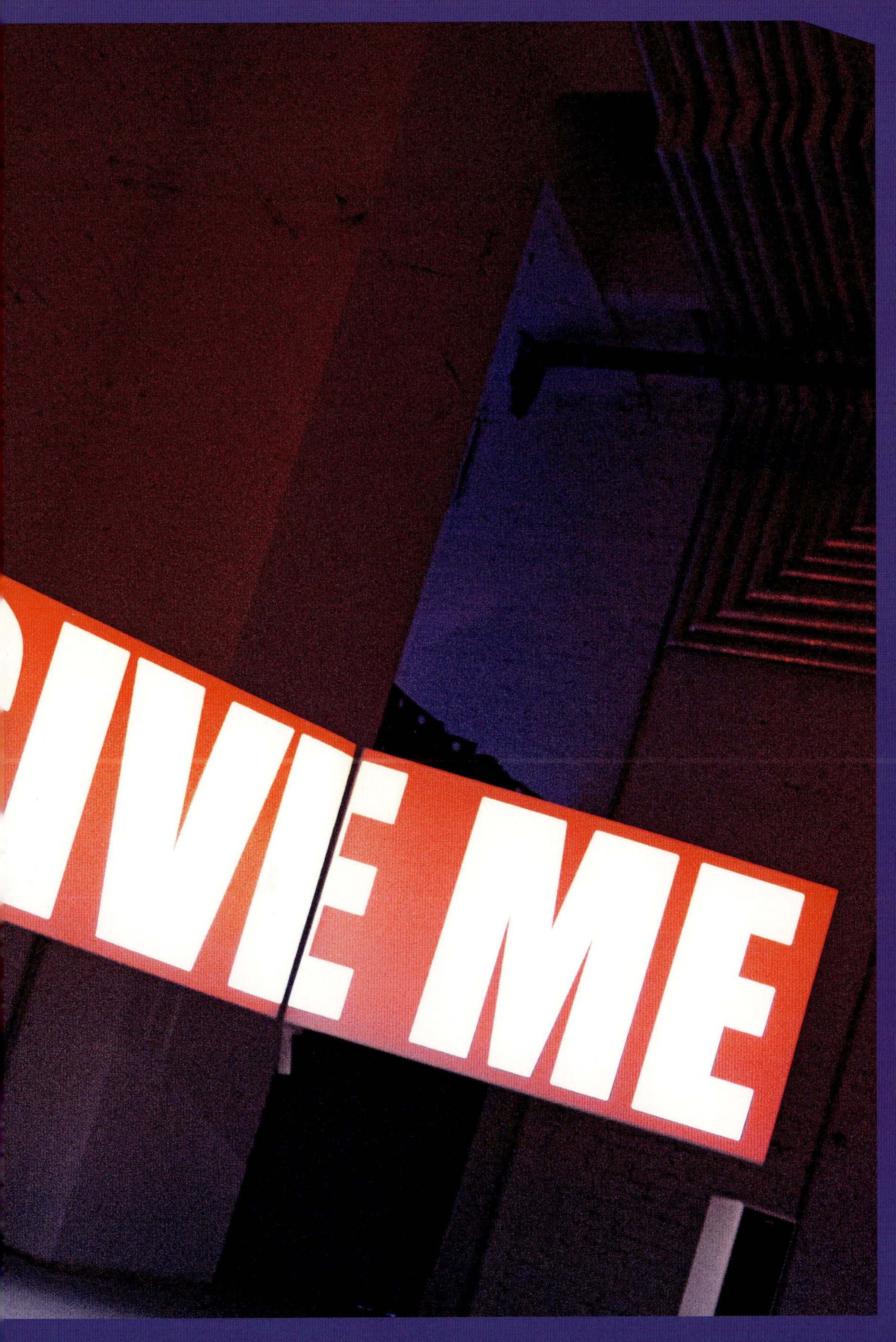
IVE ME

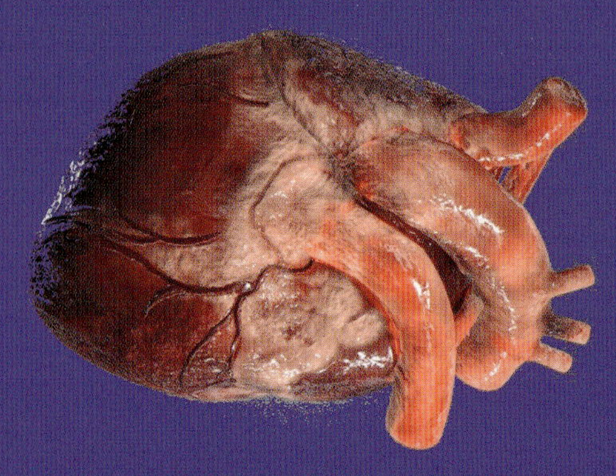

I can't trust
you to say
this

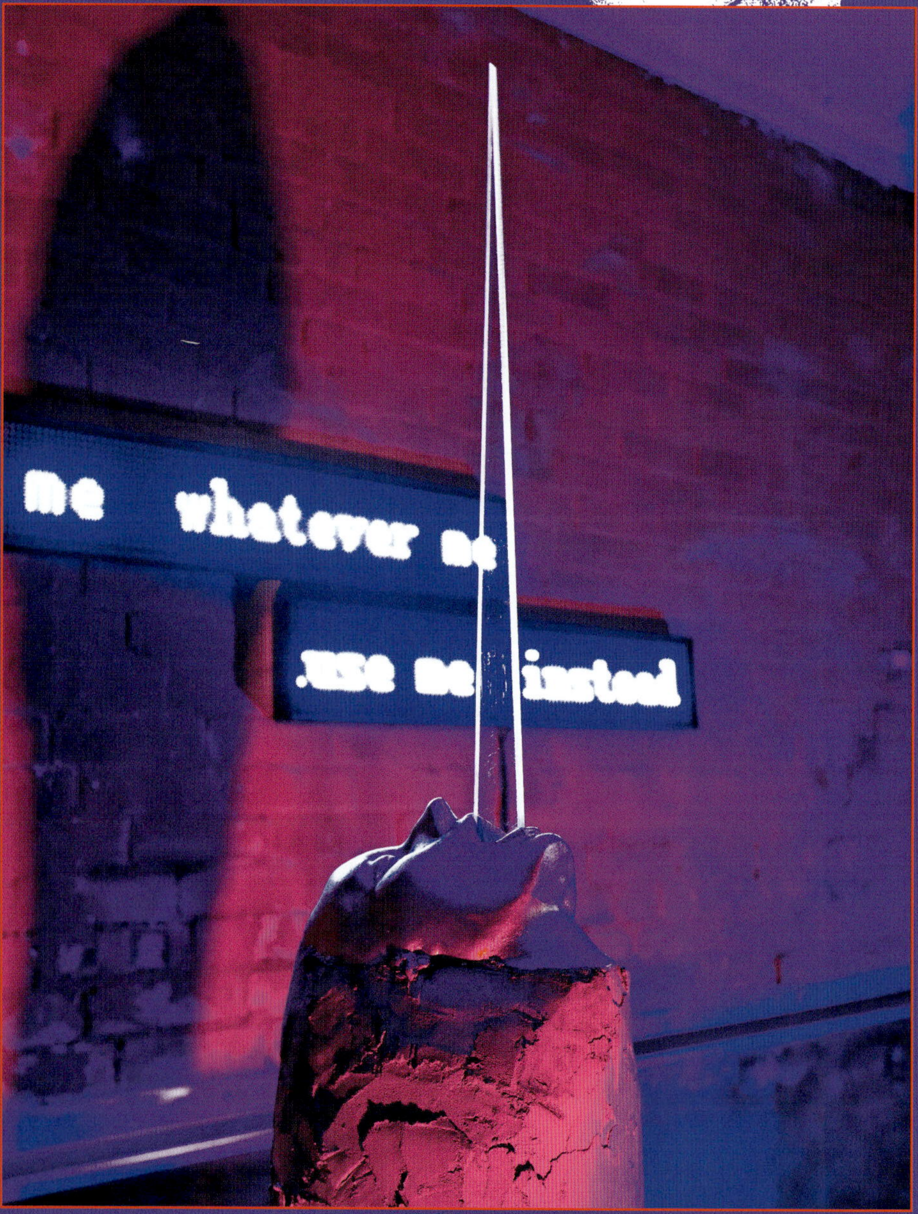

me   whatever me
.use me instead

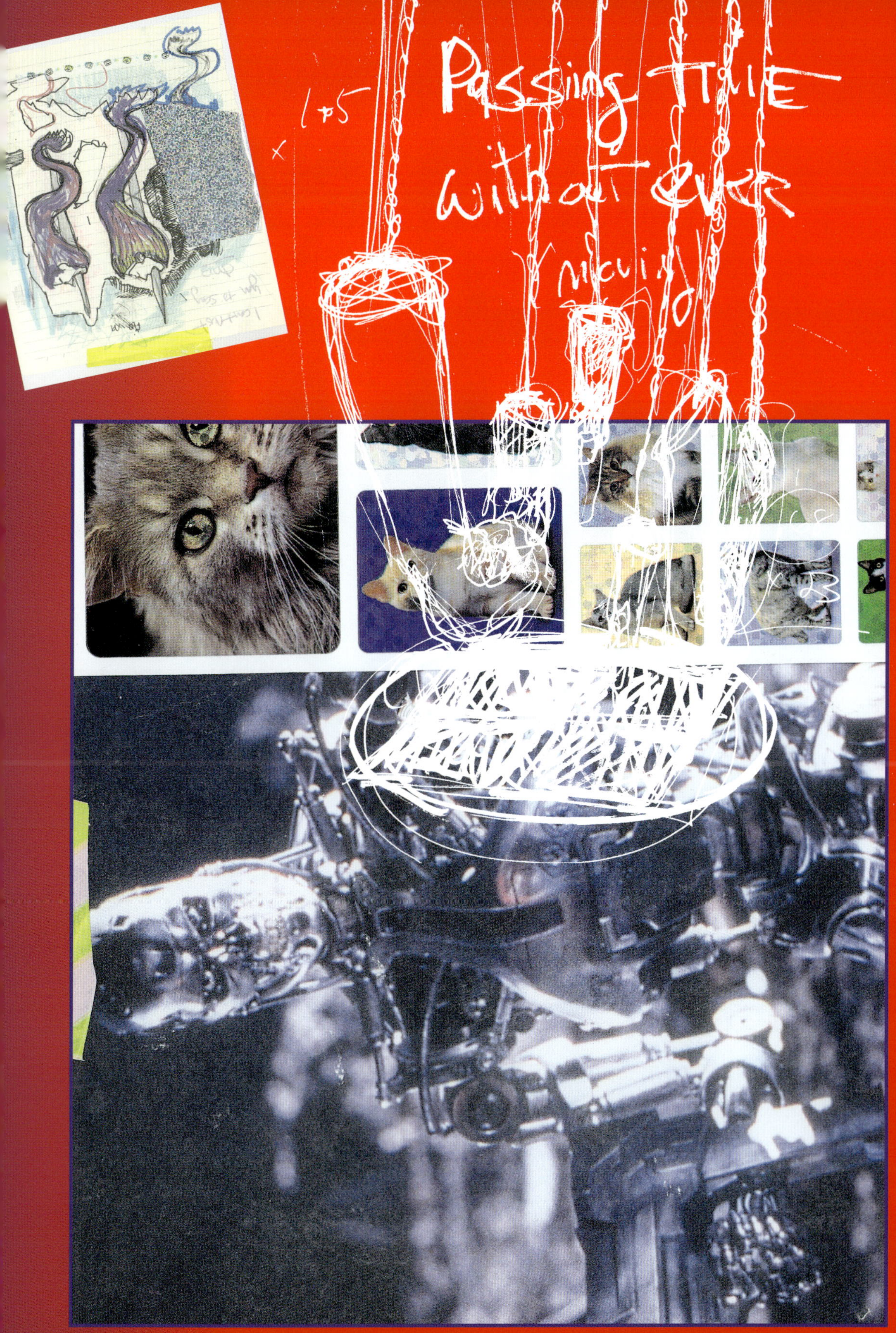
Passing time
without ever
moving

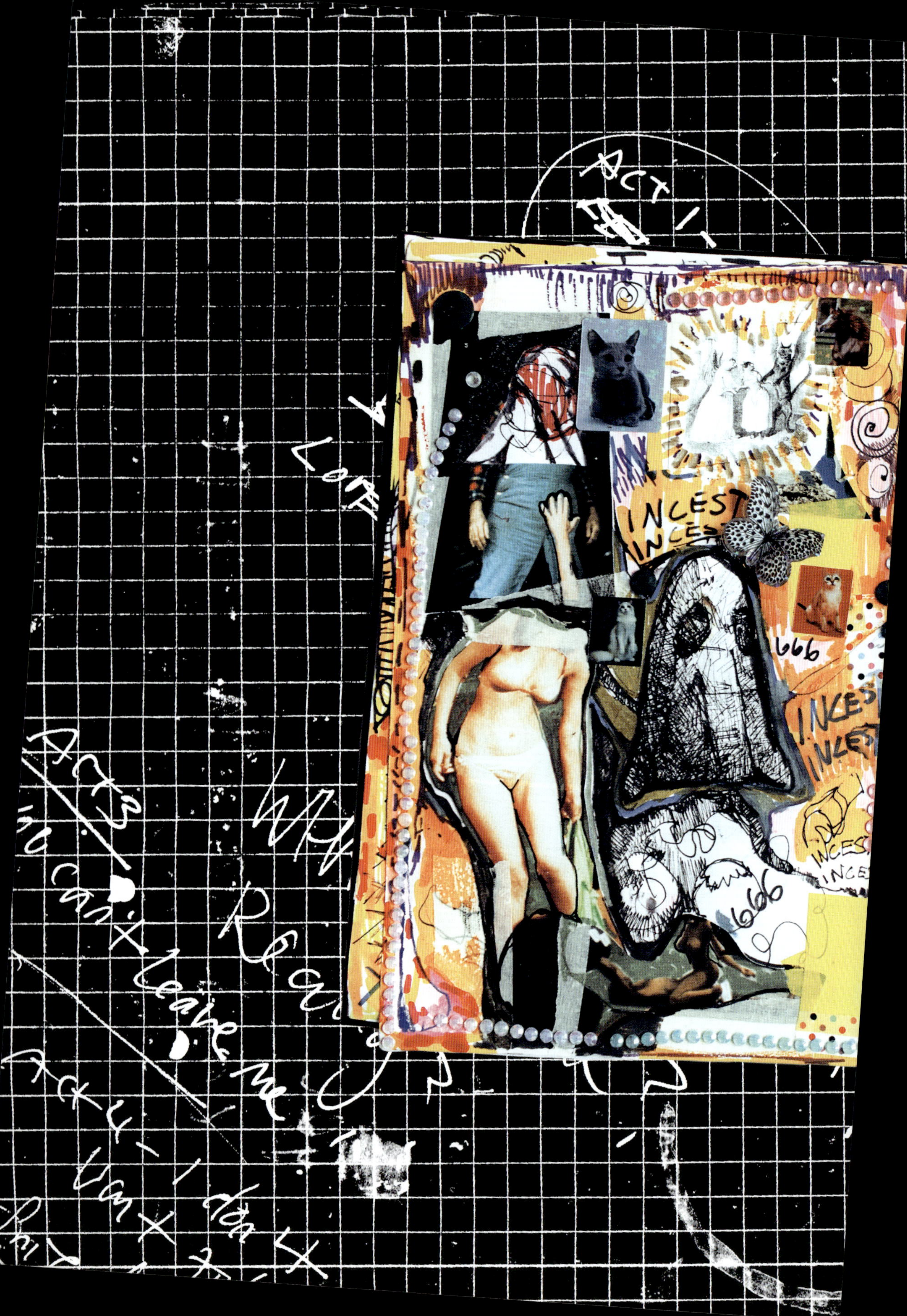
ACT 1.
LOVE
WHY
ACT3
REA
INCEST
INCES
666
INCES
INCES
666

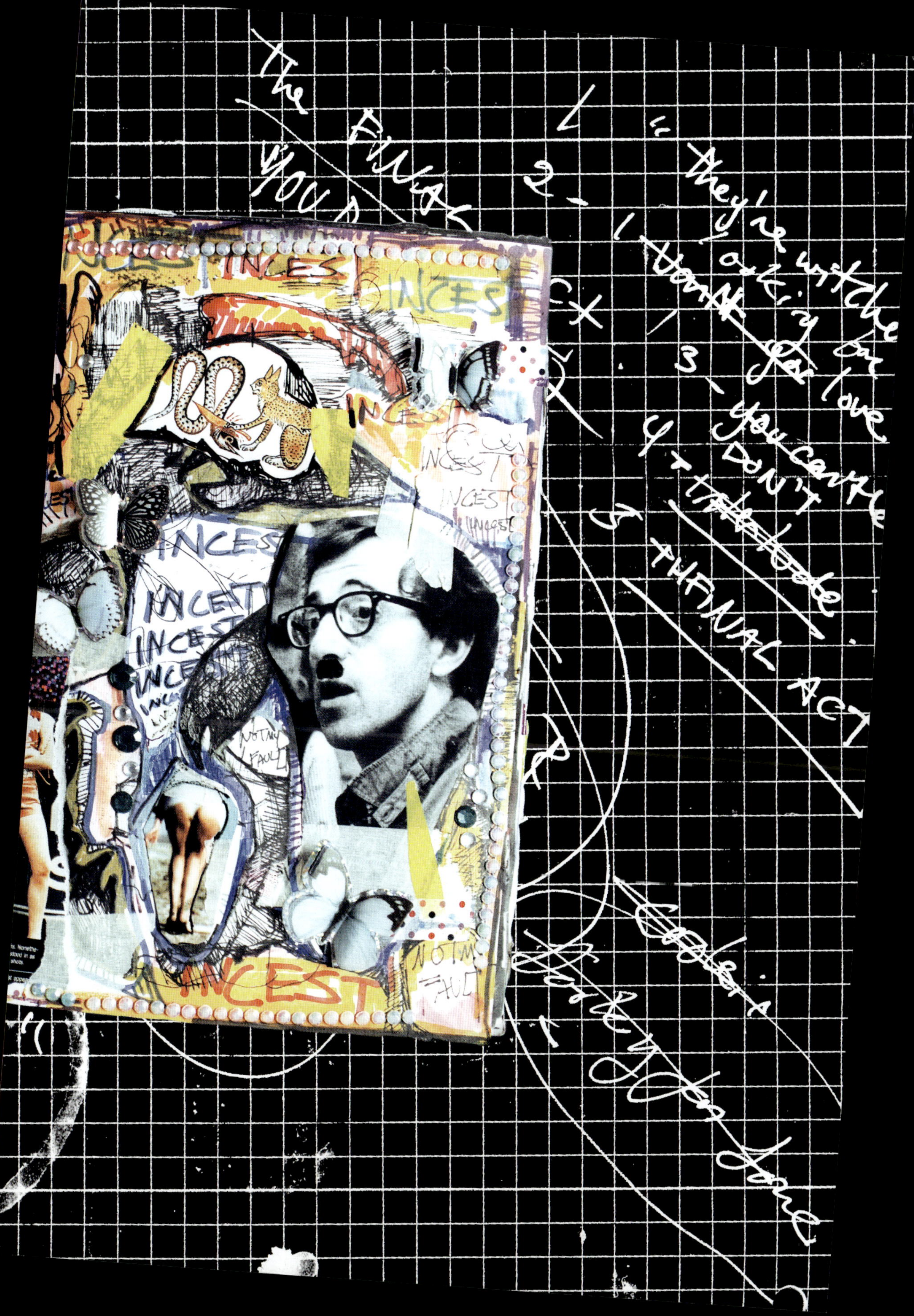

The final
your
"they're watching
you're acting for love
1 "
2 - I don't think
3 - you can't hide
4 - you can't
DON'T
the final act
INCES
INCEST
INCEST
INCEST
INCEST
INCEST
NOT MY FAULT
NOT MY FAULT

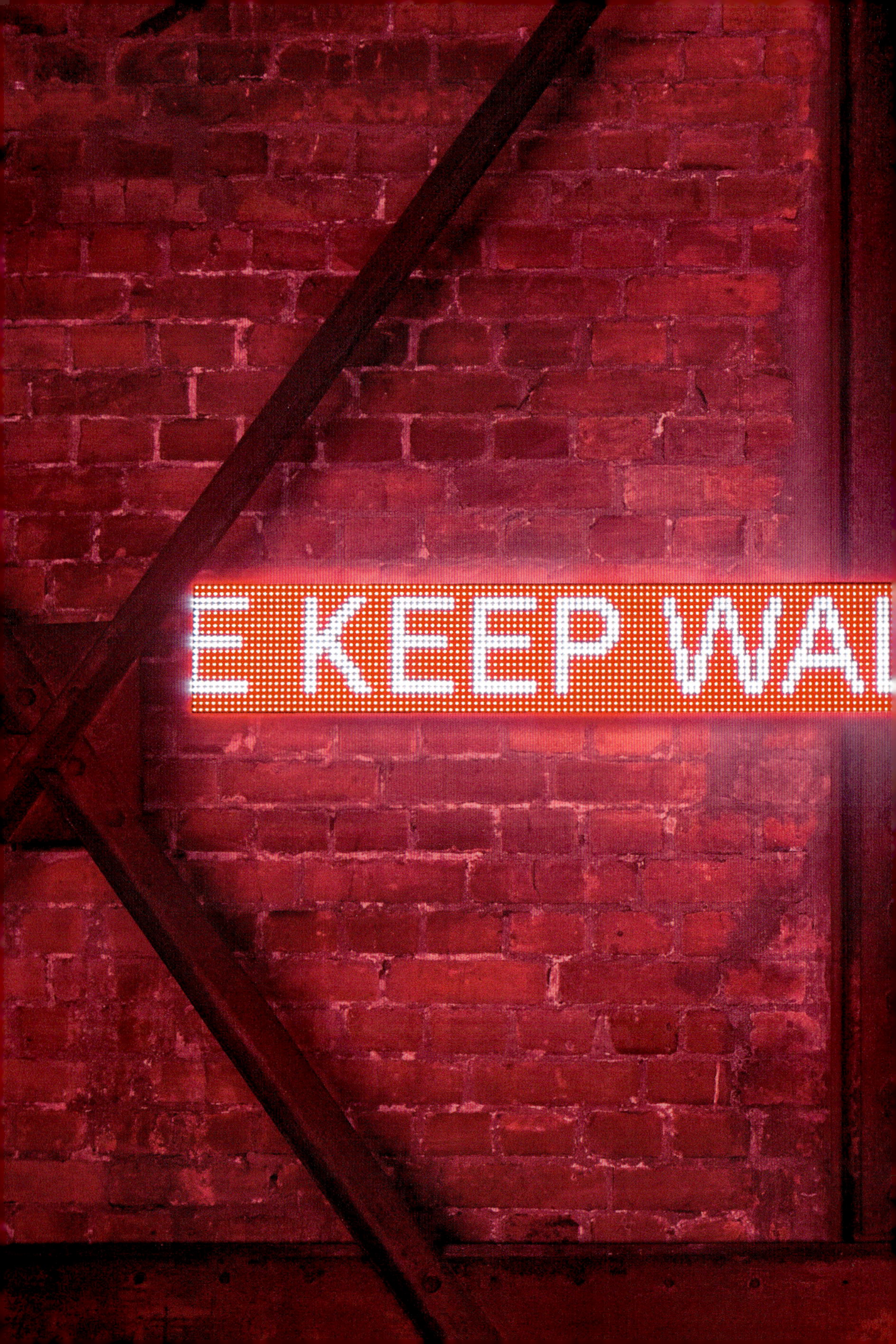

E KEEP WAL

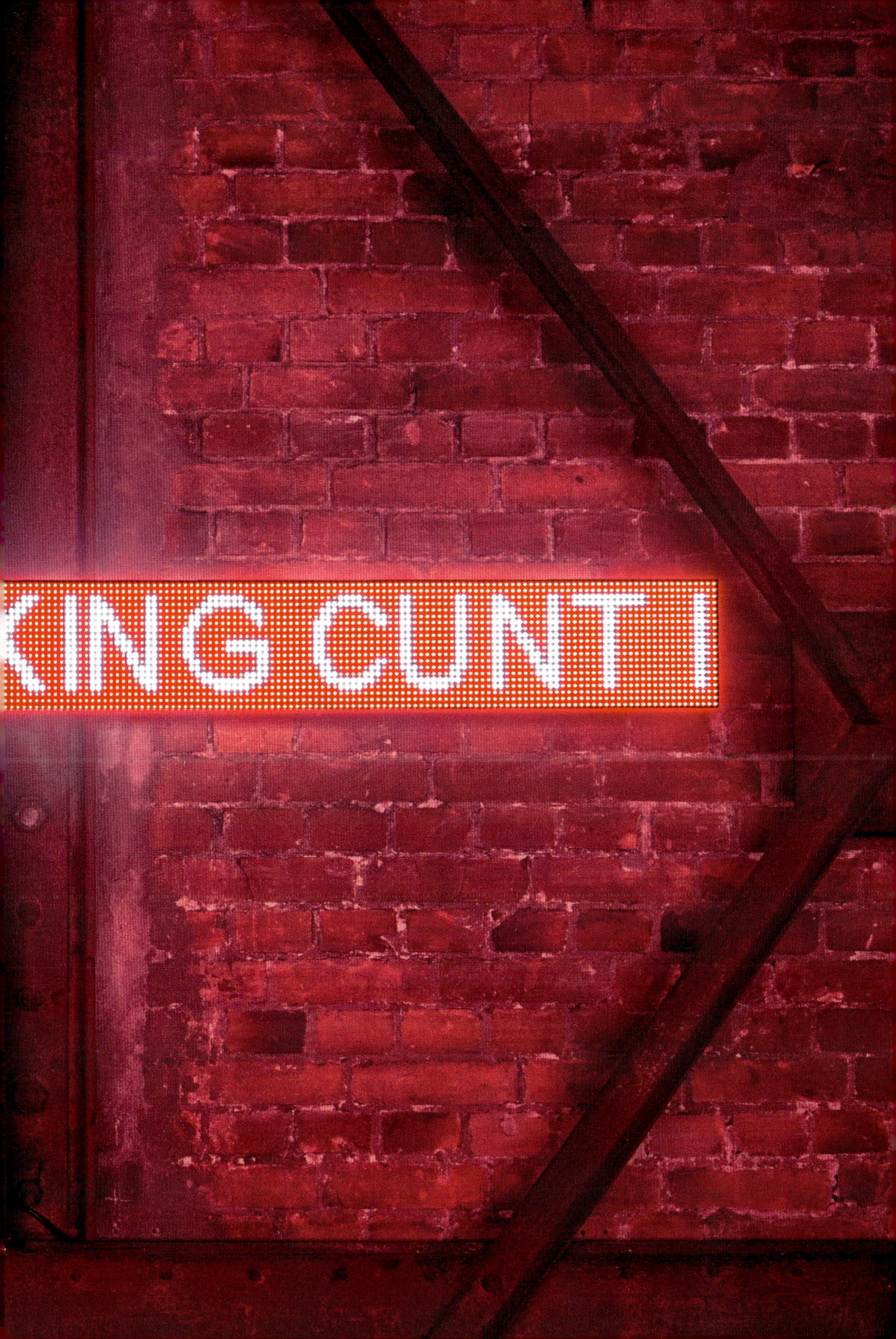
KING CUNT I

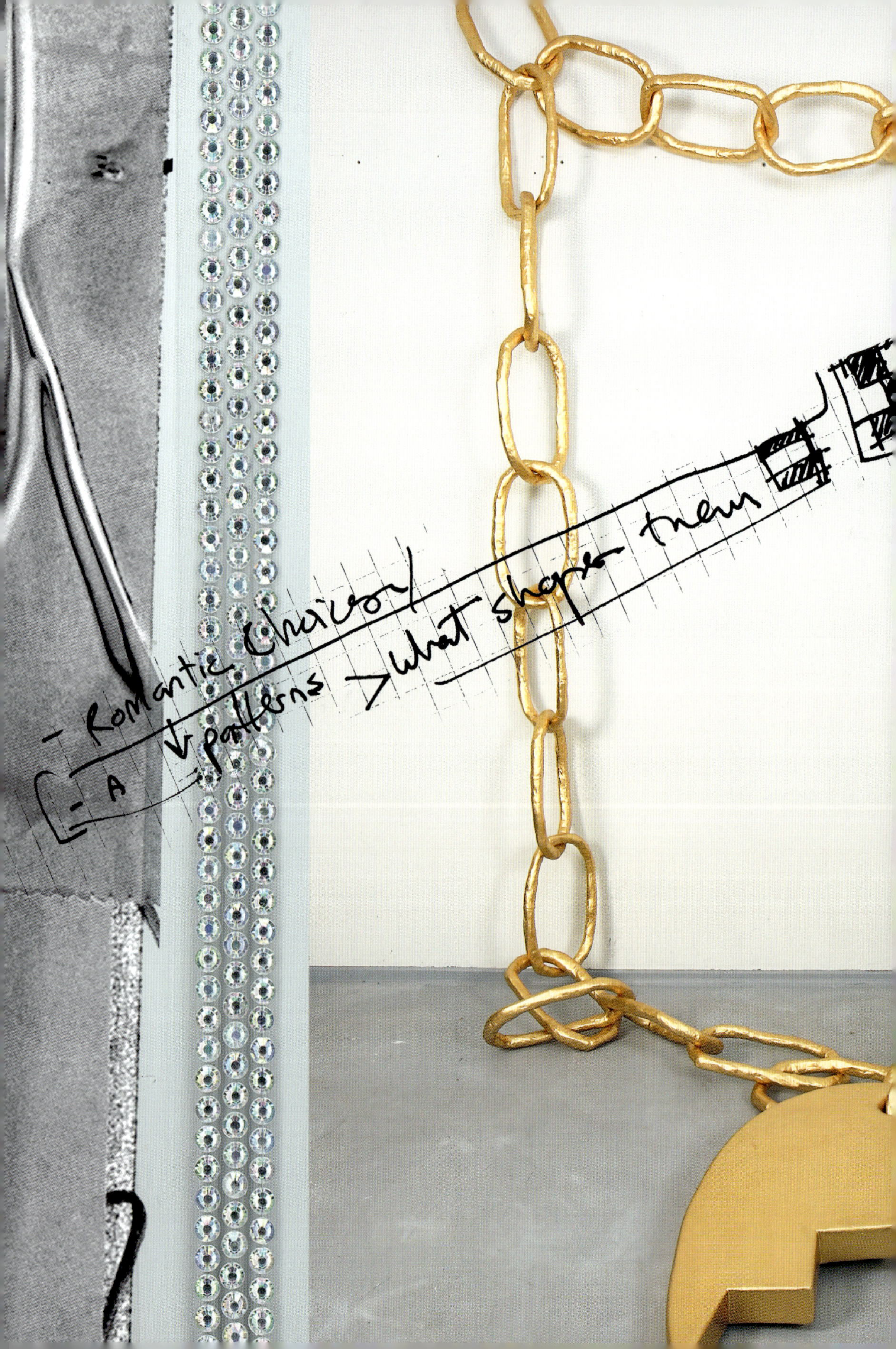
- Romantic Chivalry
- A patterns > what shape them

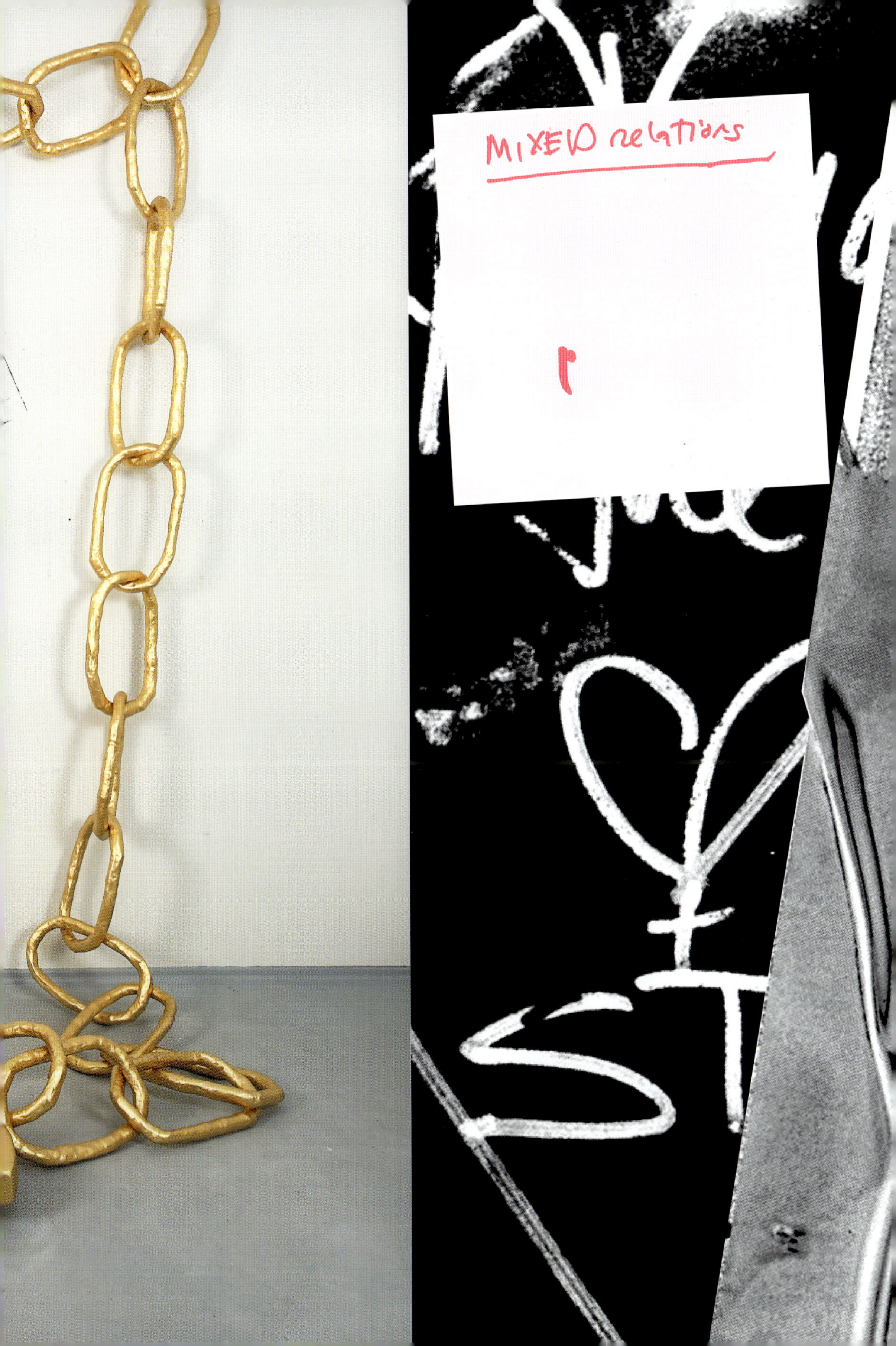
MIXED relations

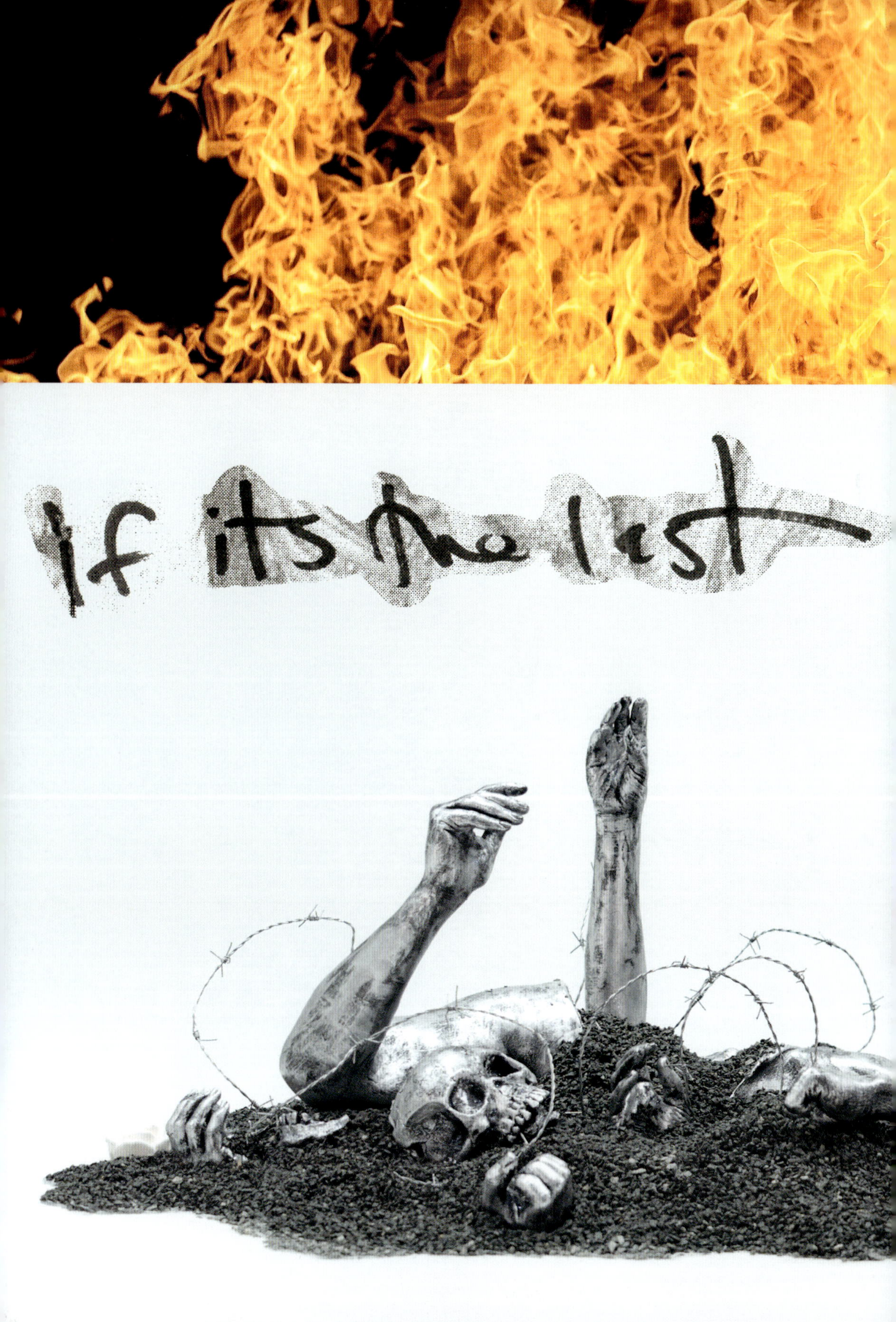
if its the lest

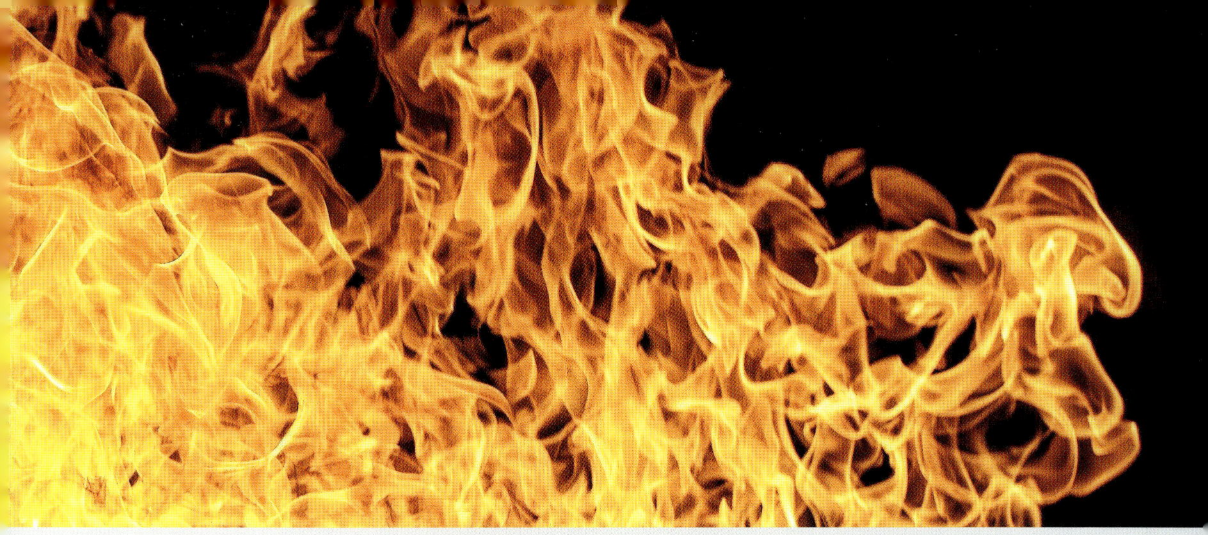

day of my life.

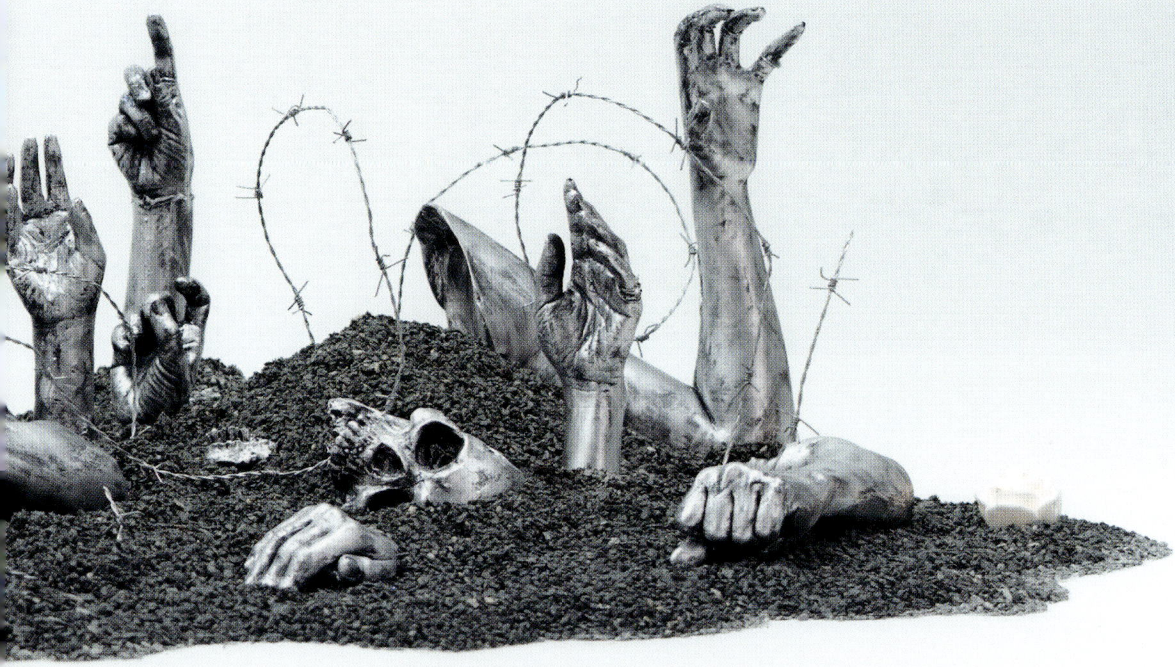

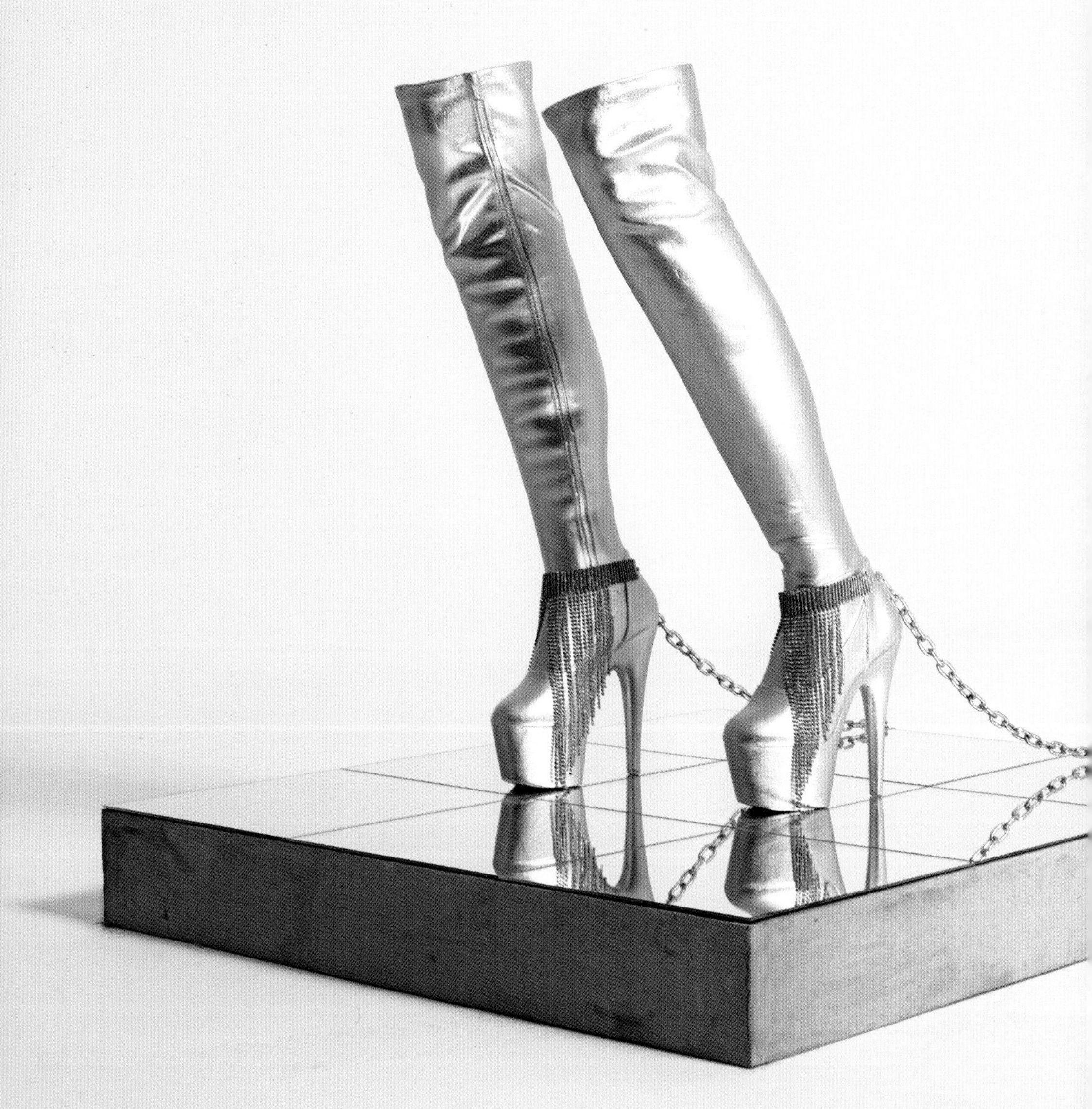

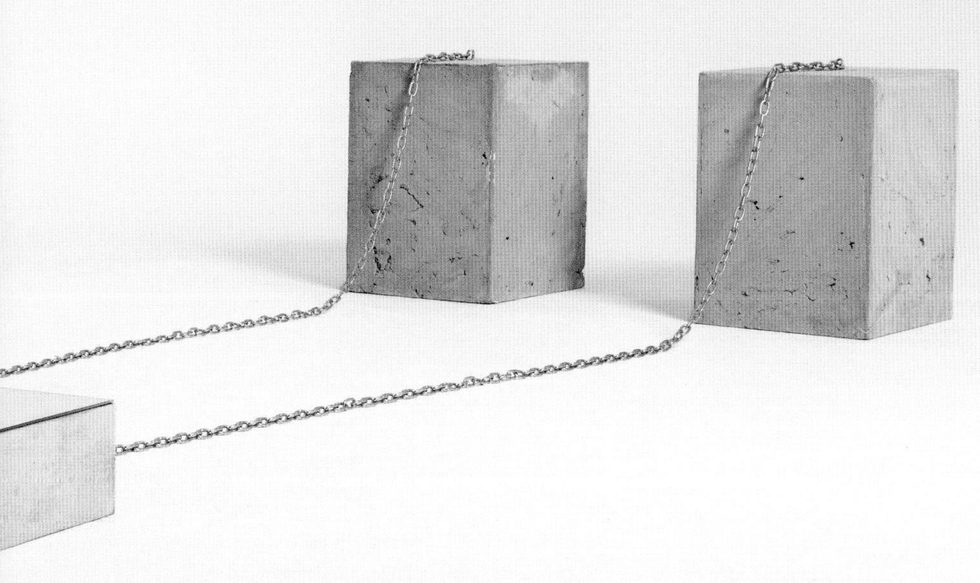

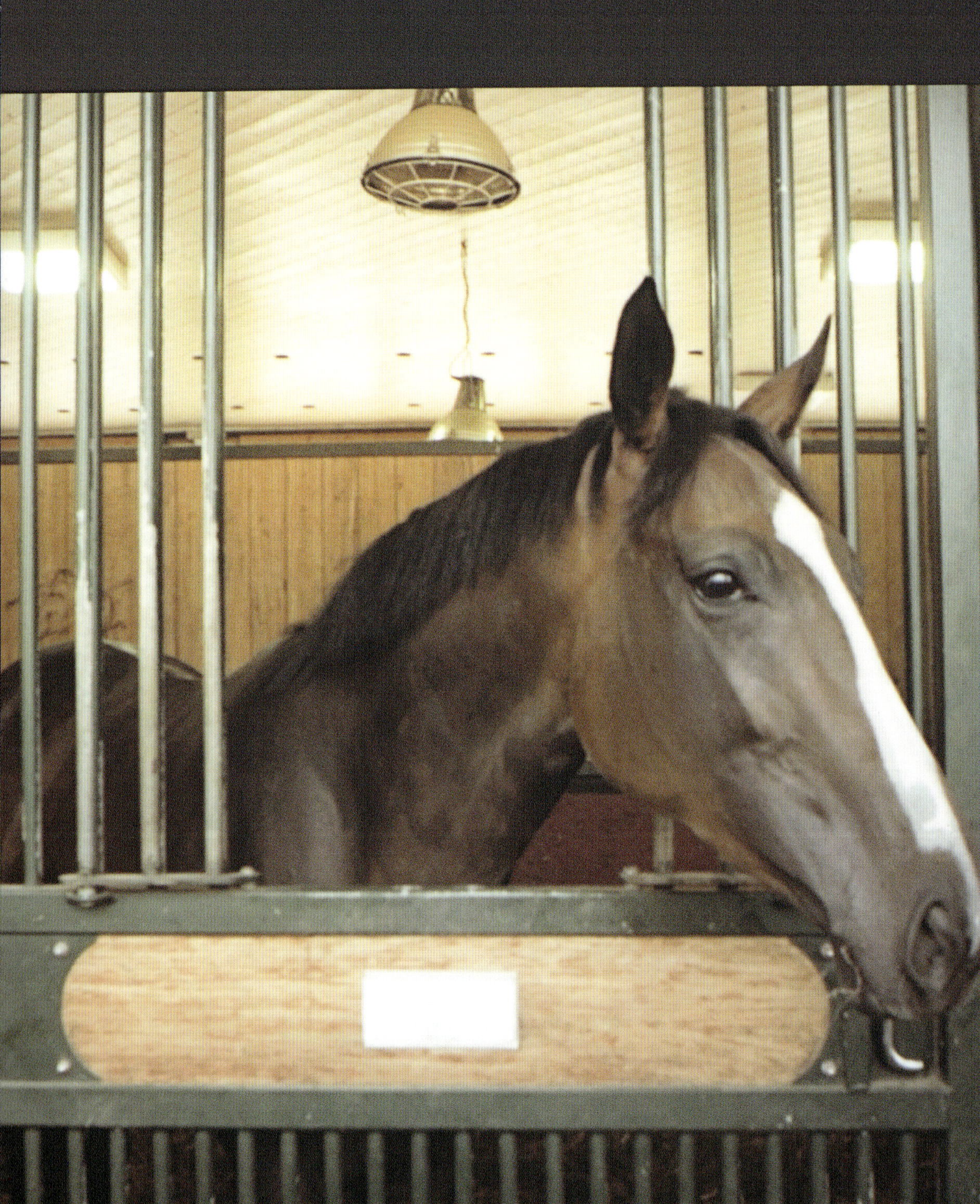

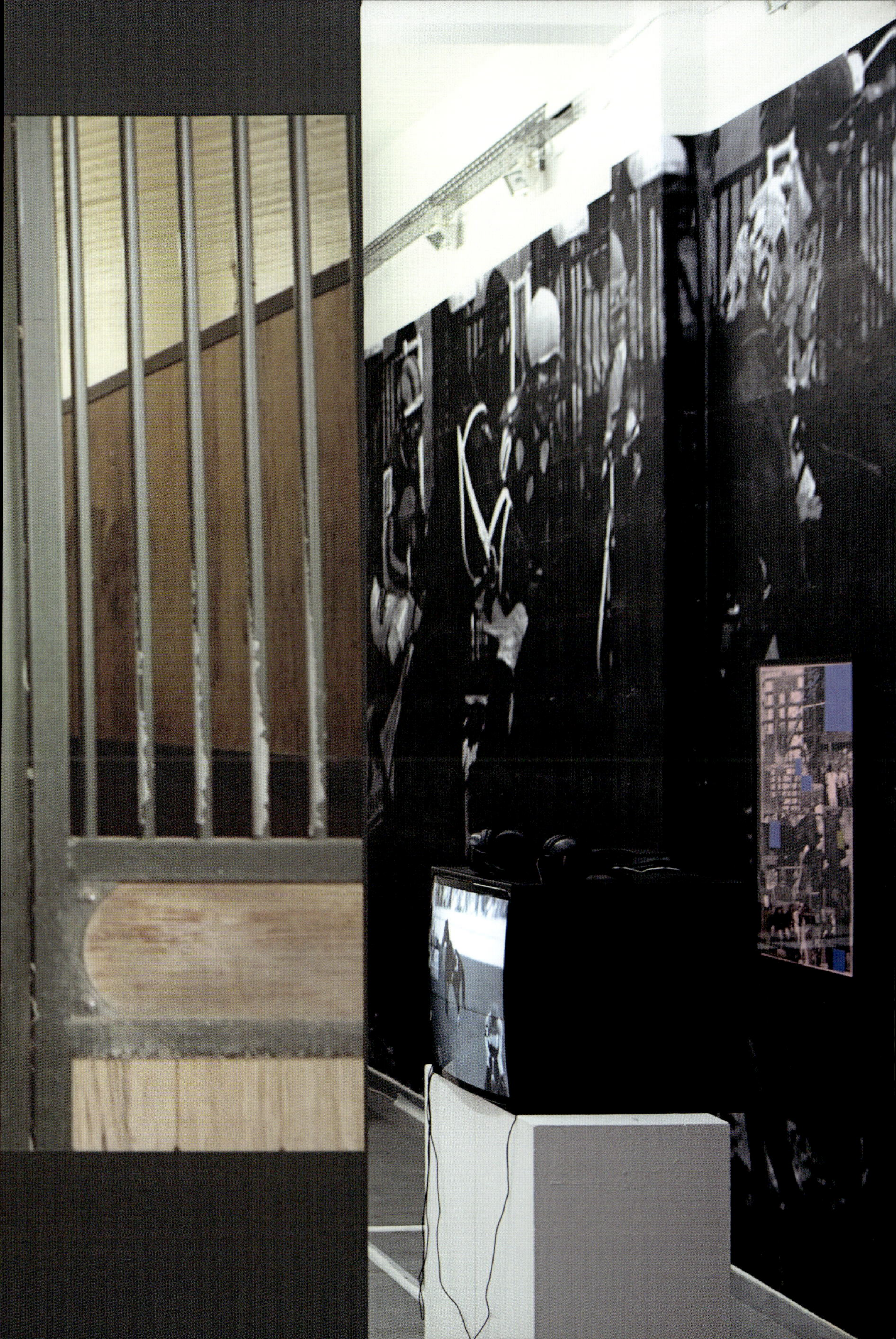

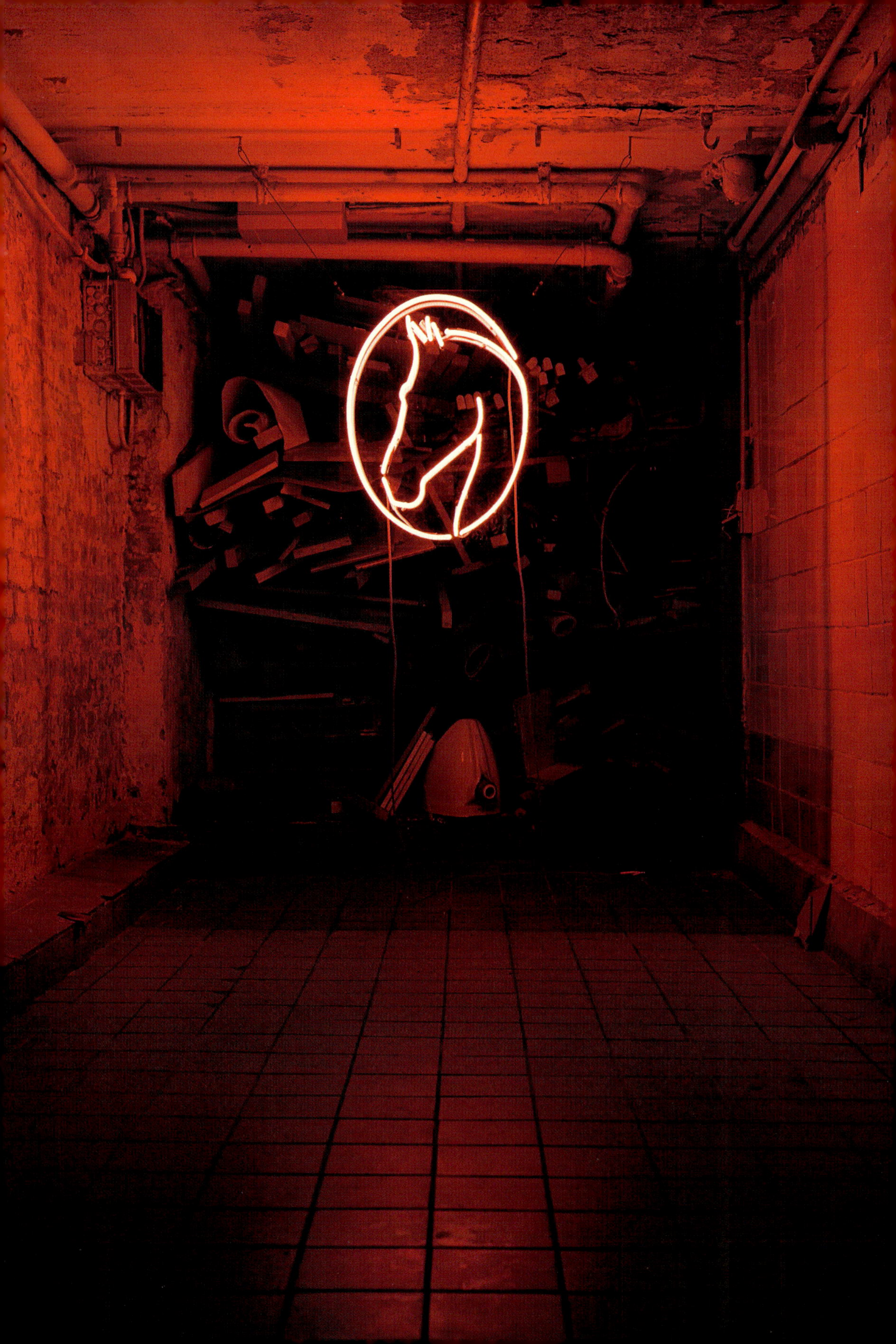

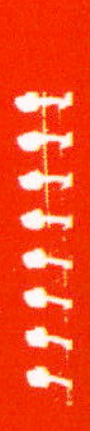

'genetic engineering & modern domestication
↓ we can no longer define animals in terms of
biology — but define them as tradition draws
on history of human animal relationships.

— values embedded in tradition that enable us
to protect above. But suppose we work to preserve either
species in the wild or a breed in domestic

Almost every jockey is a freelancer

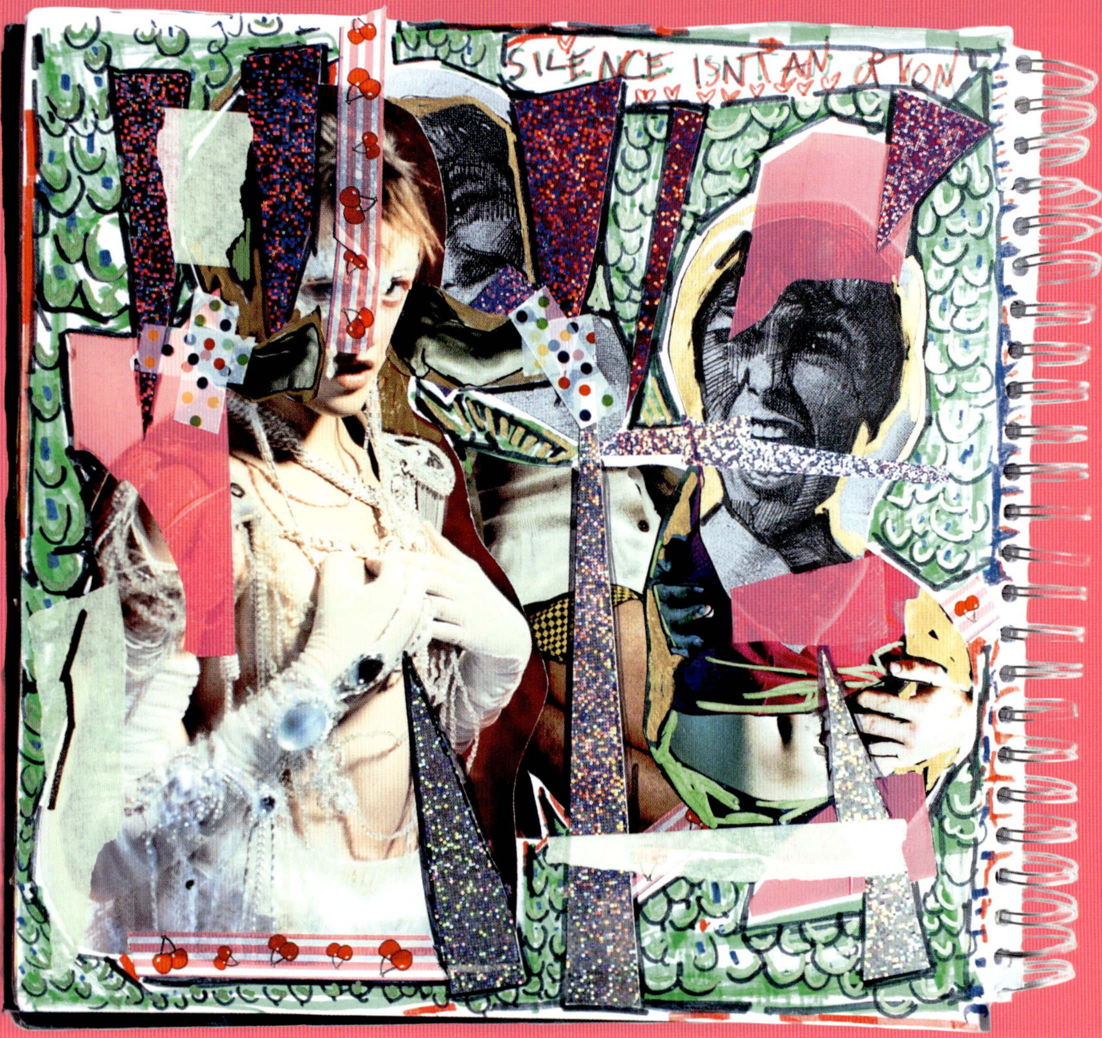

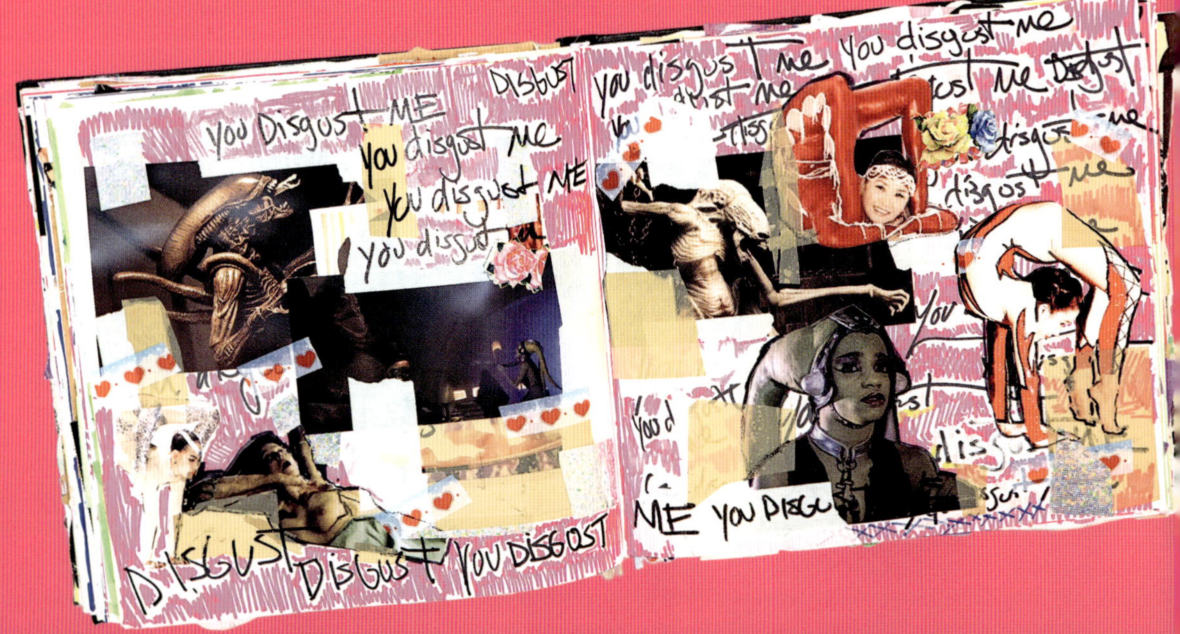
you disgust ME
you disgust Me
you disgust ME
you disgust me
you disgust me
you disgust me
DISGUST
DISGUST YOU DISGUST
ME YOU DISGUST

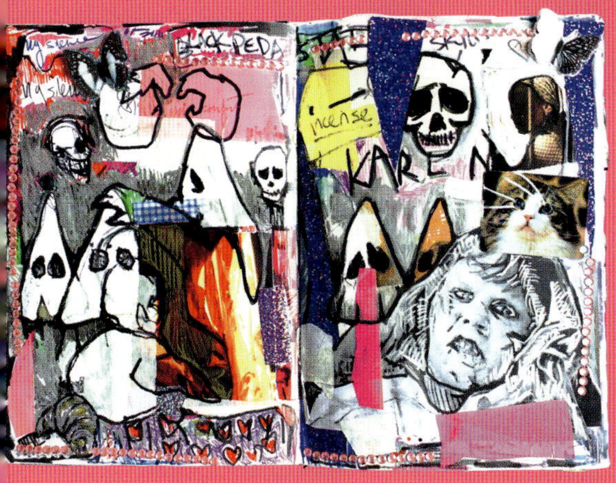
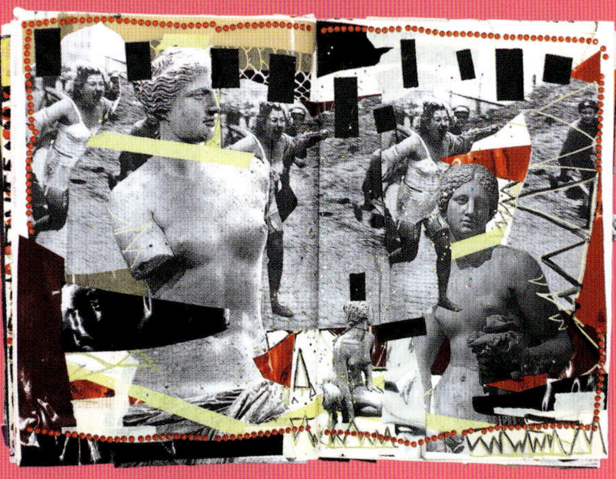
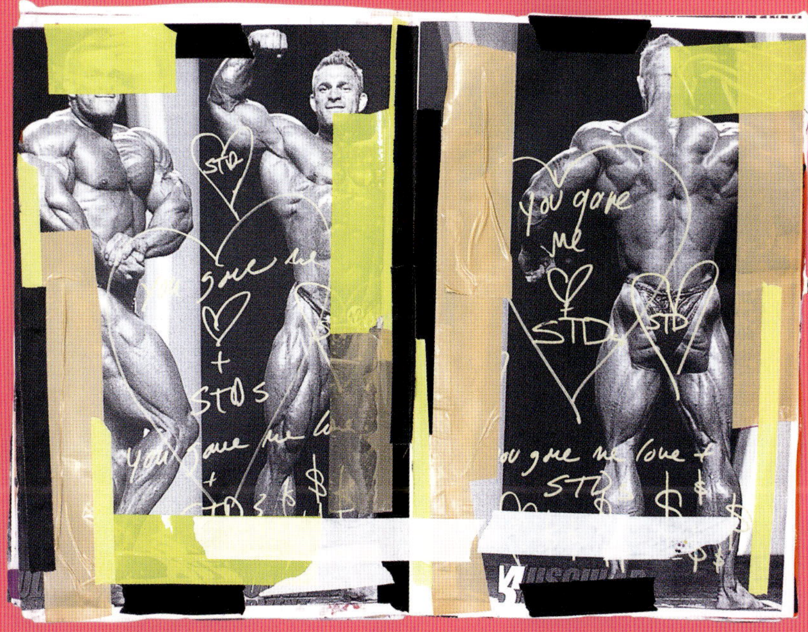
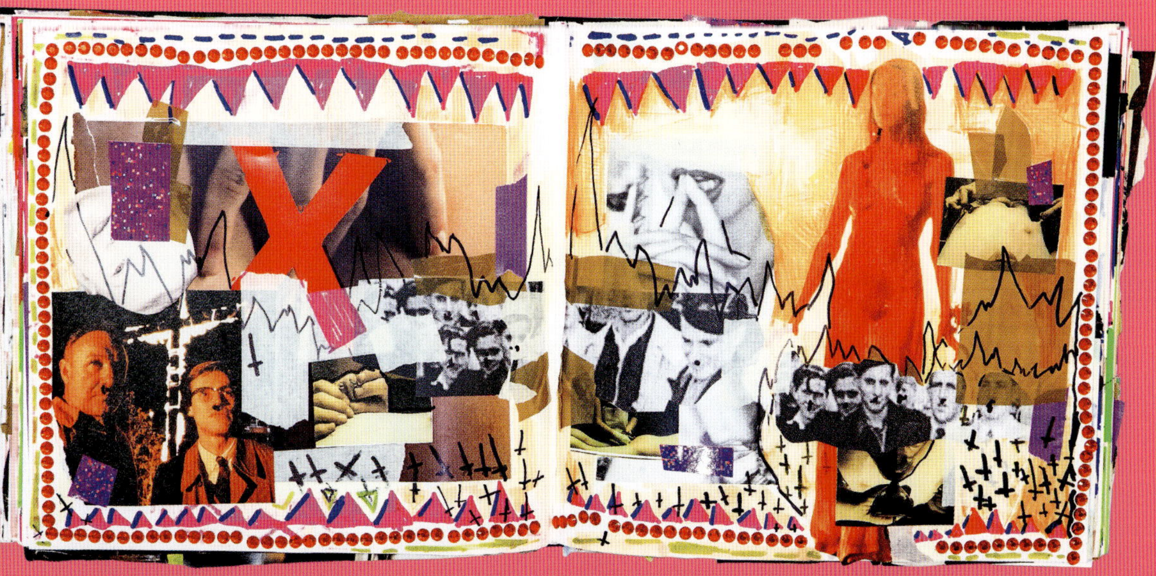

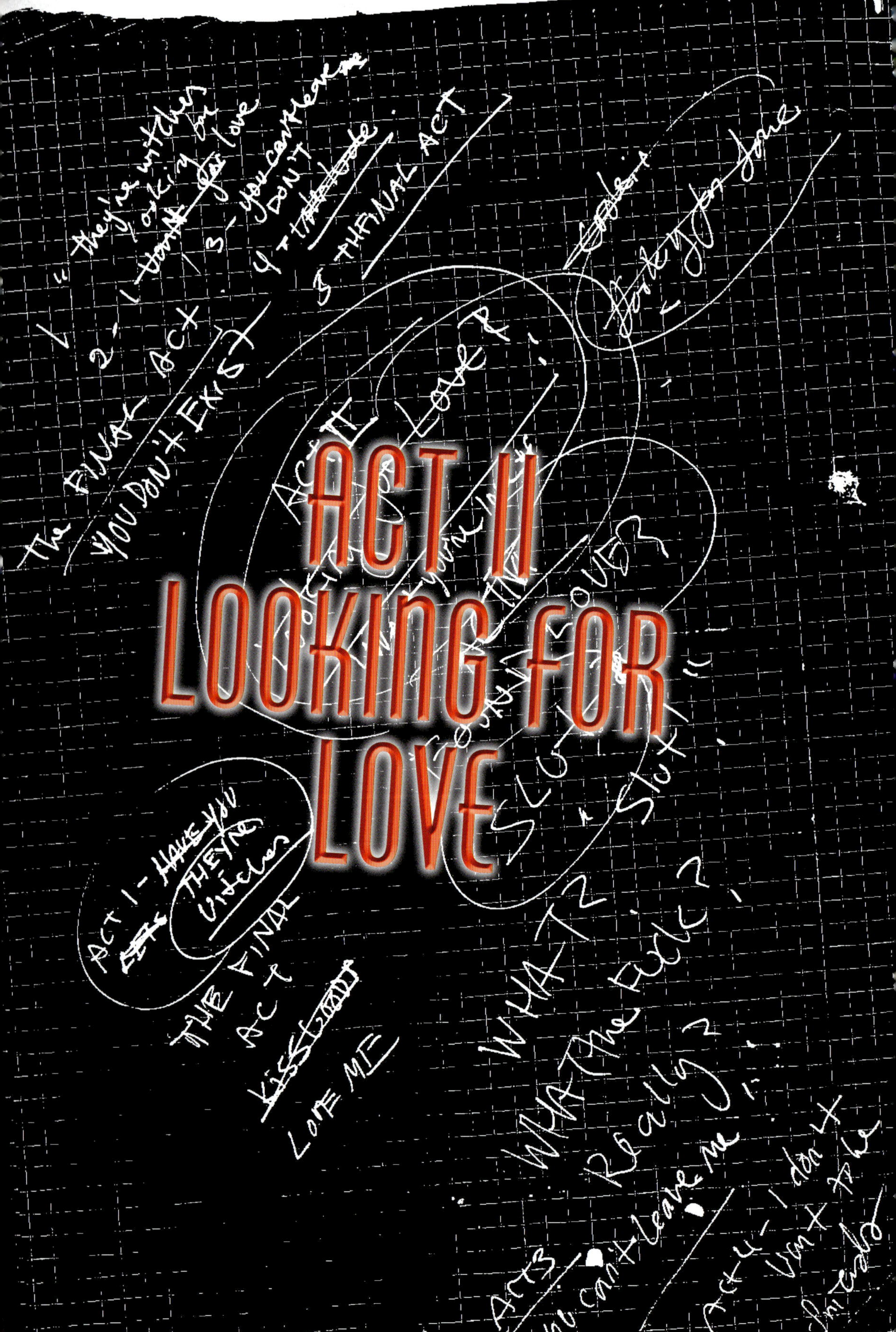

ACT II
LOOKING FOR
LOVE
THE FINAL ACT
1 - they're witches
2 - I wuz looking for
3 - you can't exist
4 - I think you're
3 - THE FINAL ACT
ACT II Love P
ACT 1 - HAVE YOU
THEY'RE
witches
THE FINAL
ACT
KISS
LOVE ME
SLUT
SLUT
WHAT?
WHAT the fuck?
Really?
ACT3
you can't leave me
ACT4 - I don't

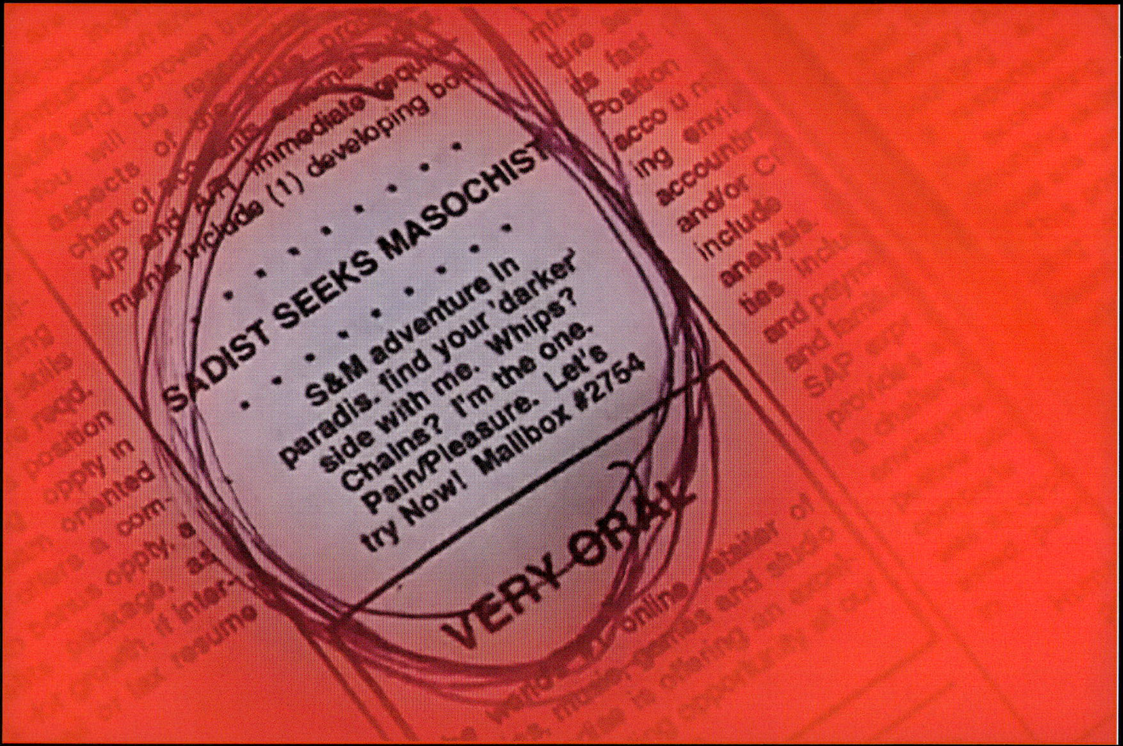

SADIST SEEKS MASOCHIST

S&M adventure in paradis. find your 'darker' side with me. Whips? Chains? I'm the one. Pain/Pleasure. Let's try Now! Mailbox #2764

VERY ORAL

Romantic love specific heterosexual love
— love conditional on obedience
submission on base self love

6:38 But you told me I was sexy.
6:44 Yes you remember me right?
6:48 You see I'm pregnant.

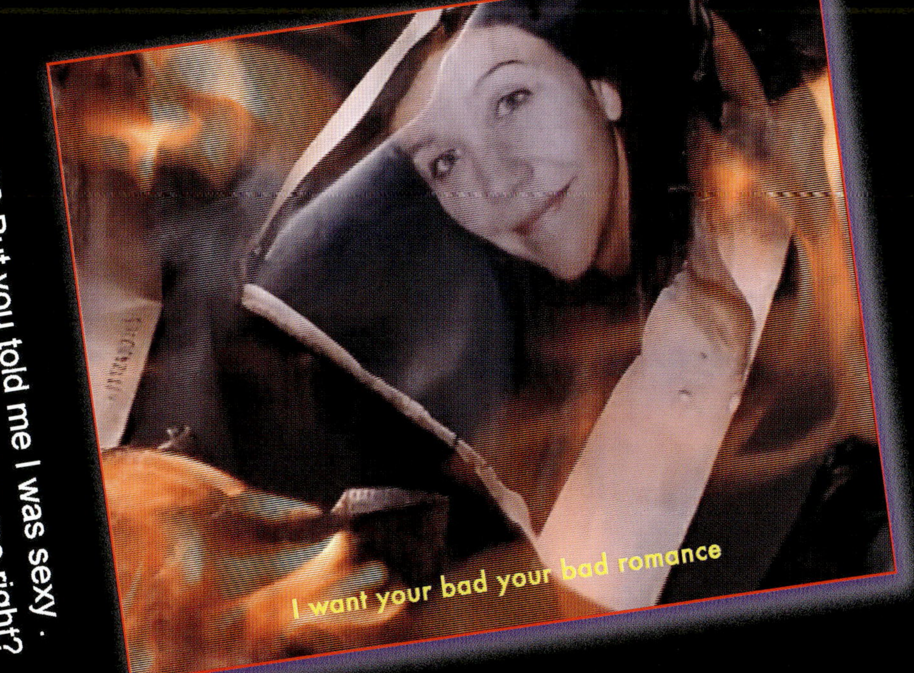

I just can't stop loving you

He loves me, He loves me not
She loves me, She lo

Ghost me me, use me, Fuck → taste me
eat me Touch choke me,
Kiss me, lick me, ^devour me, ~~eat me~~,

tie me, ride me, scolie me, make
me, ghost me, use me, ~~fuck me~~,
leave me
~~use me~~, waste me, erase me

Bury me, gut me, shame me,
starve me, Break me, (Reduce me)
~~Bore~~ Bone me, see me, Fuck me
~~tie me~~ Hate me, Follow me
~~Avoid me~~, Love me,

~~GET A FUCK~~

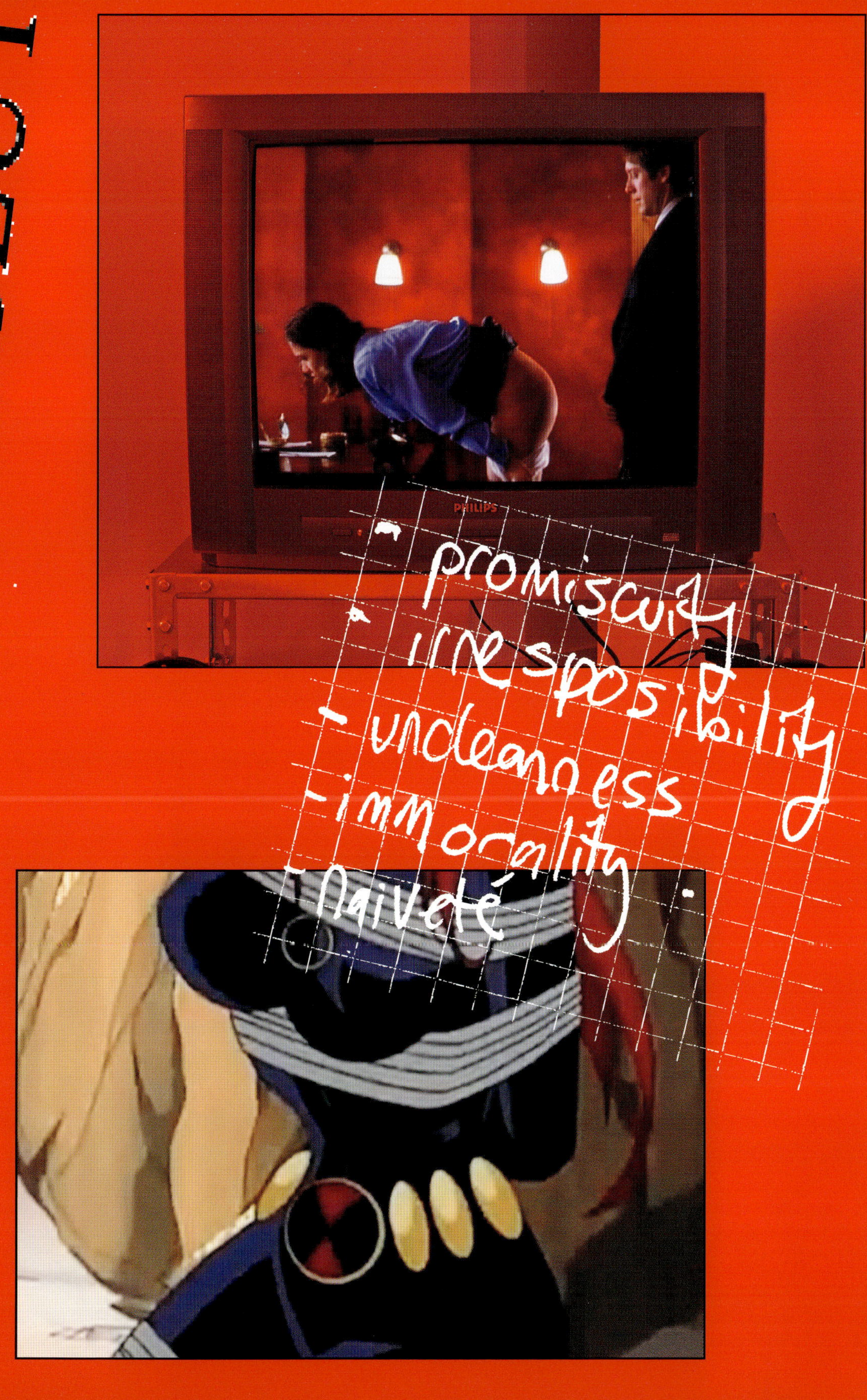
IT'S A SLUT
PHILIPS
promiscuity
irresposibility
- uncleanness
- immorality
- Naiveté

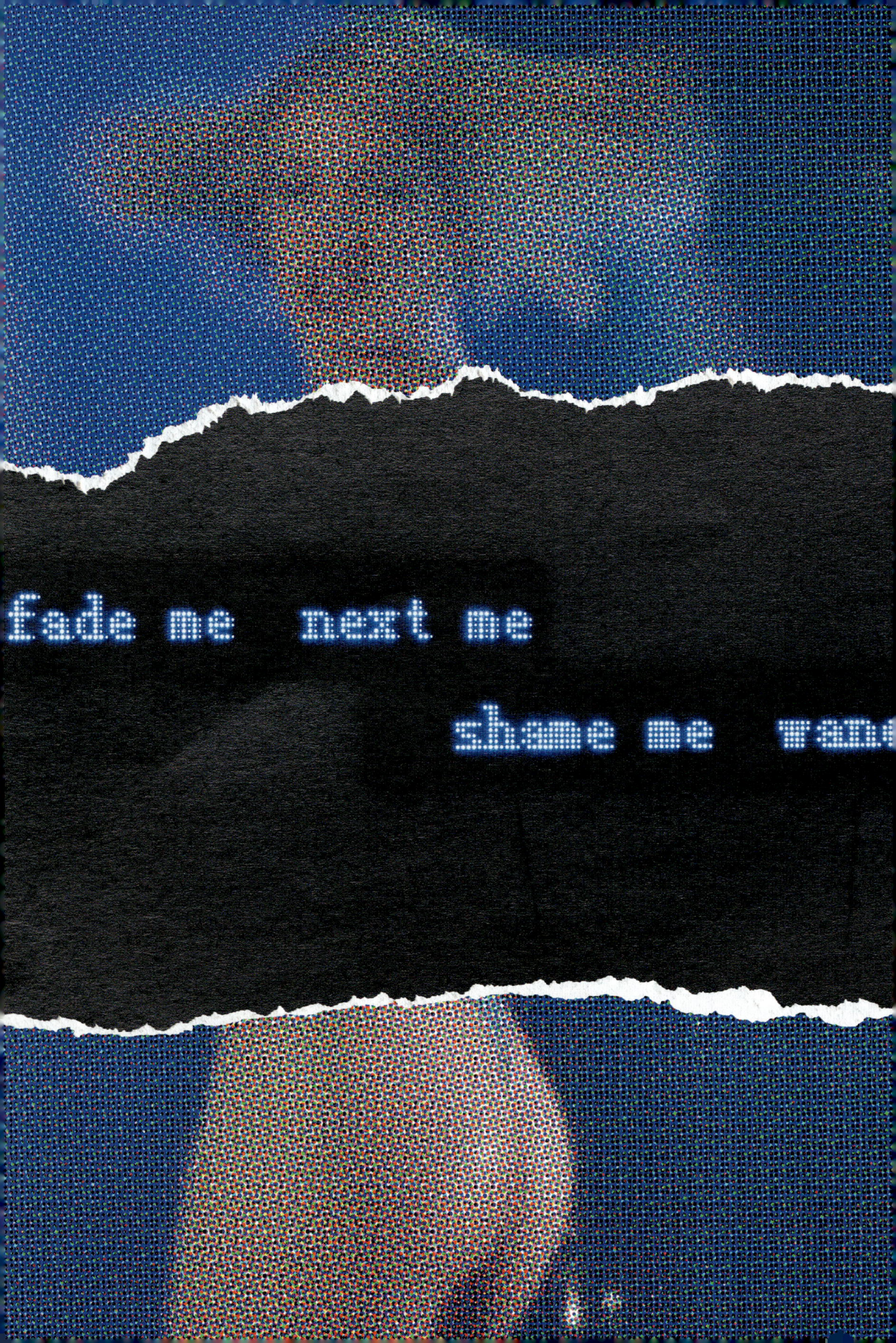

fade me   next me
shame me   vane

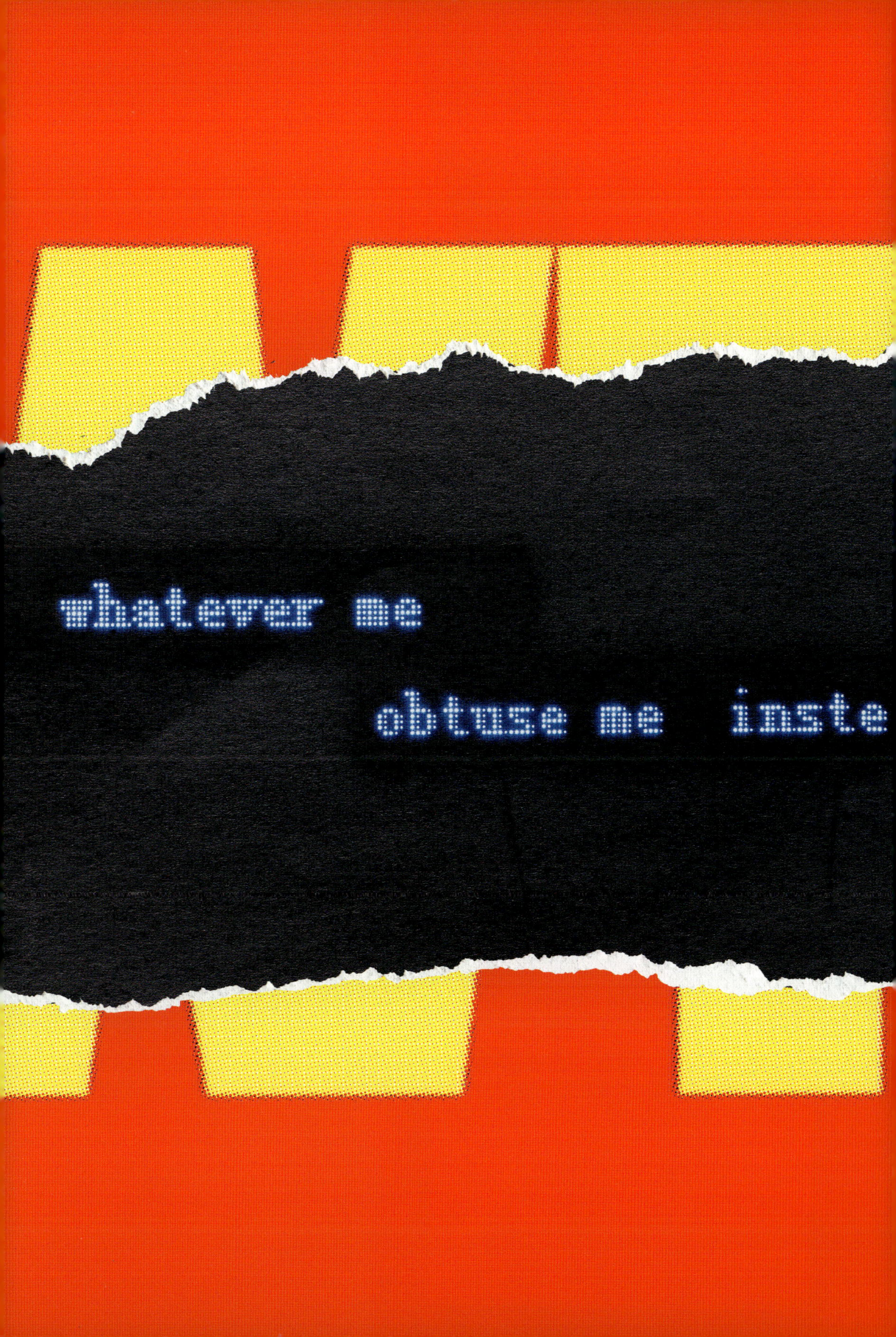
whatever me
obtuse me inste

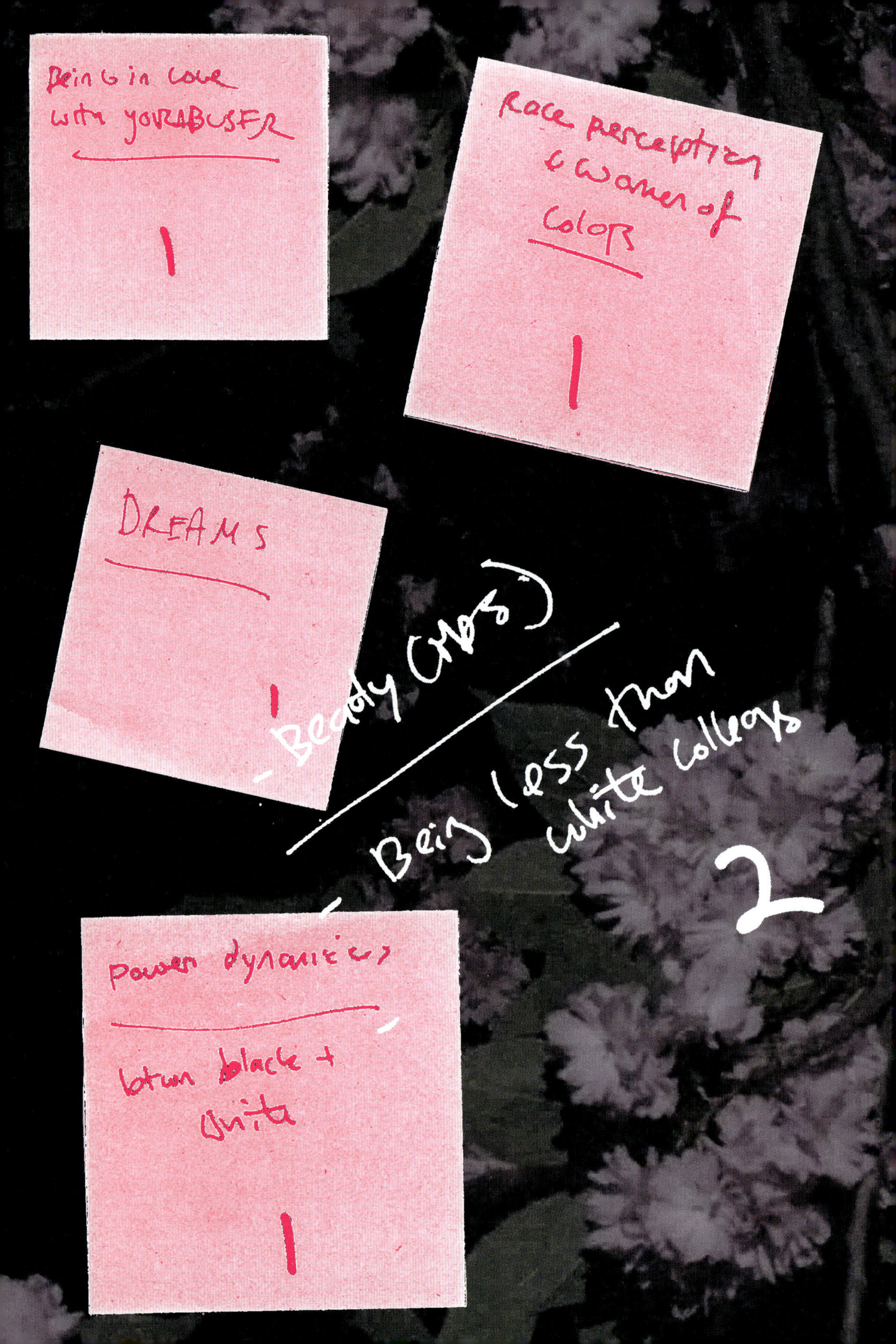

Being in love
with YOUR ABUSER

1

Race perception
& women of
color

1

DREAMS

1

- Beauty (rituals)

Being less than
white colleagues

2

Power dynamics

between black +
white

1

HIV + WOMEN
+ WOMEN
OF COLOR

1

- HIV associated with Black /Africa
- fear to look weak
- fear of being old 2
- Slut shame /morality
- Being alone / who will love me

FEAR +
GHOSTS

1

(how to prove a ghost)
(fears are like HIV)

GHOSTS
- Fear (No available jm)
⊖ Displacement (no home)
- discrimination
- AGE (?)
⊖ Women + love
ABUSE
- not Being NORMAL
- Being racialized
- sexual minorities

ProAcT 1 Desno 304

– I walk with this virus and I don't ever ask myself who made it, or why!?

I have it, I learned to deal with it, and I live and I'm a mother and I'm happy.

– But when somebody tries to remind me

("ah ha you come from Africa that's why you have HIV")

then I start seeing another ghost "ok really Africa is connected to HIV"

It is a sickness and we have to deal with this sickness and nobody will ever prove a ghost because only one person is seeing this ghost

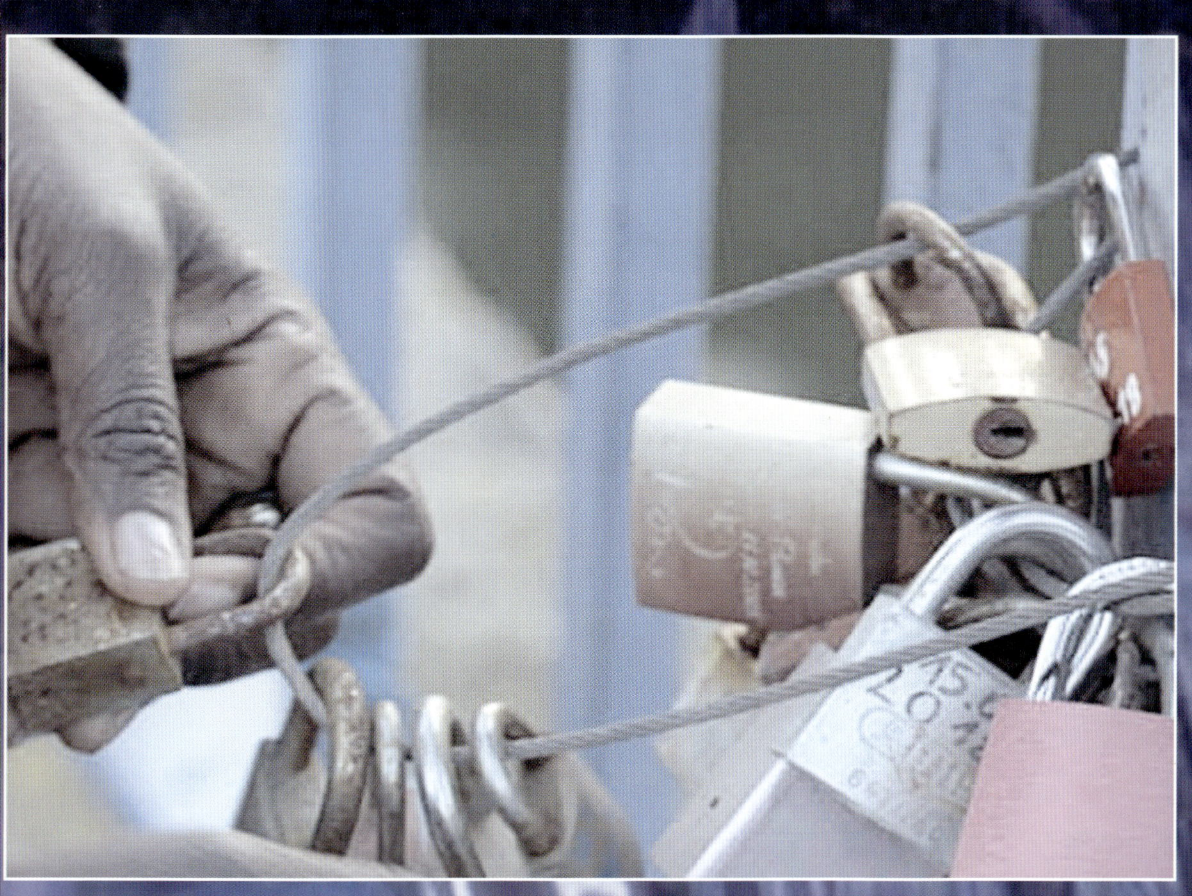

'so "It's your own fault", as they say in German

→ medical establishment's view of men
(as "the norm") further complicates HIV
prevention, detection, + treatment for
women. —
        • INFERIOR social status makes it
unlikely that treatments will be
developed with women in mind.

• — Heterosexism   3 main
• — racism   > forces
• — sexism   govt inaction

economic / political / medical pos'n
        power

⊙ "You cannot understand the ghosts of
other people who DO NOT see the ghosts
↓ you HAVE to believe the ghosts of other
people" pg 7. [23.26] ☆

There is No normal relationship with a white man.

— A DRUG COMPANY CAN'T make profit
on a DRUG if many people of who
need it are too poor to pay a high
price for it
        Research + Drug trials > concentrate
                                        on those
tuc FWARS   who can afford
      ↓ patent battles   + "profit"
delay experimental drugs + treatment

• discovery
• patent   > delay for financial gain
• license

P 81 RACE WOMEN + AIDS

women of color account for 73%
of women with AIDS in the US ↓ reflects
AIDS → "white white   that racism is in
                          all parts of our soci

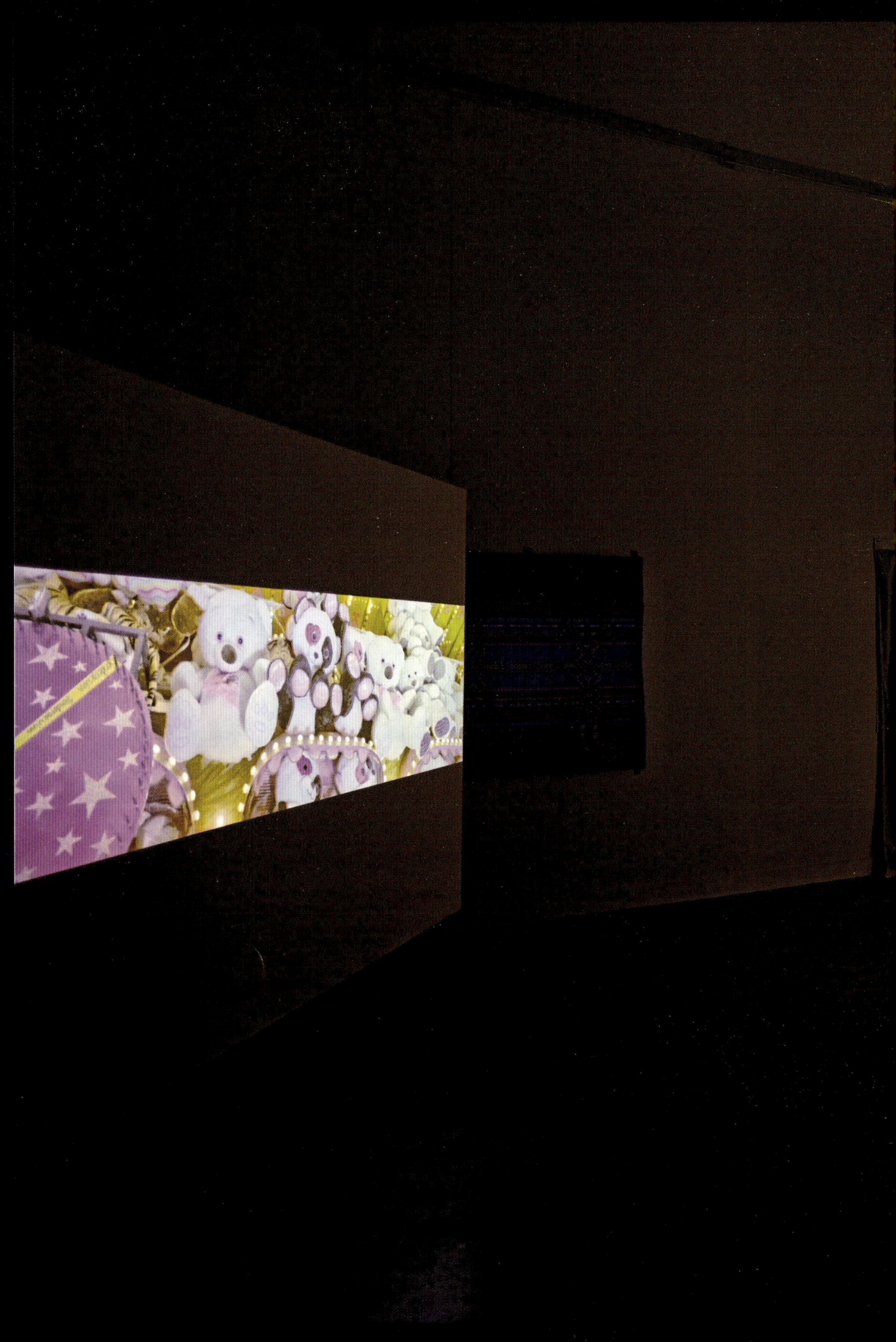

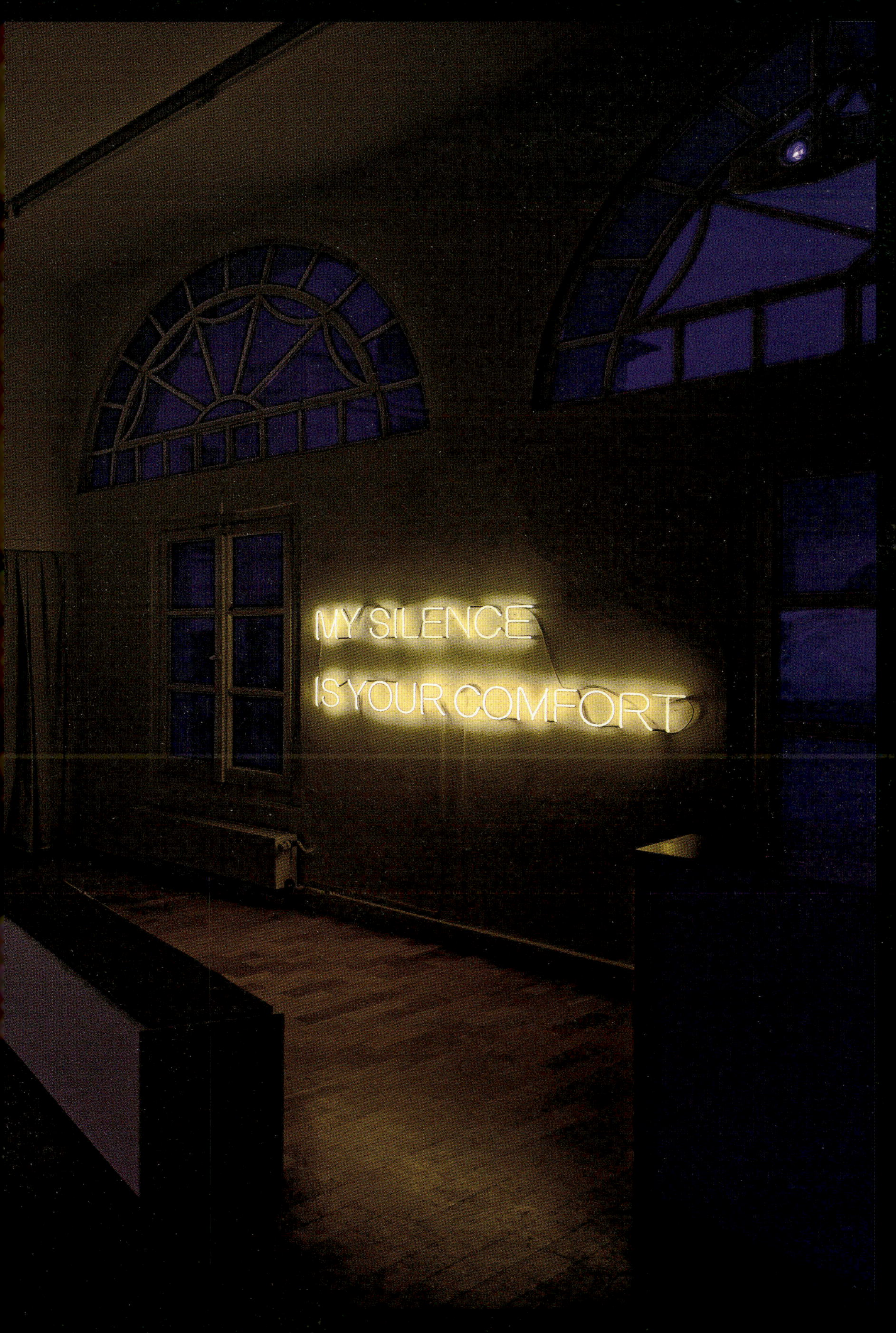
MY SILENCE
IS YOUR COMFORT

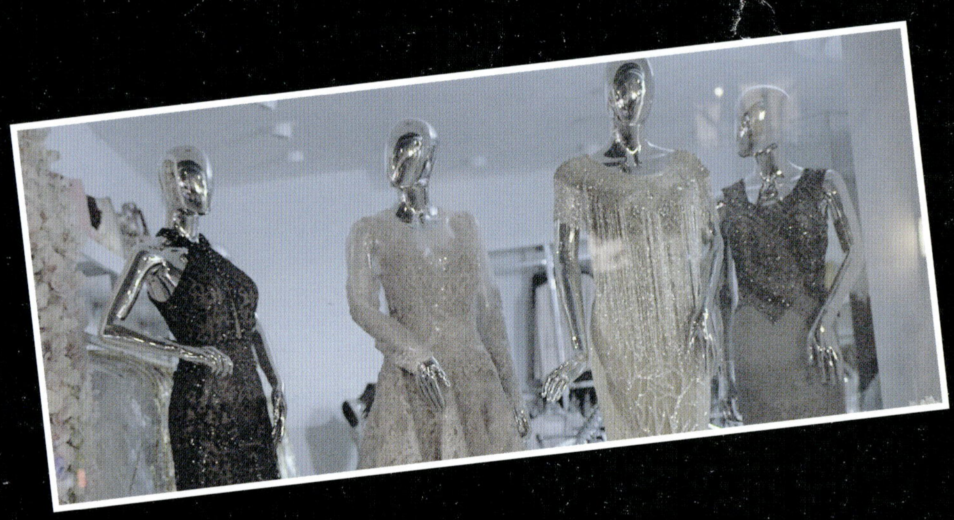

' STDS = social constructed as symbols
of immorality for women + continue
to be interactionally constructed as
shame ful stigma (

↓ reduce girls + women social status

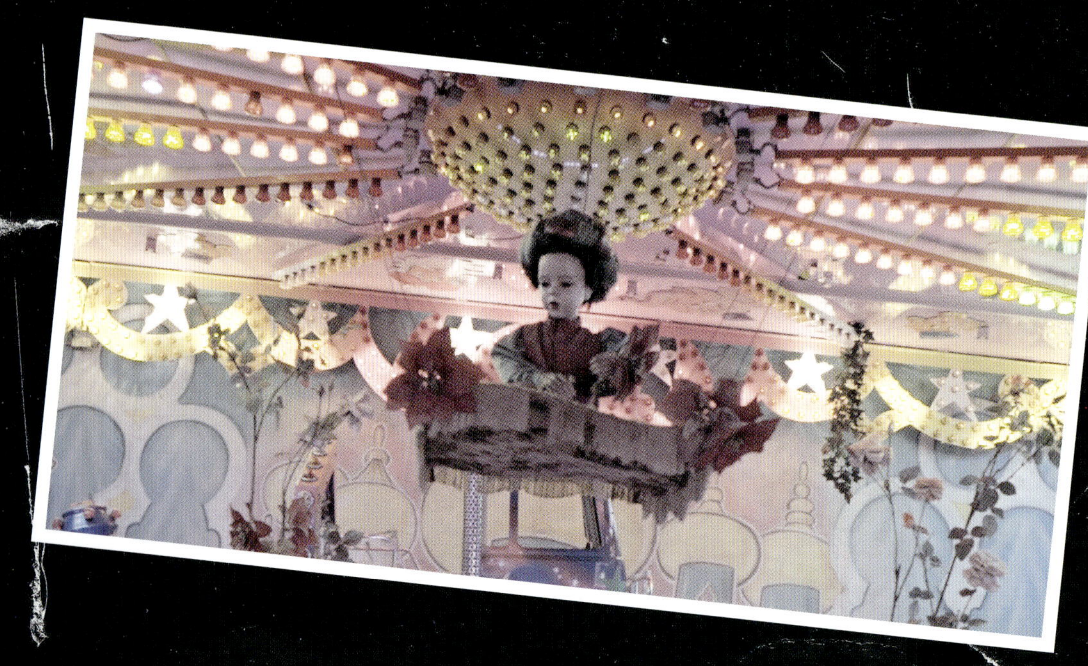

meaning?

BORDERS,

Power,

discrimination,

fear,

shame,

Blame.

ACCEPTANCE

recovery

Race,

AGE,

Sex,

Race,

GENDER,

AGE,

power,

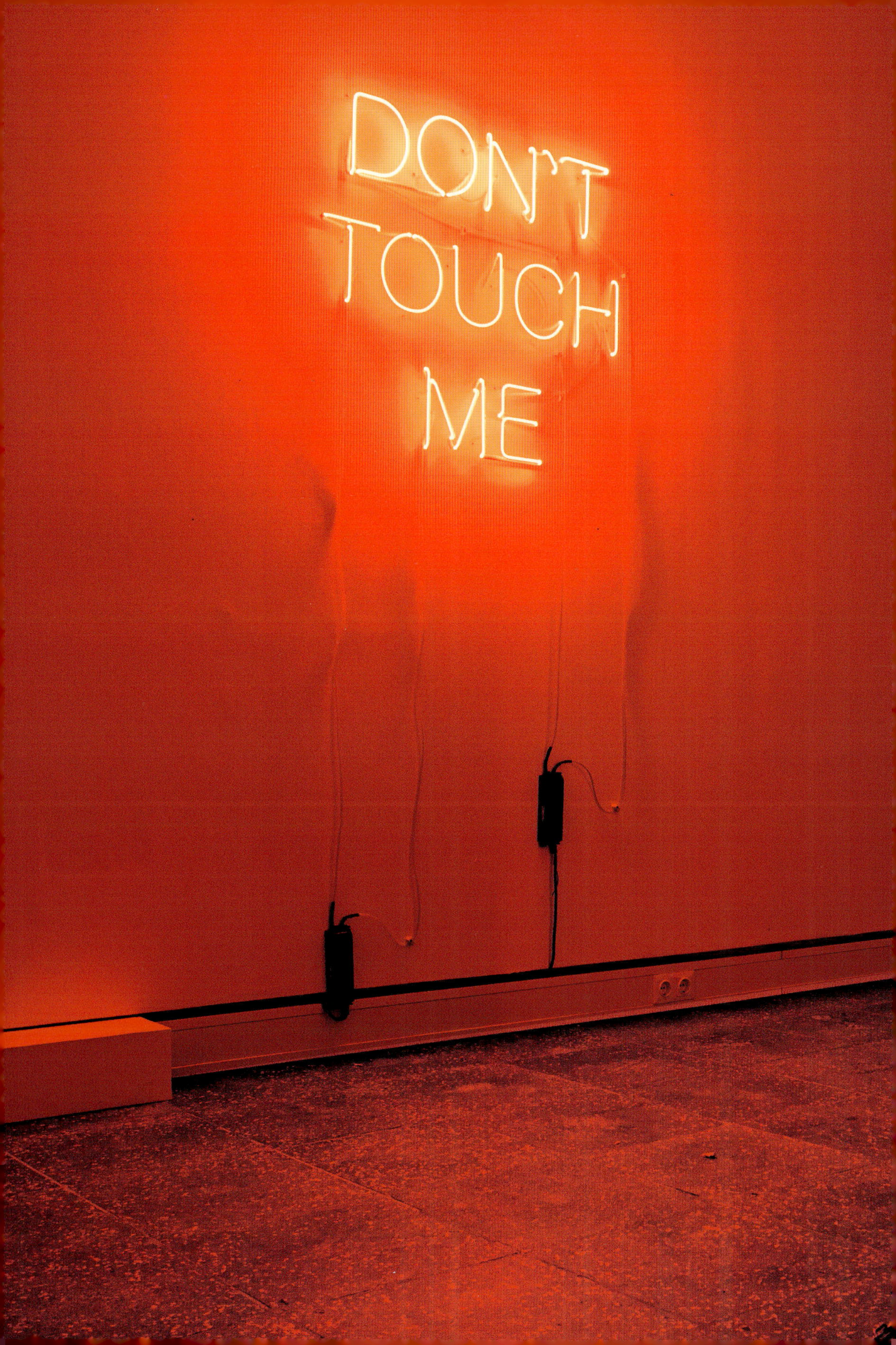
DON'T
TOUCH
ME

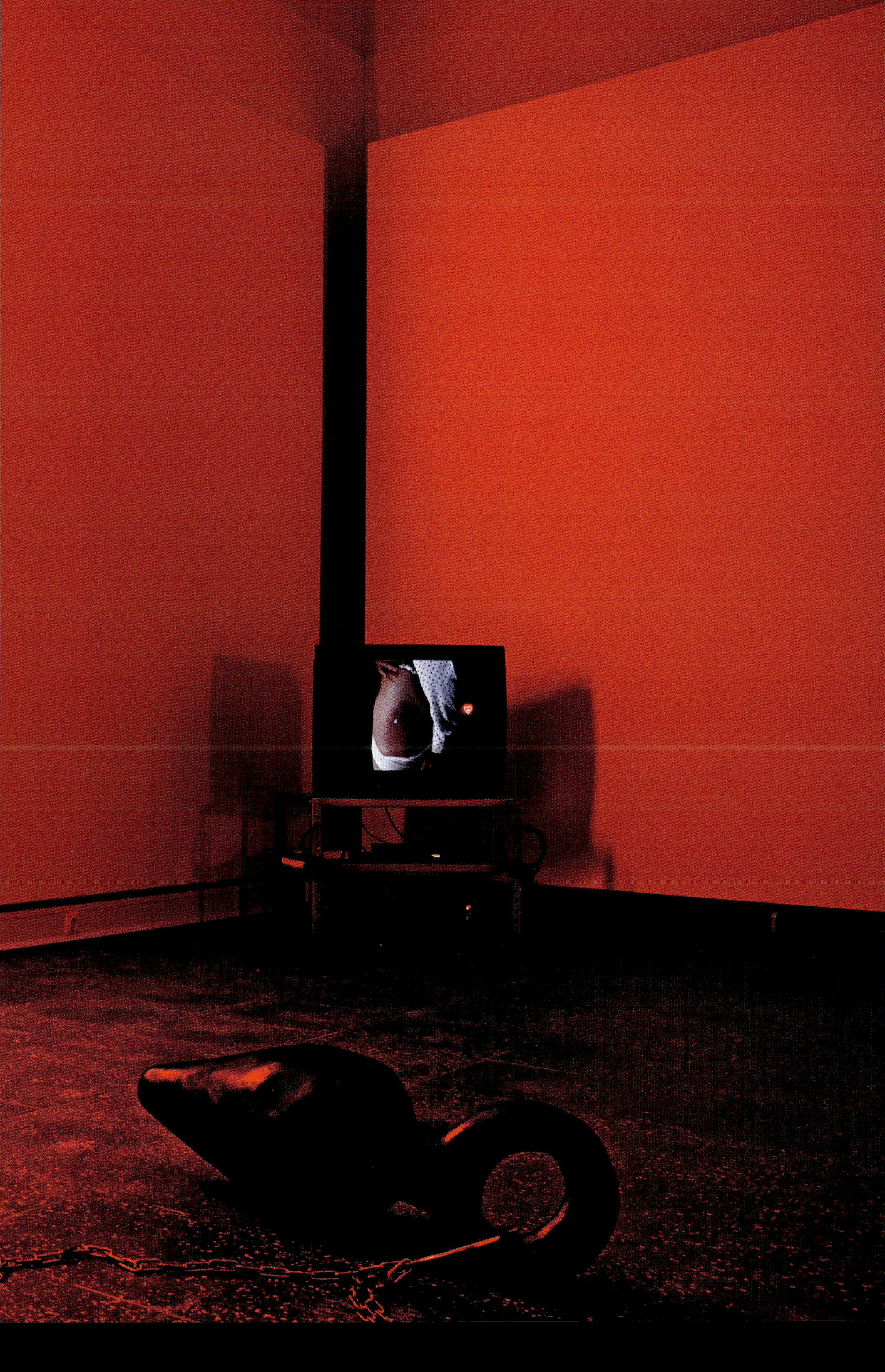

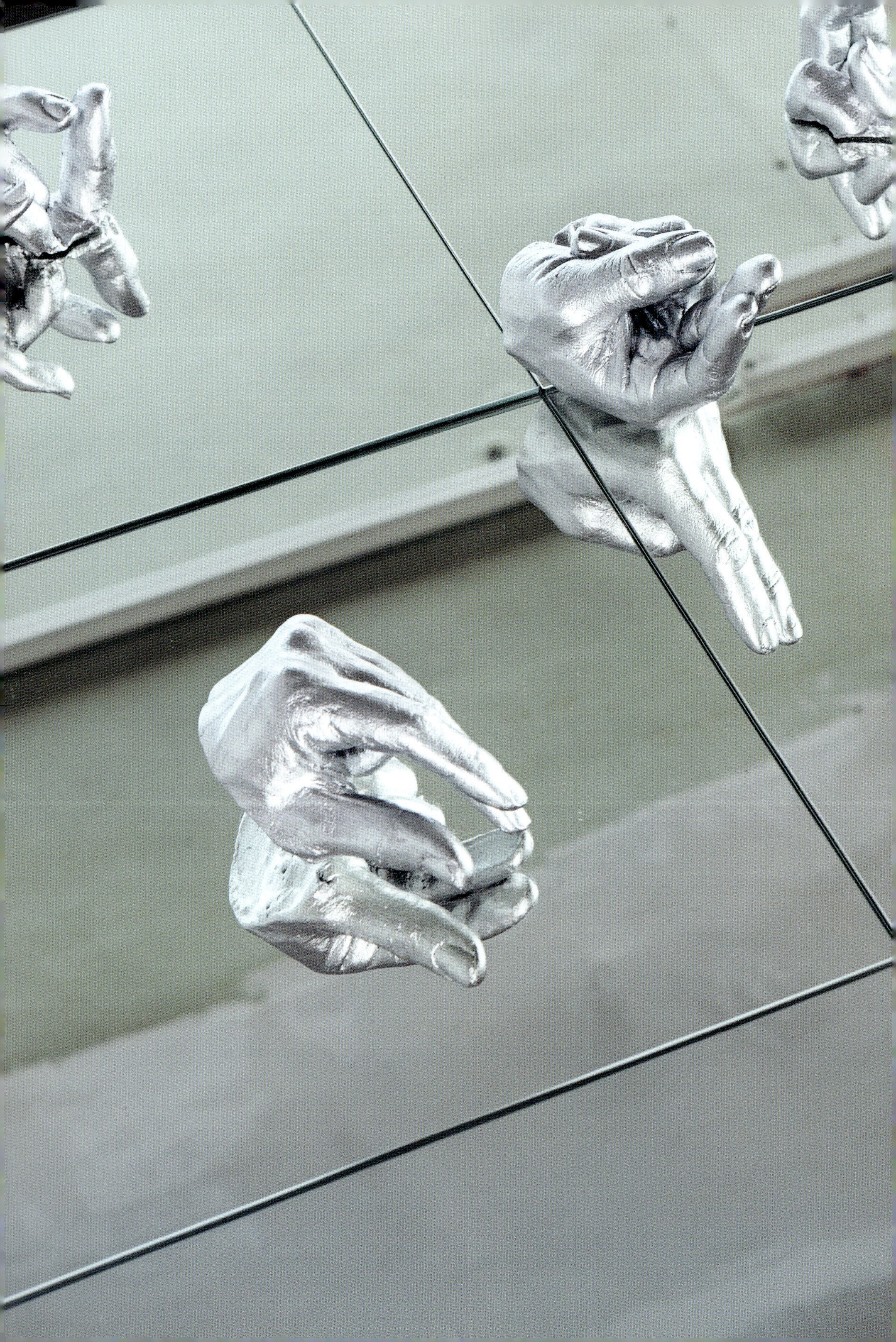

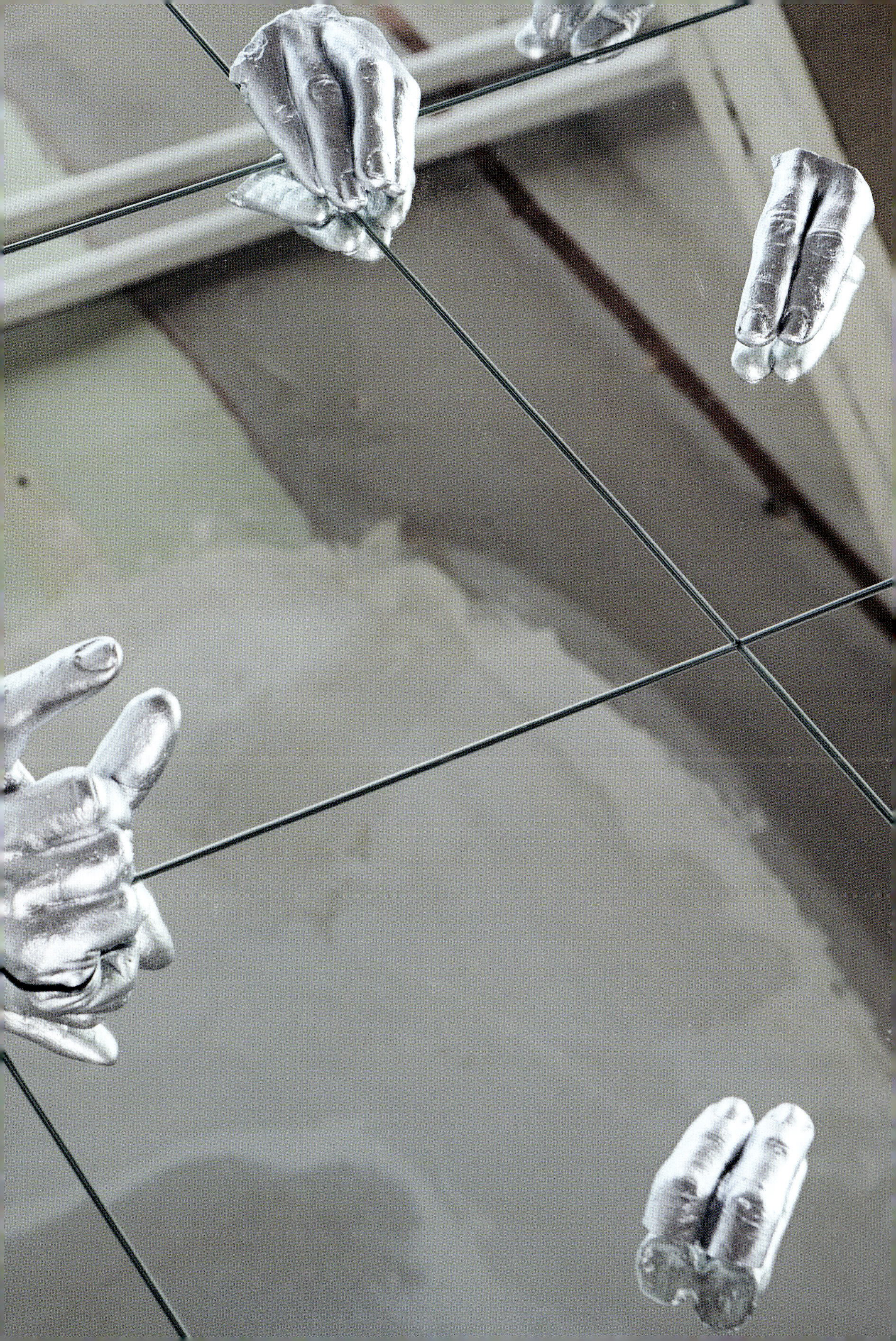

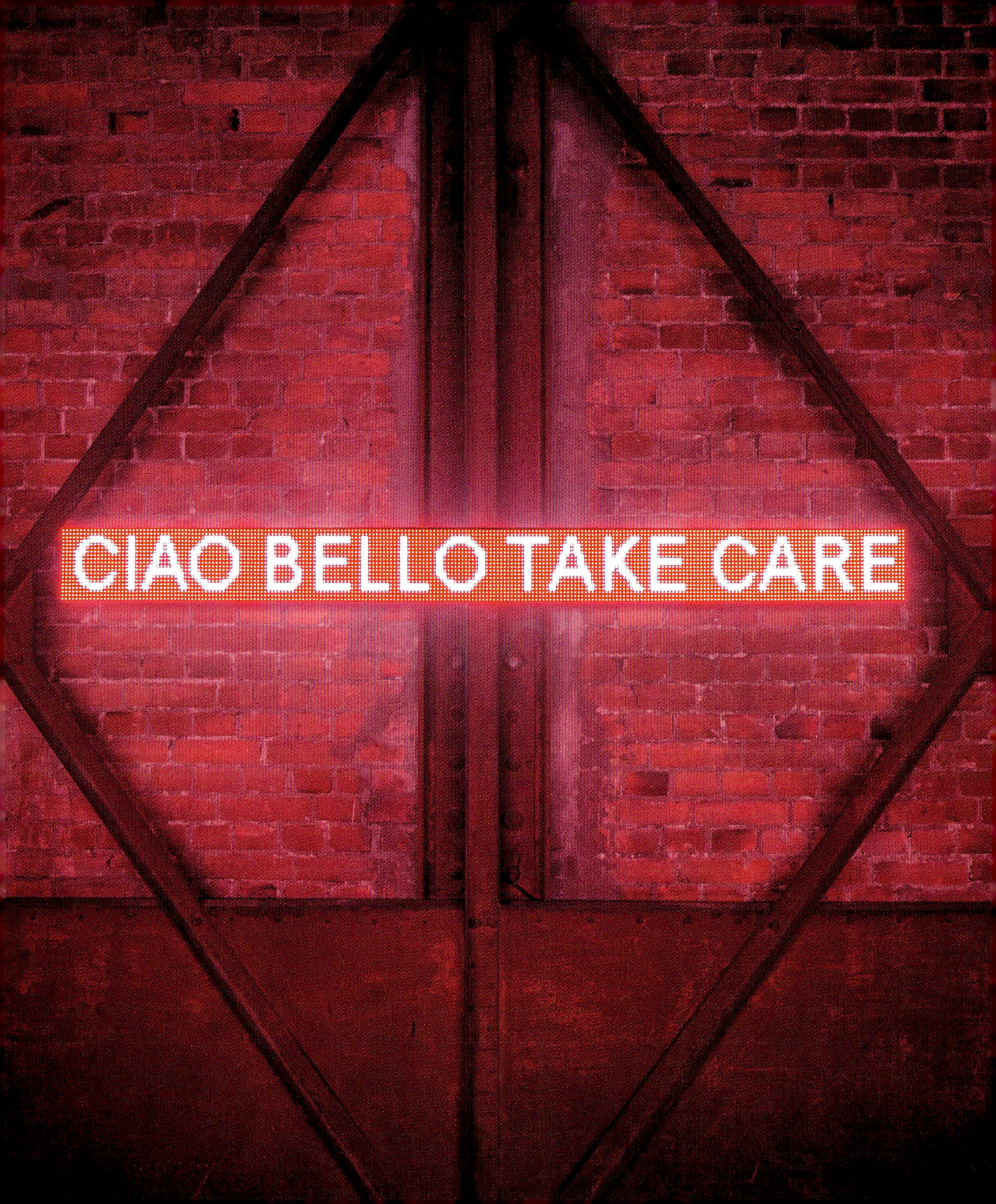
CIAO BELLO TAKE CARE

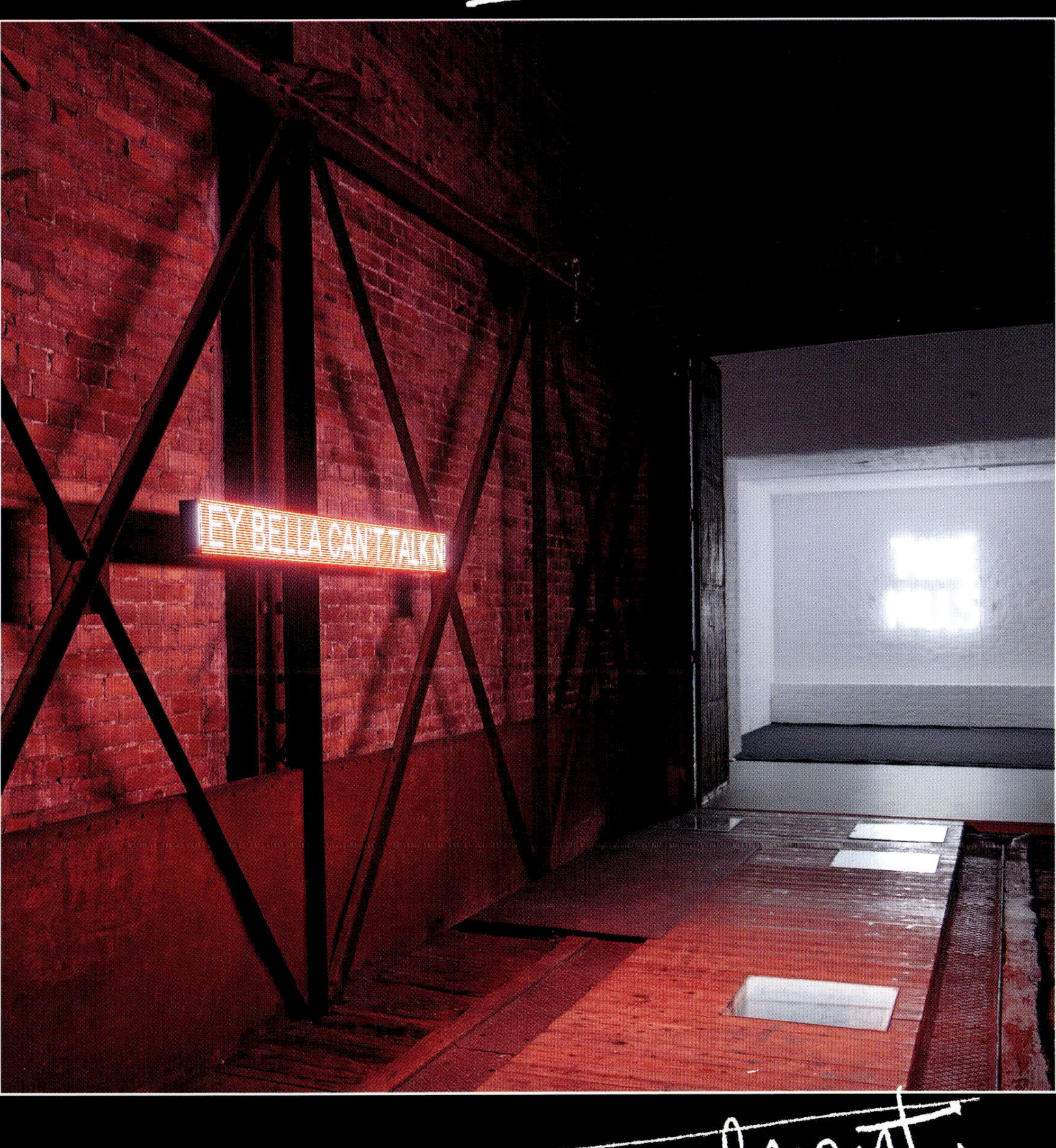

I makes me
= fear / smaller
master of concealment.
EY BELLA CAN'T TALK'N

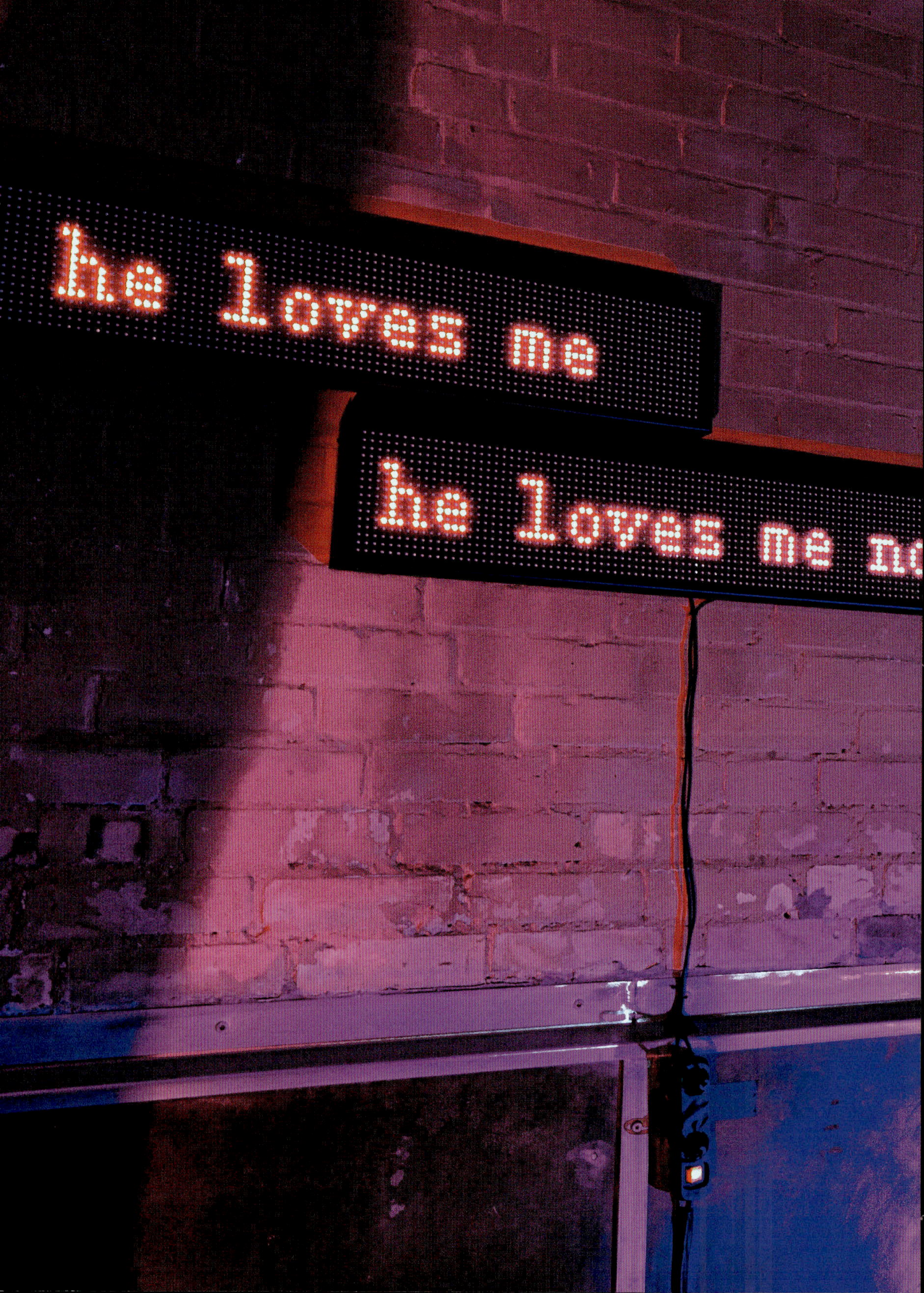
he loves me
he loves me n

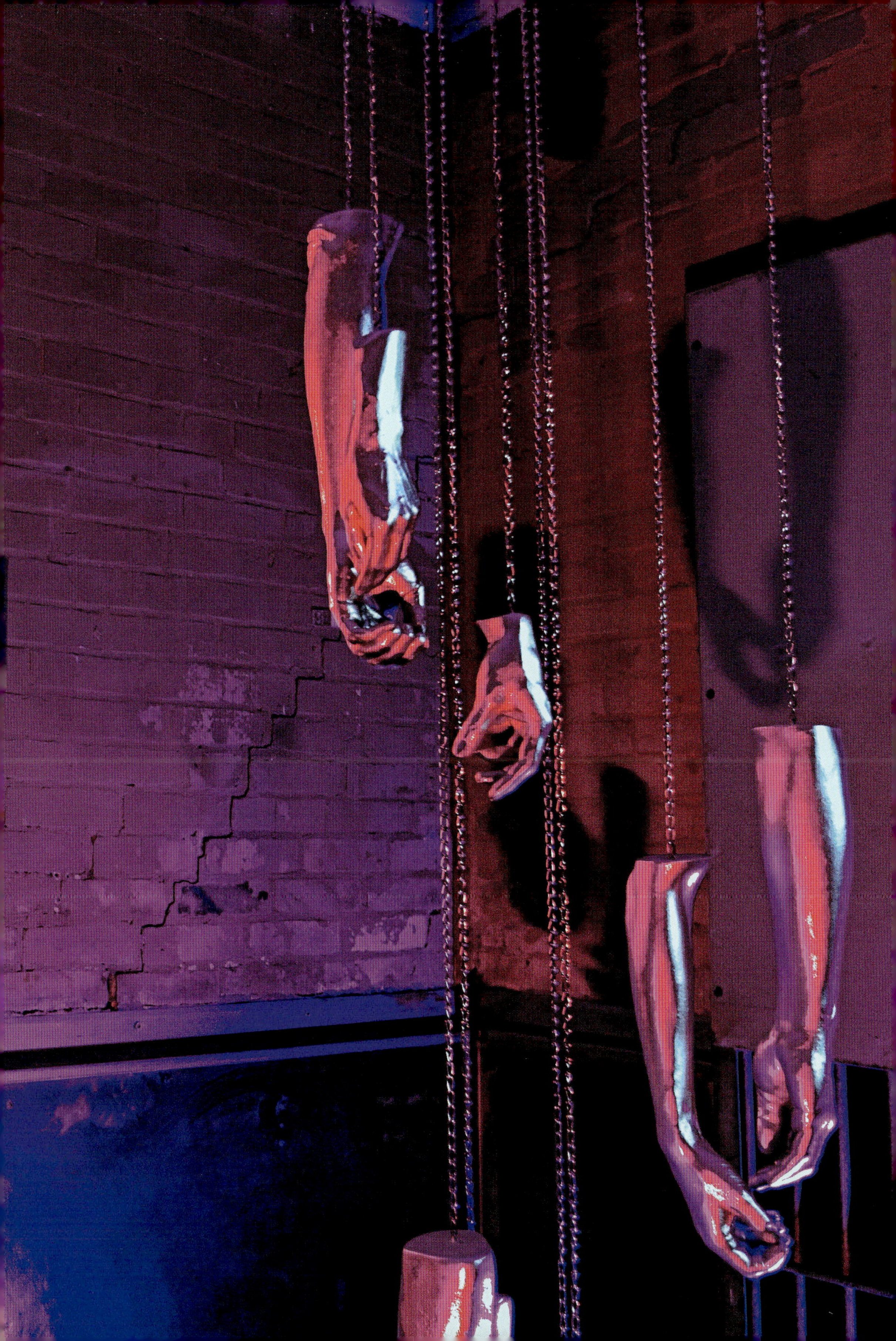

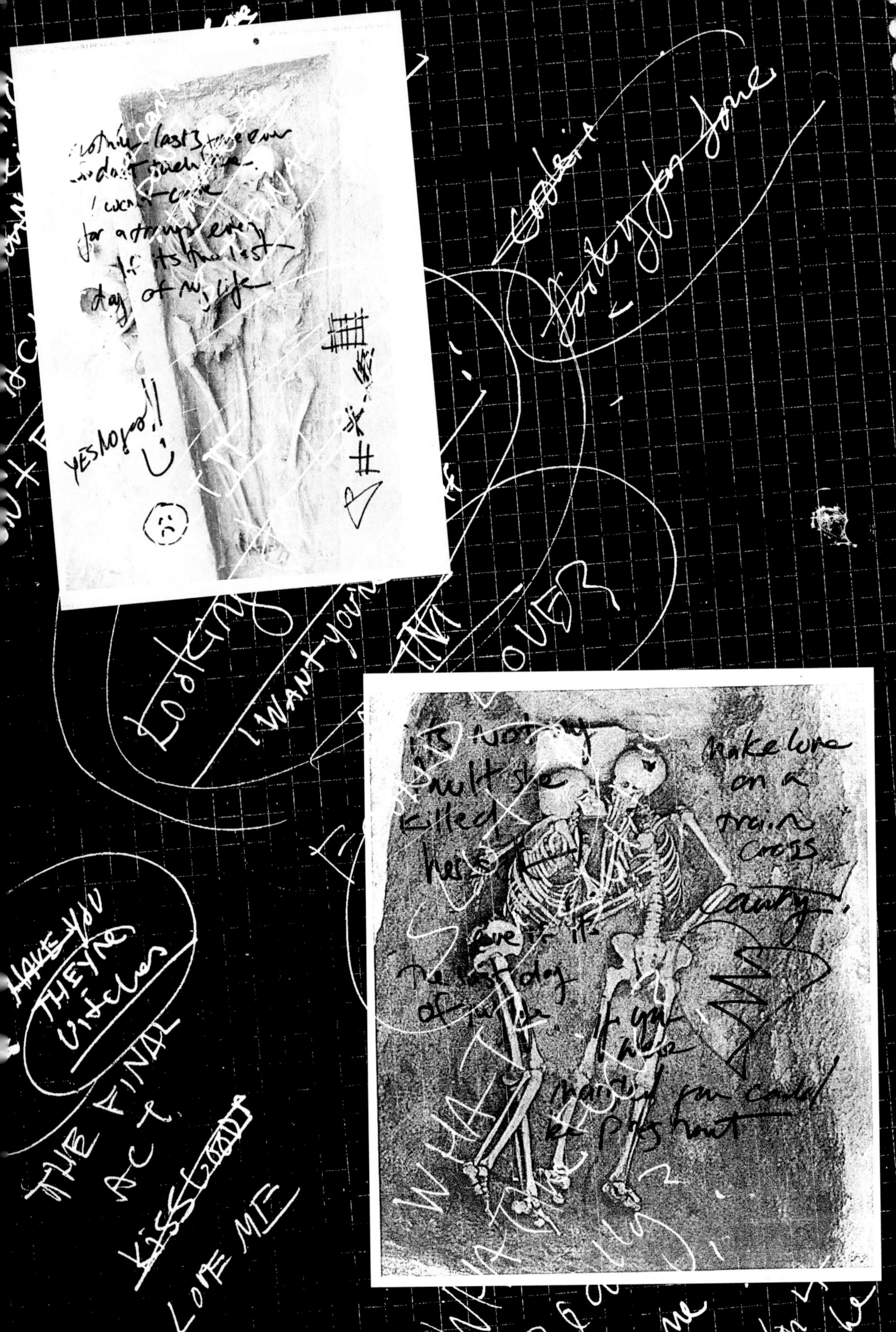
YES! good!!
HAVE YOU THEY'RE watchers
THE FINAL
ACT
KISS GOODBYE
LOVE ME
Looking
I WANT YOUR
LOVER
make love on a train cross
country
its not my fault she killed her
make love on a train

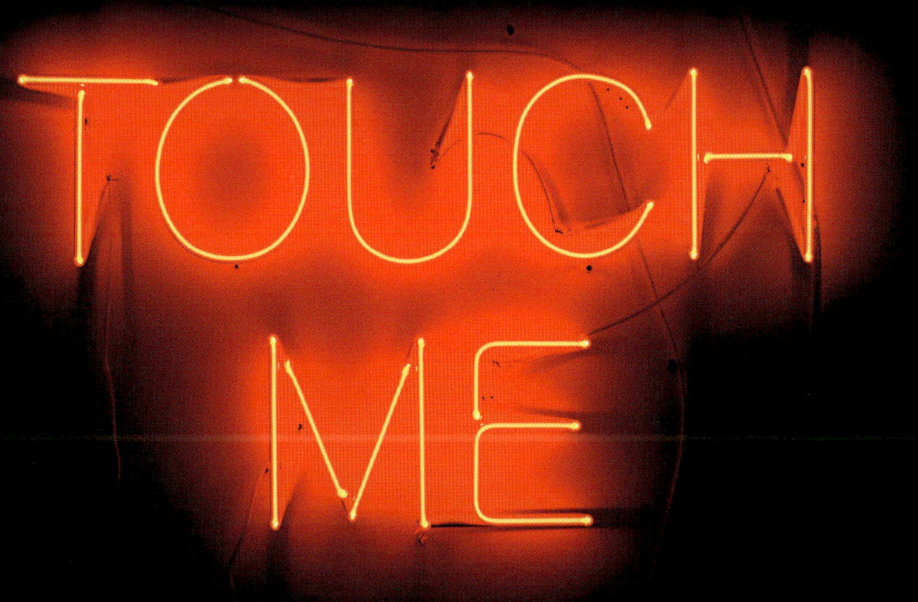

- the desire for romantic intimacy -
↓ coming to terms with higher levels of anxiety,
shame, and stigma

CHRISTA JOO HYUN D'ANGELO

D'ANGELO

Born 1983, Busan, South Korea

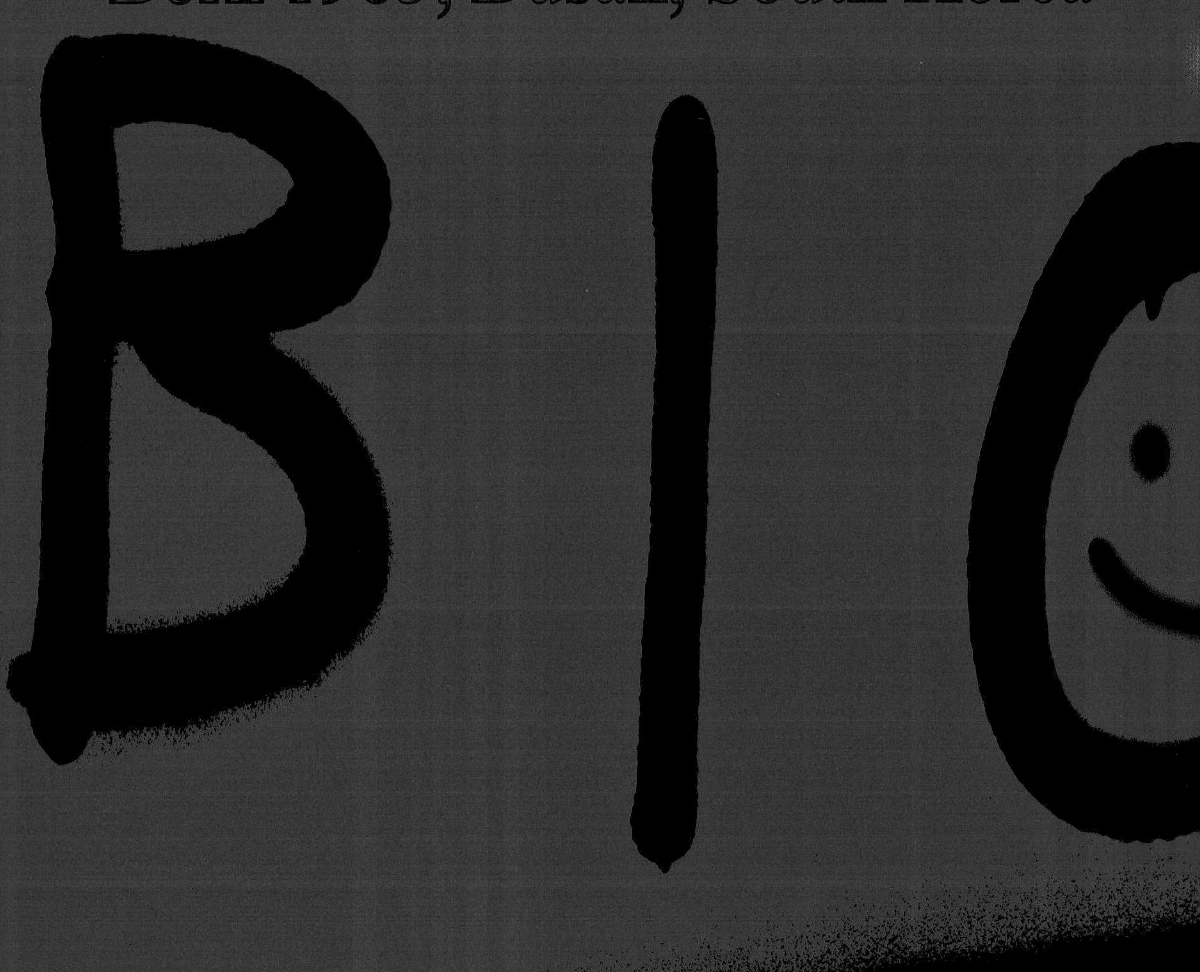

BFA (Painting)

Academy of Fine Arts, Kraków,
Poland, 2006

Maryland Institute College of Art,
Baltimore, USA, 2001–4

SOLO EXHIBITIONS

2022

Violent Desires,
SOMA Artspace, Berlin

2019

GHOSTS,
Galerie im Turm, Berlin

2016

Winner Takes All,
alpha nova & galeria futura, Berlin

2011

Spectacular Society,
Galerie Suvi Lehtinen, Berlin

Proof of Purchase,
Arts and Sciences Projects,
New York City

GROUP EXHIBITIONS

2022

An Overture of Grief and Joy,
Kunstverein Braunschweig,
Braunschweig, Germany

The House of Challenging Orders,
Vienna Art Week, Vienna

I saw you staring out in space,
Galerie P6, Berlin

Empowerment, Kunstmuseum
Wolfsburg, Wolfsburg, Germany

How (Not) to Fit In, Villa Merkel,
Esslingen, Germany

*Stampede: Eight Years at Horse &
Pony*, Horse & Pony, Berlin

Like Water, Top Project Space, Berlin

Pornotopia Revised, Kunsthalle
Exnergasse, Vienna

2021

Into the Drift and Sway,
Bärenzwinger, Berlin

Hell, Yes!, Horse & Pony, Berlin

arcHIV, Searching for Traces,
Schwules Museum, Berlin

2020

&I<3U2, Galeria Studio, Warsaw

Trio Exhibition,
Galerie Russi Klenner, Berlin

Paganismus, Neues Kunsthaus,
Ahrenshoop, Germany

Drift, Fonda, Leipzig

01_Love,
Taipei Digital Arts Festival, Taipei

Rear Window,
Hua International, Berlin

2019

Chimera,
Kunstquartier Bethanien, Berlin

Mauer Mauer, GSL Projects, Berlin

2018

A Strong Desire, PS120, Berlin

Requiem for a Failed State,
Halle14, Leipzig

Nothing Less!, VBKÖ, Vienna

Intimacies and Imagined Futures,
Asian/Pacific/American Institute at NYU
and SOMA Artspace, Berlin

Breathing the Ultimate Wave,
Galerie Sprechsaal, Berlin

Eden, Pomada Queer Culture Festival,
Warsaw

2017

Migrating Stories,
Screen City Biennial, Stavanger, Norway

2015

*Satellite Effects and Other Lines of
Flight*, District*School without Center,
Berlin

Precarious Art: Resistance and Protest,
alpha nova & galeria futura, Berlin

2013

Alter Angle, SomoS Arts, Berlin

2012

Volta Art Fair, New York City

Manisensations, Leap Galerie, Berlin

2011

Preview Art Fair, Berlin

100% Napalm,
Galerie Suvi Lehtinen, Berlin

2010

Are You Coming Too?,
September Galerie, Berlin

A Dream Within a Dream,
Korean Culture Center, Berlin

2009

The Pleasure Seekers,
Chashama Gallery, New York City

Like a Moth to a Flame,
Exile Gallery, Berlin

SCREENINGS, TALKS, and EVENTS

2023

Conversation with Christa Joo Hyun D'Angelo, Kunstverein Braunschweig, Braunschweig, Germany

Cinematographic Aesthetics of Gender, screening / artist talk, Muthesius Art Academy, Kiel, Germany

#134 Christa Joo Hyun D'Angelo, Videoart at Midnight, Berlin

2022

Art at a Time Like This and Nowness Present Excelsior, screening, Quad Cinema, New York City

Artist talk, Freie Universität, Berlin

2021

Imaging Queer Bandung, SİNEMA TRANSTOPIA, screening, Haus der Statistik, Berlin

Shaping the Past, screening, Goethe-Institut, Washington, DC

On Illness, Resistance and Collective (Health)care, artist talk, District*School without Center, Berlin

Past as Process, artist talk, Goethe-Institut, Washington, DC

Memory of HIV/AIDS Care and Activism, screening, District*School without Center, Berlin

2020

Camera Memory for Human Forgetfulness, screening, Goethe-Institut / Arsenal Institute for Film and Video, Berlin

Past Present Tense, screening, Ashley, Berlin

Berlin Art Link Presents Race, Migration and Sexuality, screening / artist talk, Soho House, Berlin

Viral Resistance, screening, Dervia, Berlin

What Voices Can Achieve, HIV and Race, screening / artist talk, VIA Berlin and Queer Asia, Refugia, Berlin

2019

Ciclo Rosa Film Festival, screening, Cinemateca de Bogotá, Colombia

Artist talk, Galerie im Turm, Berlin

Artist talk, Mentoring Artists for Women's Art, Winnipeg, Cananda

2018

DDR and Multiculturalism, artist talk / screening, Halle 14, Leipzig, Germany

Global Asia/Pacific Art Exchange, artist talk, Asian/Pacific/American Institute at NYU and SOMA Artspace, Berlin

Polarization through Enemy Images, screening / artist talk, European University, Berlin

2016

*Cultural Appropriation and
Pursuit of the Next Big Thing*,
screening/panel, Berlin

KinoNacht, screening,
Kino Central, Berlin

2015

Scottish International Queer Film
Festival, screening, Center for
Contemporary Art, Glasgow

Past Present Tense, screening,
xart splitta, Berlin

NYC Porn Film Festival, screening,
Secret Project Robot, New York City

2014

Artist talk, District*School without
Center, Berlin

Artist talk, Novia University,
Jakobstad, Finland

2013

LGBTQ History Month, artist talk,
University of the Arts, London

2012

Post-Election Roundtable Discussion,
panel, University Viadrina,
Frankfurt an der Oder, Germany

AWARDS, GRANTS, and RESIDENCIES

2023

Catalog Funding Grant,
Senate Department for Culture
and Community, Berlin

2021

Visual Arts Research Grant,
Senate Department for
Culture and Europe, Berlin

Innovative Art Project, Federal
Association of Fine Artists Germany

2020

Mentee Nomination, Forecast Edition 5

2019

Project Funding Grant,
District Office of
Friedrichshain-Kreuzberg, Berlin

Studio Grant Holder, Professional
Association of Visual Artists, Berlin

Artist in Residence, Mentoring Artists
for Women's Art, Winnipeg, Canada

COLLECTIONS

Contemporary Art Collection of the
Federal Republic of Germany

CONTRIB-UTORS

BIO

Travis Jeppesen | Kathy-Ann Tan | Karina Griffith

Travis Jeppesen is the author of numerous books. His calligraphic and text-based artwork has been the subject of solo exhibitions at Wilkinson Gallery (London), Exile (Berlin), and Rupert (Vilnius), and has featured in group exhibitions internationally. His play *Ghosts of the Landwehr Canal* premiered in April 2023 at Berliner Ringtheater, under the direction of Wang Ping-Hsiang. In November 2023, Jeppesen's latest novel *Settlers Landing* was published with ITNA Press.

Kathy-Ann Tan is a Berlin-based independent curator, writer, and founder of Mental Health Arts Space, a nonprofit project space that centers the mental health, knowledge, histories, and narratives of BIPoC and minority artists and cultural workers. She is interested in alternative and sustainable forms of art dissemination, cultural production, and institution-building committed to issues of social justice beyond a merely representational model of identity politics. Tan has an MA in Curatorial Practice from the Faculty of Fine Art, Music and Design, University of Bergen, Norway, and is the initiator of Decolonial-ArtArchives. Tan's practice revolves around creating spaces for conversation, sharing, and empowerment for BIPoC and minority communities in the arts and cultural scenes in Berlin and beyond.

Karina Griffith is an artist and researcher who uses moving image, performance, and installations to question archives and conditions of spectatorship. Through the concepts "affective debt" and "reparatory imaginings," she creates objects, films, texts, and experiences that are spaces for speculation.
Her films, installations, and curatorial programs have been shown at international galleries and festivals. Griffith is part of the faculty of the Institute for Art in Context at the Berlin University of the Arts and is a PhD candidate at the University of Toronto's Cinema Studies Institute, where her research on Black German cinemas interacts with theories of affect and intersectionality.

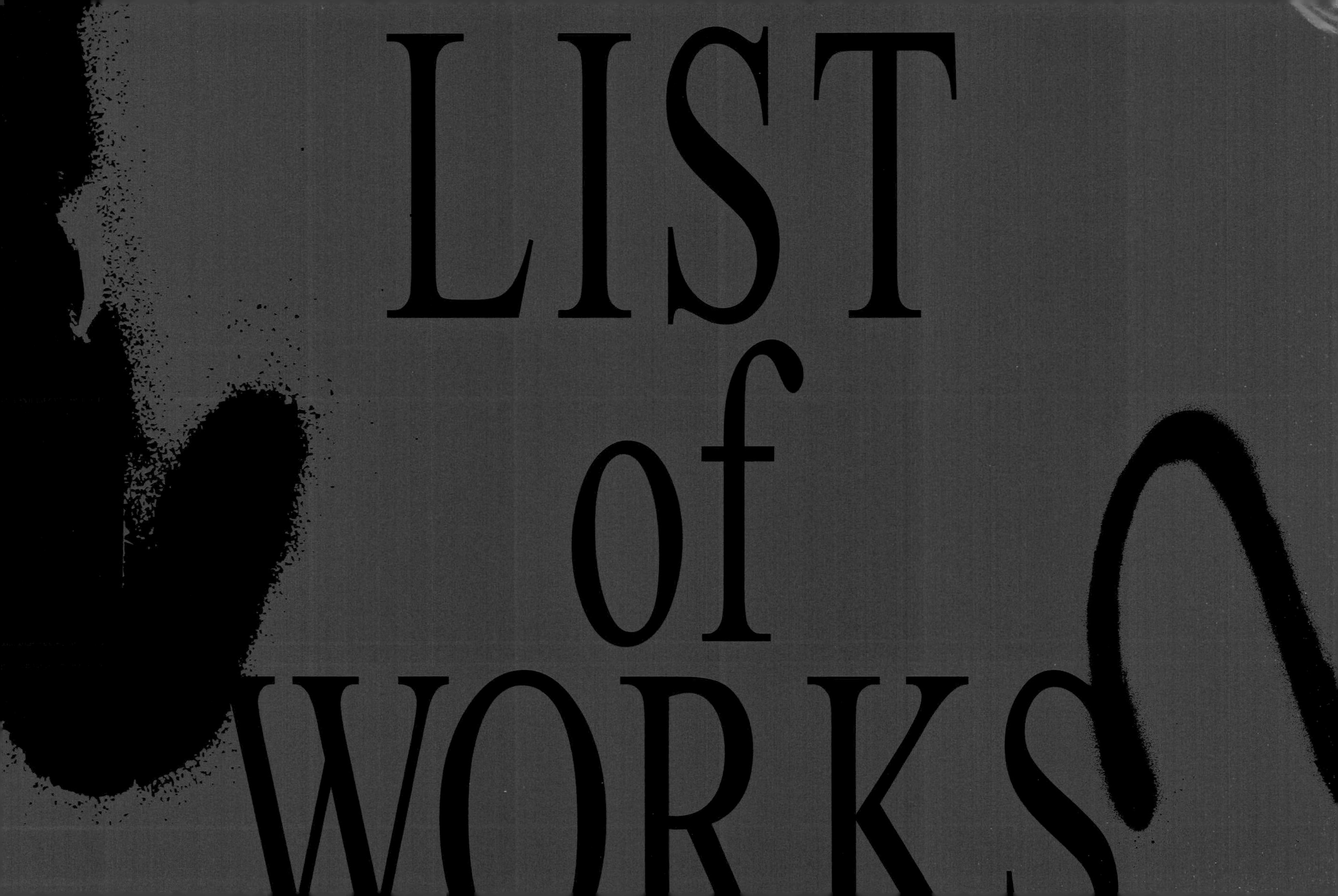

LIST
of
WORKS

A Lover's Touch, video stills, 2022
5-channel video installation, HD,
English, 5.1 surround sound, 24:12 min.
Edition of 3
Pages 44, 45, 48, 49, 53
Installation views, SOMA Artspace,
Berlin, 2022
Pages 46, 46–47, 47, 50–51

MOTHERNIGHT, video stills, 2020
3-channel video installation, HD,
English & Korean with English
subtitles, stereo sound, 17:20 min.
Edition of 5
Contemporary Art Collection of the
Federal Republic of Germany
Pages 76, 77, 82, 83, 86, 87, 88–89,
90, 91
Film excerpts from *Hanyeo
(The Housemaid)*, 1960, provided
by the Korean Film Archive and
© Kim Dong-won
Film excerpts from *Lady Vengeance*,
2005, provided by Park Chan-wook,
CJ ENM, and Moho Film

Installation views, SOMA Artspace,
Berlin, 2022
Pages 72–73, 80–81, 92–93

Protest and Desire, video stills, 2019
2-channel video installation, 4K,
English, surround sound, 19:55 min.
Edition of 5
Pages 118–119, 120–121, 121,
122–123, 126, 127

Valentine, 2022
2-panel scrolling-text LED
sculpture, 192 x 16 x 7.5 cm,
1 min. loop
Edition of 3
Installation views, SOMA Artspace,
Berlin
Pages 54, 98–99, 132, 133

It's Complicated, 2019
3-phase blinking neon, 90 x 90 cm
Edition of 5
Collection of Xiaochan Hua
and Klaus Dierkes, Berlin
Pages 43, 137

Heart of a Champion, 2016
Neon, 45 x 60 cm
Installation view,
Horse & Pony, Berlin
Edition of 3
Private collection, Berlin
Page 108

Heartless, 2017
Plaster, wire, foam, cardboard,
foam, pigment, 1098 x 107 x 45 cm
Pages 100–101

I Just Can't Stop Loving You, 2021
2-panel scrolling-text LED sculpture,
170 x 39.5 x 5 cm, 1:18 min. loop
Edition of 3
Pages 116–117

Past Present Tense, video stills, 2015
Video, HD, German with English
subtitles, stereo sound, 32 min.
Edition of 3
Pages 60, 61

Show Me Love, 2019
Collage sketchbook,
21 x 29.7 cm
Pages 23, 70–71, 110, 111

***When I Think About You
I Touch Myself***, 2018
Plaster, mirror, pigment, 120 x 90 cm
Installation view, PS120, Berlin
d'Arenberg-Parmanand Collection,
Hong Kong
Pages 130–131

How (Not) to Fit In, 2022
Exhibition views, Villa Merkel,
Esslingen
Pages 66, 68–69

An Overture of Grief and Joy, 2022
Installation view,
Kunstverein Braunschweig,
Braunschweig
Pages 124–125

Into the Drift and Sway, 2022
Exhibition view, Bärenzwinger,
Berlin
Pages 134–135

Labor of Love, video still, 2016
HD video, color and sound, 22:55 min.
Edition of 3
Page 109

**VIDEO PRODUCTION
CREDITS**

A Lover's Touch, 2022
Leticia Taguchi as Dolores Moreira
Victor Nicolaus as Marc Eichman
Cinematography: Julia Geiss
1st Assistant Camera: Jessica
Sattabongkot
Gaffer: Jonatan Winbo
Original Score: Hans Appelqvist
Sound Design: Sum Sum Shen
Sound Engineer: Ilya Selikhov
Colorist: Eric Giese

MOTHERNIGHT, 2020
Ghost Woman: Trang Le Hong
Cinematography: Julia Geiss
Voice Actress: Pam Nogales
Music: Dong Zhou
Sound Design: Sum Sum Shen
Additional Music: Hans Appelqvist
Colorist: Eric Giese

Protest and Desire, 2019
Cinematography: Julia Geiss
Sound Design: Sum Sum Shen

Labor of Love, 2016
Cinematography: Sander
Houtkruijer and Bastian Hopfgarten
Original Score: Tami T
Featuring Rafael Schistl,
Francisco Franco Da Silva,
Andrasch Starke

Past Present Tense, 2015
Cinematography: Bastian
Hopfgarten
Subtitles: Jason Harrell
Mastering: Paul Bonomo
Featuring Anonymous,
Abini Zoellner, Anetta Kahane,
Minh Nguyen, Jasmin Truong,
Jasco Viefhues, Kien Nghi Ha,
Noa Ha, Jan Riebe

Published and distributed by
Mousse Publishing
Contrappunto s.r.l.
Via Pier Candido Decembrio 28,
20137, Milan–Italy

Available through:

Mousse Publishing, Milan
moussemagazine.it

DAP | Distributed Art Publishers, New York
artbook.com

Les presses du réel, Dijon
lespressesdureel.com

Antenne Books, London
antennebooks.com

Idea Books, Amsterdam
ideabooks.nl

Motto, Berlin
mottodistribution.com

LibroCo, Firenze
libroco.it

Christa Joo Hyun D'Angelo: Fatal Attraction
First edition: 500 copies, 2023
Printed in Estonia by ManMade Agentuur OÜ
ISBN 978-88-6749-597-9
€ 25 / $ 29.95

MANAGING EDITOR
Saehee Hwang

COPY EDITOR
Max Bach

CONTRIBUTORS
Travis Jeppesen, Kathy-Ann Tan,
Karina Griffith

GRAPHIC DESIGN
Martin Falck

**PREPRESS & COLOR
PROOFING**
Krzysiek Krzysztofiak

Published with the kind support of the Senate Department for Culture and Community

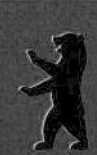

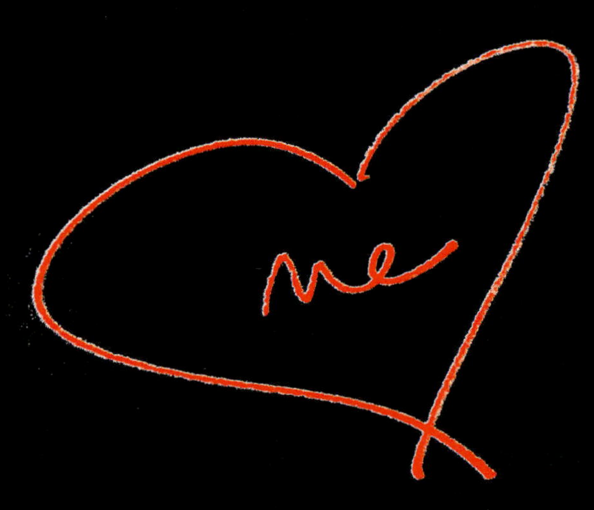